APPROXIMATE JUSTICE

Studies in Social, Political, and Legal Philosophy

General Editor: James P. Sterba, University of Notre Dame

This series analyzes and evaluates critically the major political, social, and legal ideals, institutions, and practices of our time. The analysis may be historical or problem-centered; the evaluation may focus on theoretical underpinnings or practical implications. Among the recent titles in the series are:

Faces of Environmental Racism: Confronting Issues of Global Justice
    edited by Laura Westra, University of Windsor, and Peter S. Wenz, Sangamon State University
Plato Rediscovered: Human Value and Social Order
    by T. K. Seung, University of Texas at Austin
Liberty for the Twenty-First Century: Contemporary Libertarian Thought
    edited by Tibor R. Machan, Auburn University, and Douglas B. Rasmussen, St. John's University
In the Company of Others: Perspectives on Community, Family, and Culture
    edited by Nancy E. Snow, Marquette University
Perfect Equality: John Stuart Mill on Well-Constituted Communities
    by Maria H. Morales, Florida State University
Citizenship in a Fragile World
    by Bernard P. Dauenhauer, University of Georgia
Critical Moral Liberalism: Theory and Practice
    by Jeffrey Reiman, American University
Nature as Subject: Human Obligation and Natural Community
    by Eric Katz, New Jersey Institute of Technology
Can Ethics Provide Answers? And Other Essays in Moral Philosophy
    by James Rachels, University of Alabama at Birmingham
Character and Culture
    by Lester H. Hunt, University of Wisconsin–Madison
Same Sex: Debating the Ethics, Science, and Culture of Homosexuality
    edited by John Corvino, University of Texas at Austin
Approximate Justice: Studies in Non-Ideal Theory
    by George Sher, Rice University
Living in Integrity: A Global Ethic to Restore a Fragmented Earth
    by Laura Westra, University of Windsor

APPROXIMATE JUSTICE

Studies in Non-Ideal Theory

George Sher

ROWMAN & LITTLEFIELD PUBLISHERS, INC.
Lanham • Boulder • New York • Oxford

ROWMAN & LITTLEFIELD PUBLISHERS, INC.

Published in the United States of America
by Rowman & Littlefield Publishers, Inc.
4720 Boston Way, Lanham, Maryland 20706

12 Hid's Copse Road
Cummor Hill, Oxford OX2 9JJ, England

British Library Cataloguing in Publication Information Available

Library of Congress Cataloging-in-Publication Data
Sher, George.
    Approximate justice : studies in non-ideal theory / George Sher.
        p.   cm.—(Studies in social, political, and legal philosophy)
    Includes bibliographical references and index.
    ISBN 0-8476-8753-8 (cloth : alk. paper).—ISBN 0-8476-8754-6
(pbk. : alk. paper)
    1. Criminal justice, administration of—Philosophy.   2. Criminal
justice, administration of—Moral and ethical aspects.   I. Title
II. Series.
HV7419.S54   1997
364—dc21   97-26344
                                                                             CIP

ISBN 0-8476-8753-8 (cloth : alk. paper)
ISBN 0-8476-8754-6 (pbk. : alk. paper)

Printed in the United States of America

⊗ ™ The paper used in this publication meets the minimum requirements of
American National Standard for Information Sciences—Permanence of Paper
for Printed Library Materials, ANSI Z39.48–1984.

For Sally

Contents

Preface

When I was a student in the 1960s, late positivism and "ordinary language philosophy" were still highly influential philosophical movements. In ethics the main orientation was linguistic and metaphilosophical; substantive normative inquiry played a secondary role. In that atmosphere I found ethics boring, and to this day I have never taken a course in it.

But even then, things were changing. The great storm of the 1960s, though destructive in many respects, had the salutary effect of stimulating urgent moral debate that eventually roiled even the backwater of academic ethics. Substantive normative discussion became legitimate, then dominant, as the new journal *Philosophy and Public Affairs* provided a lively and quickly prestigious outlet for it. At that point, I got interested.

In particular, I began to think about preferential treatment for blacks and women, which was then being debated in that journal and elsewhere. My first idea was that this policy was obviously and completely wrong, and because its wrongness seemed less obvious to others than it did to me, I thought there might be some benefit to pointing this out. I quickly discovered, though, that there was nothing at all obvious about the topic and that before we could reach any conclusions about it we had to understand various other issues, among them the scope, nature, and theoretical underpinnings of compensatory justice, the moral claims of the best qualified, and the meaning and justification of equal opportunity. As a result, I ended up writing a paper very different from the one I first set out to write—a hedged and qualified defense of preferential treatment, but a defense nevertheless. Many of the papers I have written since then, and more than half of the essays in this volume, continue (and I hope deepen) my investigation of the issues that that first paper raised.

As a group, the papers go against today's academic grain. There is, to be sure, a defense of preferential treatment, but there are also arguments that diversity has less educational value than many suppose, that social arrangements that cause women to prefer traditional lives need not be unjust, that poor women have no right to be provided with elective abortions, and that wrongdoers deserve to be punished. I am not unhappy to be taking these unpopular positions, but neither have I done so merely to be contrarian. Instead, I have simply tried to follow the arguments wherever they lead.

Because the essays were written over a twenty-five year period, I was pleasantly surprised to see how well they fit together. There are of course discrepancies—I briefly explore one in the book's introduction—but the essays display both thematic continuity and a continuing commitment to a single set of core values. Although I have long since recanted my philistine rejection of metaethics, and although I now take my defense of preferential treatment to have few policy implications—to apply it, we would need far more information than we can ever hope to possess—I remain convinced by the book's central arguments. For better or worse, they say what I believe.

I have made only minor stylistic changes, and no substantive ones, in nine of the book's twelve essays, but three other essays are altered or new. "Effort, Ability, and Personal Desert" amalgamates material from two previously published developments of a single line of thought, one that appeared in *Philosophy and Public Affairs*, the other from my book *Desert*. Another essay, "Preferential Treatment, the Future, and the Past," is a completely rewritten and much augmented version of what was originally entitled "Reverse Discrimination, the Future, and the Past." Only a few sentences of the original remain unaltered. A final essay, "Deserved Punishment Revisited," was newly written for this volume. It first summarizes the theory of punishment that I advanced in *Desert* and then elaborates and amends that theory in light of what some critics subsequently said.

I incurred many intellectual debts when writing these essays, and it is a pleasure to acknowledge these again. Early on, I received helpful comments from Edward Erwin, Gertrude Ezorsky, and Michael Levin. I wrote most of the papers at the University of Vermont, where my ideas were tested and refined by criticism from gifted colleagues including Steven M. Cahn, Richard Hinman, Patricia Kitcher, Philip Kitcher, Hilary Kornblith, and William E. Mann. At Rice University, where I now teach, Baruch Brody and Larry Temkin have been similarly helpful. I owe a special debt to two other former colleagues from Vermont, Arthur Kuflik and Alan Wertheimer, both of whom commented on many of the papers and were wonderfully generous with their advice and encouragement. As always, my greatest debt is to my wife, Emily Fox Gordon, on whose insight and judgment I can always rely. She understands my daily struggles with language and ideas as only another writer can, and her companionship makes the writing life a joy.

Acknowledgments

The author and publisher gratefully acknowledge permission to reprint the following material.

Chapter 1, "Ancient Wrongs and Modern Rights," originally appeared in *Philosophy and Public Affairs* 10, no. 1 (Winter 1981): 3–17. Copyright 1981 by Princeton University Press. Used by permission of Princeton University Press.

Chapter 2, "Compensation and Transworld Personal Identity," originally appeared in *The Monist* 62, no. 3 (July 1979): 378–91.

Chapter 3, "Justifying Reverse Discrimination in Employment," originally appeared in *Philosophy and Public Affairs* 4, no. 2 (Winter 1975): 159–70. Copyright 1975 by Princeton University Press. Used by permission of Princeton University Press.

Chapter 4, "Groups and Justice," originally appeared in *Ethics* 87, no. 1 (October 1977): 81–87. Copyright 1977 by the University of Chicago. All rights reserved.

Chapter 5, "Effort, Ability, and Personal Desert," originally appeared in *Philosophy and Public Affairs* 8, no. 4 (Summer 1979): 361–76. Copyright 1979 by Princeton University Press. An altered version appeared under the title "Rawls's Attack on Desert" in George Sher, *Desert* (Princeton, N.J.: Princeton University Press, 1987), 22–36. Copyright 1987 by Princeton University Press. The current chapter incorporates material from both versions; used by permission of Princeton University Press.

Chapter 6, "Preferential Treatment, the Future, and the Past," is a completely rewritten and much expanded version of an essay entitled "Reverse Discrimination, the Future, and the Past," which originally appeared in *Ethics* 90, no. 1 (October 1979): 81–87. Copyright 1979 by the University of Chicago. All rights reserved.

Chapter 7, "Right Violations and Injustices: Can We Always Avoid Trade-Offs?" originally appeared in *Ethics* 94, no. 2 (January 1984):

212–24. Copyright 1984 by the University of Chicago. All rights reserved.

Chapter 8, "Our Preferences, Ourselves," originally appeared in *Philosophy and Public Affairs* 12, no. 1 (Winter 1983): 34–50. Copyright 1982 by Princeton University Press. Used by permission of Princeton University Press.

Chapter 9, "Predicting Performance," originally appeared in *Social Philosophy and Policy* 5, no. 1 (Autumn 1987): 188–203.

Chapter 10, "What Makes a Lottery Fair?" originally appeared in *Nous* 14, no. 2 (May 1980): 203–16.

Chapter 11, "Subsidized Abortion: Moral Rights and Moral Compromise," originally appeared in *Philosophy and Public Affairs* 10, no. 4 (Fall 1981): 361–72. Copyright 1981 by Princeton University Press. Used by permission of Princeton University Press.

Introduction

From Plato on, philosophers have sought to articulate social ideals. At its loftiest, this enterprise seeks nothing less than a complete description of the just or good society—or, alternatively, a complete set of principles, a society's complete conformity to which would *make* it just or good. Somewhat less lofty, but still high-flying, are attempts to formulate general principles for specific social domains—for example, theories of economic justice or political obligation. Operating yet closer to the actual world, some philosophers try to work their way toward universal principles by exposing the flaws of existing institutions or practices, while others contend that there *are* no universal principles— that each society's ideals must be extracted from its own culture, history, practices, or shared understandings.

Despite their differences, these approaches all have one thing in common: they all seek to describe societies as they ought to be. In this sense, they are all variants of what John Rawls calls *ideal theory*. But in addition to treating existing societies as occasions for reflection about the ideal, or as sources of materials from which to fashion it, philosophers can also treat their lapses from the ideal as independent occasions for normative reflection—as distinct new sources of normative problems. When philosophers take this approach, they engage in what Rawls calls *non-ideal theory* or *partial compliance theory*, and what others call *the theory of the second best*.

The essays in the current collection are all studies in non-ideal theory. Each takes as its point of departure some problem that is raised either by the injustice of certain past or present social arrangements or else by some limitation on what people can reasonably be expected to know or do. Moreover, when the discussion concerns human limitations, these are treated not as aspects of the human condition to be accommodated *within* a theory of the ideal, but rather as impediments to fully *realizing* some ideal. Thus, each essay treats some contingent or

1

necessary deviation from the ideal as an independent source of distinct normative problems.

Many of those problems are instantly recognizable. For example, most thoughtful people have at some point wondered:

1. When we try to move from unjust to (more) just social arrangements, which methods of promoting social change may we legitimately employ? Which sacrifices may we inflict on whom, and which moral prohibitions, if any, may we infringe?
2. Given the existence of widespread injustice, what may, or must, be done to compensate its victims? What are the practical and theoretical limits on our efforts to compensate? By what moral constraints must those efforts be hedged?
3. Given our limited information, how can we know what it is just for any individual to have or do? When we cannot know this in detail, what simplifying devices may we use?
4. Given the lack of consensus about what is right, should we, as individuals or a society, ever refrain from acting on our convictions in deference to those who disagree?

Needless to say, these questions are illustrative but far from exhaustive.

Despite the clarity of the distinction between ideal and non-ideal theory, the line that divides the two is not rigidly fixed. Various human limitations, such as our inability to keep track of the endless flow of transactions between individuals, can be regarded either as barriers to implementing ideals that require detailed information or as reasons for adopting ideals that do not. Robert Nozick's "entitlement theory," which implies that we cannot know whether someone is entitled to his holdings without knowing how he acquired them, embodies the first attitude toward our cognitive limitations; theories such as Rawls's, which focus not on any individual's holdings but on the justice of the whole system of institutions that *determines* who has what, embody the second. Yet even if many ideal theories do manage to coopt some potential impediments to their own implementation, no ideal theory can coopt them all. Any theory that tried would be so deracinated as not to specify *any* ideal. For this reason if for no other, the distinction between ideal and non-ideal theories remains real and useful.

Like its ideal counterpart, non-ideal theory is essentially normative. Indeed, in many non-ideal discussions, normative considerations enter twice, once in the specification of whatever wrong or injustice is said to pose the problem and again in whatever solution is proposed. Let me therefore put some of my own normative cards on the table.

In a word, my approach is pluralistic. I believe that considerations of efficiency and social utility often provide good reasons to conduct social policy in one way rather than another, but that fairness, desert, and individual rights often provide good reasons too. Because I assign weight to all these considerations and a variety of others, and because I have no simple (or even complex) formula for integrating them, my approach is unlikely to satisfy anyone who insists on referring all policy questions to some single principle or small set of principles, or to some overarching theory. It is, for this reason, unlikely to prove satisfying to many orthodox utilitarians, Rawlsians, or libertarians.

Yet while an undisciplined pluralism certainly has its dangers—perhaps the most obvious is the temptation to treat the available principles as so many tools in a kit, to be used or set aside according to whether they support an antecedently favored view—the urge to unify has its dangers too. Preeminent among these is the danger of premature systematization. Anyone whose first priority is theoretical unity will be tempted to ignore, rather than incorporate or otherwise accommodate, any relevant but recalcitrant phenomena. I know of no better way to avoid this danger than to open oneself to all the considerations that seem pertinent and to sort out their roles and weights by remaining similarly open at higher justificatory levels. If a unified account eventually emerges, so much the better. In any event, my commitment to pluralism is rooted less in antipathy to system than in a belief that the definitive systematization has yet to be produced.

With these preliminaries discharged, let us turn next to the essays themselves. Because (serious) deviations from ideal justice are injustices and because injustice cries out for rectification, one especially salient branch of non-ideal theory is compensatory justice, and it is with that topic that the book begins. At first glance, the basic idea of compensation seems straightforward. Fully to compensate a victim of injustice is to "make him whole again"; and to do that is to make him as well off as he would have been had no injustice occurred. However, as soon as we look more closely at this attractive idea, daunting problems emerge.

The most obvious problems are epistemic. Because we are hopelessly ignorant about most wrongs done in the past, we also lack detailed knowledge of most of their effects. This means that for any past time t, we have no idea which of the holdings that prevailed at t were the results of wrongdoing and which were not. Thus, when we rectify a past wrong by restoring the holdings that prevailed when the wrong occurred (or when we do so by restoring the holdings that would now prevail if the original holdings had been used legitimately), we cannot assume that we are making the prevailing distribution more just. Instead, we may actually be making it *less* just by restoring holdings to which the victim (or his descendants) would not have been entitled had the wrong not occurred.

If no one can know when compensation is warranted, there is no point in trying to compensate. However, upon closer inspection, such pessimism will not be warranted unless claims to compensation retain their force indefinitely. If, instead, they eventually lose their force—if claims to compensation fade with the passage of time, as law and common opinion suppose—then the danger that compensating for a recent injustice will only restore an older one will be less pressing. But is the supposition that claims to compensation fade with time anything more than a mere prejudice?

In the collection's first essay, "Ancient Wrongs and Modern Rights," I argue that it is—that this view can indeed be given a theoretical defense. My argument turns on two principles, each of which limits the degree to which the level of well-being that a person would have enjoyed in a world without the relevant injustice (call this *the rectified world*, or W_r) can provide a basis for compensation in the actual world (call this W_a). The two principles are

1. Differences between a person's levels of well-being in W_r and W_a that are traceable to his failure to perform certain (readily available) acts in W_a are not compensable; and
2. Differences between a person's levels of well-being in W_r and W_a that are traceable to his performing certain productive or otherwise meritorious acts in W_r are also not compensable.

Both principles, I argue, are independently defensible. The first implies that persons should not be compensated for wrongful losses they could easily have avoided, while the second implies that they should not be compensated for holdings that would have resulted from efforts they did not actually make. When they are conjoined with plausible further assumptions, the two principles imply that claims to compensation do fade with time. This in turn explains why compensating only victims of recent wrongs is indeed likely to lead to a more just overall distribution.

By invoking principles 1 and 2, I have already abandoned the idea that compensating someone is simply making him as well off as he would be if no wrong had been done. But another problem may compel a further retreat. To make sense of someone's level of well-being in a rectified world, we need some way of specifying which inhabitant of that world he is. We need, in other words, a criterion of transworld personal identity. But of the available criteria, each has the disturbing implication that some victims of wrongdoing do not exist at all in the relevant rectified worlds. Suppose, for example, that a developer builds on land that he knows to be seriously polluted; that because the houses are so cheap, a couple who purchases one can afford to have a child; and that, as a result of the pollution, the child is born with serious defects. If this child has a claim to be compensated by the developer, the reason cannot be that he would have been better off if the developer had not sold the tainted house; for if the house had not been sold, then that child would not have existed at all.

One response, of course, is simply to deny that the child *has* a claim to be compensated. But such responses are not always plausible, so in "Compensation and Transworld Personal Identity" I take a different tack. There I tentatively suggest that when a victim of wrongdoing does not exist in W_r, what matters from the standpoint of compensation may be not *his* level of well-being in W_r but rather that of certain related others. Because those others are assumed to exist in W_r, this suggestion secures the possibility of compensating the defective child.

At the same time, however, it also raises new questions. The most obvious, of course, are who the related others are and why their well-being in W_r should be relevant to what the child ought to have in W_a. But other, less obvious problems arise when we consider this suggestion in conjunction with the argument of the previous essay.

For in "Ancient Wrongs," I try to explain why claims to compensation fade with time by invoking two principles, each of which applies only when a victim of wrongdoing exists in both W_a and W_r. Thus, if a current victim would *not* now exist if the original wrong act had not been performed—and this, of course, becomes increasingly likely as the original wrong act recedes into the past—then principles 1 and 2 will not imply that *any* part of the difference between that victim's level of well-being in W_a and that of the relevant others in W_r is non-compensable. This means that to preserve our explanation, we must either revise principles 1 and 2 so that they too apply even to a victim of wrongdoing who does not exist in W_r, or else revise our assumption that W_r is simply the closest possible world in which the wrong act is not performed. A natural alternative, briefly mentioned in "Ancient Wrongs," is that W_r is instead the closest possible world in which the wrong act is not performed *and the victim exists*.

Whichever solution we adopt, the need to square the two proposals illustrates the complexity of compensatory justice. A comprehensive and integrated theory—something no one has come close to producing—would require many similar adjustments. But the problems raised by compensation are not confined to the level of high theory: many further complications arise when we focus on specific injustices and specific ways of compensating for them. Some of these new complications are explored in the book's next group of essays. Their main topic is the dominant injustice in this country's history—the great wrong of slavery and its legacy of suffering and discrimination—and the guiding question is whether past discrimination justifies preferential treatment now.

That it does is an assumption of many who favor affirmative action programs. These programs benefit the current members of groups whose past members were the victims of discrimination—primarily blacks, but also women and others—by giving them preference in competition for jobs, admission to educational institutions, and contracts to provide services. Because past discrimination has many lingering effects, one way to defend preferential treatment—though not the only way—is to construe it as compensation *for* (some of) those effects. However, against this suggestion, some argue that preferential treatment benefits only a small proportion of any group's current members (and, in general, that it benefits just the group members who were harmed the least). More importantly, preferential treatment is said to be unfair because it imposes the whole burden of compensation on a relatively small number of best-qualified candidates. This, indeed, is said to be unfair for two distinct reasons: first, because these best-qualified candidates are not relevantly different from most others of their race and gender, and, second, because they were not the perpetrators of the original discrimination.

But, at least in theory, these objections can be met. In "Justifying Reverse Discrimination in Employment," I argue that preferential treatment is best viewed as compensation, not for any and all harmful effects of past discrimination, but only for the single effect of being rendered less able to compete. To give an applicant preference, on this account, is simply to nullify whatever portion of his competitive disadvantage is due to past injustice. Because nullifying an unjustly produced competitive disadvantage may not tip the balance in a given applicant's favor—because many group members would not have been best qualified even if their qualifications had *not* been reduced—this way of narrowing our focus nicely explains why only some group members should actually receive positions. It also nicely explains why preferential treatment does not unfairly burden the best-qualified candidates whom it bypasses. The explanation here is that because only these best-qualified candidates are in line to acquire positions as a result of injustice—because they alone stand to gain from the relevant effects of discrimination—it cannot be unfair to ask them alone to forgo those gains.

Once again, this reasoning requires some adjustment in light of our other results. For one thing, given principles 1 and 2, what requires offsetting is evidently not the whole difference between any victim's current competitive position and the position he would have had in the absence of injustice, but only whatever part of the difference cannot be attributed either to his omissions in W_a or to his actions in W_r. More seriously, this reasoning may not work at all when the victim himself does not exist in W_r. For even if other people's *holdings or levels of well-being* in W_r can sometimes determine what a victim should have in W_a, the *competitive positions* that others occupy in W_r may be too distant from the victim's own talents and abilities to play such a role. If they are, then my reasoning may not justify giving *any* preference to persons who were affected by discrimination, but who would not now exist if that discrimination had not taken place.

Whether or not this is true, it seems clear that my argument justifies less preference, and justifies it in fewer cases, than many supporters of affirmative action would wish. Also, to provide what the argument construes as the right amount of preference, we must know how much more competitive each individual would now be in the absence of discrimination—and, given principles 1 and 2, how much of any difference is due either to the individual's own actions in W_a or to his own omissions in W_r. Because such knowledge can never be attained, the argument implies that we cannot know how much preference is called for in any given case. However, it was just the fact that each best-qualified candidate is asked to relinquish only the portion of his competitive advantage that is traceable to injustice that allowed us to avoid the charge of unfairness. Thus, given our epistemic limitations, affirmative action programs as actually administered almost certainly *are* often unfair.

Reactions to this conclusion can be expected to vary. Some will immediately infer that preferential programs ought to be abolished, while others will argue that tolerating unrectified injustices is also unfair, so the real question is which sort of policy involves *less* unfairness. But others again will contest the charge of unfairness itself; and this more fundamental challenge sets the agenda for the next two essays.

One way to press the challenge is to construe preference as compensation for groups rather than individuals. Because discrimination itself is generally directed at groups, some argue that any compensatory efforts must have a similar focus. This suggestion, if correct, might eliminate the need to establish how much more competitive any given individual would be in the absence of discrimination. However, I argue in "Groups and Justice" that the suggestion is *not* correct—that racial and sexual groups cannot qualify for compensation because they are not the sorts of entities that can either benefit or suffer harm. Because these groups lack nervous systems, they cannot experience pleasure or pain; because they lack consciousness, their desires cannot be satisfied or frustrated; and because they cannot take purposive action, their goals cannot be furthered or thwarted. For these and other reasons, racial and sexual groups cannot fall under any principle of distibutive justice—or, therefore, under any principle of compensation for *in*justice.

Because racial and sexual groups lack moral standing, the first challenge to the charge of unfairness fails. A second challenge, however, contests not the idea that only individuals have moral standing, but rather the idea that being best-qualified for a position gives an individual a serious claim to it. By undermining the claims of the best-qualified, this approach seeks to show that awarding positions to others is not unfair. Moreover, at least when the claims of the best-qualified are said to stem from their desert, those claims may indeed seem questionable; for it is commonly believed that no one deserves the talents and natural abilities that *make* him best qualified, and from this, some conclude that no one deserves any position for which he *is* best qualified. However, in "Effort, Ability, and Personal Desert," I argue that this last step is one we should not take.

Suppose, however, that we were justified in taking it; and suppose, further, that no better defense of the claims of the best-qualified were forthcoming. Then the strongest objection to preferential treatment would be disarmed—but so too would the strongest objection to outright discrimination. However, if racial and sexual discrimination were not seriously wrong, then it would no longer be clear why their effects should warrant compensatory preference now.

Perhaps because of this, many who challenge the claims of the best-qualified go on to defend preferential treatment on consequentialist grounds. They argue for affirmative action not as compensation for any effects of past injustice, but rather as a way of promoting some desirable consequence such as utility, equality, or diversity. However, at least offhand, it is not clear how individuals are made more equal when a specially high-paying position is awarded to a woman rather than a man; and neither is it clear why a university's racial mix is more important than—or even as important as—a diverse mix of viewpoints and interests among its faculty and students. Also, even if students, professors, and workers should be drawn from diverse groups, why single out just the groups that affirmative action guidelines mention? Although various answers can be given, I argue in "Preferential Treatment, the Future, and the Past" that the most salient fact about these groups is just that their past members were often subject to discrimination. This suggests that even apparently consequentialist arguments for preferential treatment may have a hidden compensatory dimension. To the extent that they do, these arguments must assume that past discrimination was indeed wrong. However, if so, then not only the claims of its past victims, but also those of all currently best-qualified applicants, must again be taken seriously.

This returns us to the question of how to proceed when we have too little information to tailor the amount of preference that each group member receives to the specific (compensable) reduction in competitive standing that he has suffered. In general, any across-the-board increase in the amount of preference that is given will increase both the number of victims of past injustice who receive full compensation and the number who receive more compensation than is fair to their currently best-qualified rivals; while any across-the-board *decrease* in preference will both treat fewer best-qualified applicants unfairly and leave more victims of injustice uncompensated. Thus, given our unavoidable ignorance of who has been harmed to what degree, we may seem forced to minimize injustices through something like a utilitarian calculus. But is this really consistent with the widely held view that justice (and rights) are not values to be pursued but constraints on the pursuit of value? After considering several aspects of this question, I argue in "Right Violations and Injustices: Can We Always Avoid Trade-Offs?" that trade-offs are indeed inevitable, but that, properly understood, they are consistent with the role of rights and justice in our moral scheme.

In many discussions of preferential treatment, different discriminated-against groups are treated as interchangeable. However, despite their similarities, these groups can differ in important ways. For example, the reason so few blacks have historically held construction jobs is simply that until recently few construction companies (or unions) were willing to accept them. By contrast, although women have also held few construction jobs, the explanation in their case is more complicated. Here the reason is partly that until recently few construction jobs were open to women, but also partly that until recently few women wanted to *be* construction workers.

Does this mean that women suffered less injustice than blacks or only that the injustice they suffered took a different form? Were women treated unjustly not only by being barred from male-dominated fields, but also by being conditioned to prefer not to *enter* those fields? In "Our Preferences, Ourselves," I address this question by asking exactly what is wrong with women's traditional preferences for uncompetitive, family-oriented lives. Those preferences have been criticized on a variety of grounds, among them that they cause women to be less happy than men, impose arbitrary limits on women's contributions to society, deprive women of important benefits, undermine women's self-respect, and, when unreflectively internalized, render women non-autonomous. However, while each criticism raises complicated issues, I argue that each may beg the question at a crucial point. In the end, the worst thing about women's traditional preferences may be simply that they conflict with other contingent yet urgent preferences, such as aspirations to independence and achievement, that powerful economic and social forces have recently called forth.

As conceived here, preferential treatment is a mechanism for promoting equal opportunity. More precisely, I have defended it as a way of reconciling that ideal with the effects of injustice on some applicants' qualifications. But equal opportunity is also problematic for a variety of other reasons, and some of these have nothing to do with injustice. One such difficulty concerns the notion of qualifications itself.

The problem I have in mind is not how to define contested positions—whether, for example, the main task of a faculty member should be conceived as transmitting knowledge, doing research, or imparting desirable attitudes to students—but is, instead, how to predict performance at whatever tasks *are* required. Because we cannot discover how well someone will perform by peering into the future (or into other possible worlds), any such predictions must be based on indirect evidence. But on *what* evidence? The simplest answer, of course, is that we may use any evidence that supports reliable predictions. But may we really base our predictions on factors such as age or size, which may be statistically linked to performance but are beyond an applicant's control? And what if one racial or sexual group has a history of performing better at certain tasks than another? Confronted by these questions, many would draw back from the idea that all accurate predictions are equally legitimate. But what, in that case, distinguishes legitimate from illegitimate predictions?

Here one appealing suggestion is that any legitimate prediction must be based on something an applicant has *done*. This suggestion, if correct, would allow employers to use tests, auditions, and recommendations from past employers, but would disallow the use of statistics about classes or groups. Because it seems to give each applicant control over his own fate, this restriction may appear to follow from the very ideal of equal opportunity itself. But in "Predicting Performance," I argue that any gains in control would be minimal and that no other simple criterion of legitimacy is more promising. Thus, unsatisfyingly, a prediction's legitimacy may depend not on its conformity to any single principle but on a complex balancing of different factors.

Equal opportunity requires that all applicants have equal chances to compete but not that all competitors have equal probabilities of winning. However, in some contexts, it *does* seem best to allocate an indivisible good by equalizing the probability that each claimant will receive it. In particular, this seems best both when there is no plausible basis for selecting any particular claimant or type of claimant—for example, when several applicants for a position are equally qualified or several children want a single ticket to the circus—and when there *is* a plausible basis for selection but we lack the information to apply it. In both cases, the preferred method of allocation is a *randomizing device or lottery*.

Because we have little difficulty recognizing fair lotteries—because flipping ordinary coins and drawing straws are obviously fair procedures, while flipping a weighted coin is obviously not—the moral status of lotteries is not often discussed. Yet difficult problems lurk just below the surface. These begin with the fact that if determinism is true, then every lottery's outcome is entirely fixed in advance. This does not mean that we cannot equalize the probabilities that different entrants will win; but it does mean that what must be equalized are probabilities of victory *relative to available evidence*. But then relative to *whose* evidence must these probabilities be equal? And what of lotteries whose outcomes no one knows in advance, but whose victory criteria themselves seem biased—for example, a lottery whose victory criterion is having the fewest Jewish ancestors? In "What Makes a Lottery Fair?" I examine a number of such troublesome cases. Guided by the intuitions they elicit, I propose a unified analysis that explains the moral grounding of fair lotteries.

So far, we have seen that many problems of non-ideal theory are rooted in our lack of knowledge. The theme of epistemic limitation has surfaced in our discussions of compensation for ancient wrongs, the justification of preferential treatment, the assessment of qualifications, and, most recently, the fairness of lotteries. Yet even together, these discussions do not exhaust the field; for while each turns on some lack of empirical knowledge, still other problems are raised by deficiencies of *moral* knowledge.

Consider, for example, the vexed topic of abortion. When conservatives assert that abortion is tantamount to murder, they in effect claim to know that fetuses and zygotes have the moral status of persons. By contrast, when liberals compare abortion to an unproblematical surgical procedure, they in effect claim to know that fetuses are *not* persons, morally speaking. Even when liberals refuse to take a position, and argue that because the issue is so unclear the choice should simply be left to the pregnant woman, they in effect claim to know something that is incompatible with what conservatives claim to know. Of course, the mere fact that liberals and conservatives advance incompatible knowledge-claims does not show that neither side has achieved knowledge; and still less does it show that neither side *can* achieve it. But what does follow, and what in this context seems bad enough, is that *at least one side* must currently be in error. For if conservatives resist abortion with all the tactics appropriate to opposing mass murder while liberals resist their efforts with all the tactics appropriate to the defense of basic rights, acrimonious and destabilizing conflict is bound to result.

But in "Subsidized Abortion: Moral Rights and Moral Compromise," I argue that things are not this bad—that even persons who are hopelessly at odds about morality's substantive demands may agree on principles that permit or even require moral compromise. When our opponents are thoughtful and well-meaning, when the basis of our own position is murky at key points, and when there are weighty arguments on the other side, we may have good reason to moderate our moral demands if our opponents do likewise. Although no principle of moral compromise will be acceptable to everyone, something along these lines may seem reasonable to many. As one possible compromise, I suggest that conservatives may have reason not to resist abortion as strenuously as they would resist (other forms of) state-sanctioned murder if liberals will ask only that abortion remain legal but not that the state support it.

Whatever its exact requirements, moral compromise is rooted partly in awareness of one's own moral fallibility and partly in respect for the judgment of other moral agents. But neither attitude is always appropriate. When someone does something whose wrongness cannot be seriously contested, and when he does it because he is swayed by greed or does not care about others or has no use for morality, the standard response is not to accommodate but rather to punish. It is, moreover, hard to imagine any effective legal or political system that did not have some sort of coercive arm. But punishment typically deprives a person of his liberty, property, or life, and such treatment is usually itself morally impermissible. Thus, a further important question of non-ideal theory is how, if at all, punishing wrongdoers can be justified.

When punishment is judiciously administered, it may both prevent the wrongdoer from committing further crimes and deter others from committing them. But how can even these manifestly desirable goals override prohibitions whose usual task is precisely to *constrain* our pursuit of goals. To answer this question, we must somehow show that wrong acts alter the usual structure of obligations and permissions; and one well-known version of retributivism seeks to do just that. This theory takes as its point of departure the observation that when someone breaks a rule that others obey, he in effect benefits twice: once from the others' self-restraint and again from his own *lack* of restraint. Because this double benefit is unfair, it calls for some righting of the balance by an offsetting burden. This extra burden is precisely the wrongdoer's deserved punishment, and it is justified not by its desirable effects but by the demands of fairness.

Even as hastily sketched, this version of retributivism is clearly promising. But various critics have argued that it has implausible implications when the wrongdoer's extra benefit is understood as some form of psychic or material gain. To meet this objection, I have suggested that we should instead interpret the extra benefit as an extra measure of freedom *from moral restraint*; and this suggestion has been criticized in its turn. In the collection's final essay, "Deserved Punishment Revisited," I reexamine my suggestion in light of some of the criticism it has received.

Non-ideal theory is what we get when we apply philosophy's approach and techniques—its careful analysis, rational reflection, willingness to ascend to principle, and so on—to our own failures to live up to its ideals. Because many "realists" cite just these failures to show that philosophy is irrelevant, the very possibility of non-ideal theory is itself a kind of triumph. Because we are permanently flawed, we will never inhabit an ideal world; but because each flaw can be dealt with, no lapse from the ideal need be final either. The guiding question of non-ideal theory—"How can we best cope with this failure?"—can be asked again and again. It is precisely in the endless iteration of this question that any truly practical philosophy must live.

1

Ancient Wrongs and Modern Rights

It is widely acknowledged that persons may deserve compensation for the effects of wrong acts performed before they were born. It is such acts that are in question when we say that blacks deserve compensation because their forebears were originally brought to this country as slaves, or that American Indians deserve compensation for the unjust appropriation of their ancestors' land. But although some principle of compensation for the lasting effects of past wrongs seems appropriate, the proper temporal scope of that principle is not clear. We may award compensation for the effects of wrongs done as many as ten or twenty generations ago; but what of wrongs done a hundred generations ago? Or five hundred or a thousand? Are there any temporal limits at all to the wrong acts whose enduring effects may call for compensation? In the first section of this essay, I shall discuss several reasons for addressing these neglected questions. In subsequent sections, I shall discuss some possible ways of resolving them.

I

A natural initial reaction to questions about compensation for the effects of ancient wrongs is that these questions are, in the main, hopelessly unrealistic. In the case of blacks, Indians, and a few analogous groups, we may indeed have enough information to suggest that most current group members are worse off than they would be in the absence of some initial wrong. But if the wrong act was performed even longer ago, or if the persons currently suffering its effects do not belong to a coherent and easily identified group, then such information will *not* be available to us. There are surely some persons alive today who would be better off if the Spanish Inquisition had not taken place or if the Jews had never been originally expelled from the land of Canaan. However, to discover who those persons are and how much better off they would be, we would have to draw on far more genealogical, causal, and counterfactual knowledge than anyone can reasonably expect to possess. Because this information is not and never will be completely available, the question of who, if anyone, deserves compensation for the current effects of these wrongs will never be answered. But if so, why bother asking it?

This relaxed approach to compensation has the virtue of realism. The suggestion that we might arrive at a complete understanding of the effects of ancient wrongs is a philosopher's fantasy and nothing more. Nevertheless, despite its appeal, I think we cannot rest content with a totally pragmatic dismissal of the issue of compensating for ancient wrongs. For one thing, even if compensatory justice is a partially unrealizable ideal, its theoretical limits will retain an intrinsic interest. For another, even if we cannot now ascertain which persons deserve compensation for the effects of ancient wrongs, the insight that such persons exist might itself suggest new obligations to us. In particular, if the victims of even the most ancient of wrongs can qualify for compensation, and if our current compensatory efforts are therefore aimed at only a small subset of those who deserve it, then we will at least be obligated to enlarge the subset by extending our knowledge of the effects of ancient wrongs as far as possible. Alternatively, the discovery that desert of compensation is not invariant with respect to temporal distance might force us to reduce our compensatory efforts in certain areas.

These considerations suggest that clarifying the theoretical status of ancient wrongs may dictate certain (rather marginal) changes in our actual compensatory policies. But there is also another, far more significant implication that such clarification might have. Given the vastness of historical injustice and given the ramification of every event over time, it seems reasonable to assume that most or all current individuals have both benefited from and been harmed by numerous ancient wrongs. For (just about) every current person P, there are likely to be some ancient wrongs that have benefited P but harmed others, and other ancient wrongs that have benefited others but harmed P. In light of this, neither the distribution of goods that actually prevails nor that which would prevail in the absence of all recent wrongs is likely to resemble the distribution that would prevail in the absence of all historical wrongs. But if so, and if the effects of ancient wrongs do call as strongly for compensation as the effects of recent ones, then it seems that neither compensating nor not compensating for the known effects of recent wrongs will be just. On the one hand, since the point of compensating for the effects of wrong acts is to restore a just distribution of goods among the affected parties, the injustice of the distribution that would prevail in the absence of recent wrongs will undermine our rationale for restoring it. However, on the other hand, even if that distribution is unjust, the distribution that actually prevails is no better; and so a failure to compensate for recent wrongs will be every bit as unpalatable. The only strategy that *is* just is that of restoring the distribution that would have prevailed in the absence of all historical wrongs. But this, as we have seen, we will never have sufficient information to do.

How to respond to this combination of pervasive injustice and indefeasible ignorance is a complicated and difficult question. One possible strategy is to argue that even if compensating for recent wrongs would not restore full justice, it would at least bring us substantially closer to a totally just distribution than we are now. A second alternative is to revise our account of the aim of compensating for recent wrongs—to say that the point of doing this is not to restore a fully just distribution among the affected parties, but rather only to nullify the effects of one particular set of injustices. A third is to accept Nozick's suggestion that we "view some patterned principles of distributive justice [e.g., egalitarianism or Rawls's difference principle] as rough rules of thumb meant to approximate the general results of applying the principle of rectification of injustice."[1] A fourth is to abandon hope of achieving justice by either compensating or not compensating and simply start afresh by redistributing goods along egalitarian or Rawlsian lines. If their positions can be grounded in either of the latter ways, egalitarians and Rawlsians may hope to rebut the charge that they ignore such historical considerations as entitlement and desert.[2] But as interesting as these issues are, it would be premature for us to consider them further here. The choice among the suggested options arises only if ancient wrongs do call for compensation as strongly as recent ones; and so that claim must be investigated first. The discussion so far has been merely to establish the claim's importance. Having done that, we may now turn to the question of its truth.

II

Intuitively, the effects of ancient wrongs do not seem to call as strongly for compensation as the effects of recent ones. Indeed, the claim that persons deserve compensation even for the effects of wrongs done in biblical times appears to be a reductio of the ideal of compensatory justice. But we shall be wary of intuitions of this sort. It is perfectly possible that they reflect only an awareness of the epistemological difficulty of establishing desert of compensation for ancient wrongs; and if they do, then all the problems limned above will remain untouched. To clarify the force of our intuitions, we must ask whether they can be traced to any deeper source in the notion of compensation itself. Is there anything *about* compensation that reduces the likelihood that ancient wrongs may call for it? More precisely, are there any necessary conditions for desert of compensation that become progressively harder to satisfy over time?

Prima facie, the answer to this question is clearly yes. On its standard interpretation, compensation is the restoration of a good or level of well-being that someone would have enjoyed if he had not been adversely affected by another's wrong act. To enjoy (almost) any good, a person must exist. Hence, it seems to be a necessary condition for X's deserving compensation for the effect of Y's doing A that X would have existed in A's absence. Where A is an act performed during X's lifetime, this requirement presents few problems. However, as A recedes into the past, it becomes progressively more likely that the effects of the non-performance of A will include X's non-existence. If X's currently low level of well-being is due to the defrauding of his great-grandfather in Europe, the very same fraudulent act that reduced X's great-grandfather to poverty may be what caused him to emigrate to America and so to meet X's great-grandmother. Because the prevalence of such stories increases as the relevant wrong act recedes into the past, the probability that the effects of the wrong act will call for compensation must decrease accordingly. And where the wrong act is an ancient one, that probability may approach zero.

This way of explaining our intuitions about ancient wrongs may at first seem quite compelling. But once we scrutinize it more closely, I think doubts must arise. If X cannot deserve compensation for the effects of A unless X would have existed in the absence of A, then not only ancient wrongs, but also the slave trade, the theft of the Indians' land, and many other acts whose effects are often deemed worthy of compensation will turn out to be largely non-compensable. As Lawrence Davis notes, "were we to project 200 years of our country's history in a rectified movie, the cast of characters would surely differ significantly from the existing cast."[3] Moreover, even if we were to accept this conclusion, as Michael Levin has urged that we do,[4] further problems would remain. Even in the case of some wrong acts performed very shortly before their victims' existence (for example, acts of environmental pollution causing massive genetic damage), it seems reasonable to suppose that it is not the victim, but rather some other person, who would exist in the absence of the wrong act. And there are also cases in which wrong acts do not produce but rather preserve the lives of their victims, as when a kidnapping accidentally prevents a child from perishing in the fire that subsequently destroys his home. Since compensation may clearly be deserved in all such cases, it seems that the proposed necessary condition for deserving it will have to be rejected.

If we do wish to reject that necessary condition, there are at least two alternatives available to us. One is to alter our interpretation of the counterfactual presupposed by the standard account of compensation—i.e., to read that counterfactual as requiring not simply that X be better off in the closest possible world in which A is absent, but rather that X be better off in the closest possible world in which A is absent *and X exists*. A more drastic alternative, for which I have argued elsewhere, is to modify the standard view of compensation itself—i.e., to say that compensating X is not necessarily restoring X to the level of well-being that *he* would have occupied in the absence of A, but rather that it is restoring X to the level of well-being that some *related* person or group of persons would have occupied in the absence of A.[5] Although both suggestions obviously require further work,[6] it is clear that neither yields the unacceptable consequences of the simpler account. However, it is also true that neither implies that the probability of desert will decrease over time. Hence, the shift to either of them will call for a different explanation of our intuitions about compensation for ancient wrongs.

III

A more promising way of explaining these intuitions can be extracted from a recent article by David Lyons. In an important discussion of the American Indian claims to land,[7] Lyons argues that property rights are unlikely to be so stable as to persist intact through all sorts of social changes. Even on Nozick's extremely strong conception of property rights, the "Lockean Proviso" implies that such rights must give way when changing conditions bring it about that some individuals are made worse off by (originally legitimate) past acts of acquisition. In particular, this may happen when new arrivals are disadvantaged by their lack of access to established holdings. Because property rights do thus change over time, Lyons argues that today's Indians would probably not have a right to their ancestors' land even if it had *not* been illegitimately taken. Hence, restoring the land or its equivalent to them is unlikely to be warranted as compensation. But if this is true of America's Indians, then it must be true to an even greater degree of the victims of ancient wrongs. If property rights are so unstable, then rights held thousands of years ago would surely not have survived the world's drastic population growth, the industrial revolution, or other massive social changes. Hence, their violation in the distant past may appear to call for no compensation now.

Because wrongful harm and deprivation of property are so closely connected, this approach initially seems to offer a comprehensive solution to our problem. However, here again, a closer examination reveals difficulties. First, even if we grant Lyons's point that changing conditions can alter people's entitlements and that new arrivals may be entitled to fair shares of goods already held, it remains controversial to suppose that these fair shares must be equal ones. If the shares need not be equal, then the instability of property rights may well permit the preservation of substantial legitimate inequalities through both time and inheritance. Moreover, second, even if property rights do fade completely over time, there will still be many current persons whom ancient wrongs have in one way or another prevented from acquiring *new* property rights. Because these new rights would ex hypothesi not have been continuations of any earlier rights, they would not have been affected by the instability of those earlier rights. Hence, the persons who would have held them will apparently still deserve to be compensated. Finally, despite the close connection between property and well-being, there are surely many ways of being harmed that do not involve violations of property rights at all. As many writers on preferential treatment have suggested, a person can also be harmed by being deprived of self-respect, by being rendered less able to compete for opportunities when they arise, and in other related ways. Although these claims must be scrutinized with considerable care, at least some appear clearly true. Moreover, there is no reason to believe that the psychological effects of a wrong act are any less long-lived, or any less likely to be transmitted from generation to generation, than their economic counterparts. It is true that the psychological effects of wrong acts are often themselves the result of property violations; but the case for compensating for them does not appear to rest on this. Because it does not, that case seems compatible with any view of the stability of property rights.

IV

Given these difficulties, Lyons's insight about property does not itself resolve our problem. However, it suggests a further line of inquiry that may. We have seen that because property rights are not necessarily stable, we cannot assume that anyone who retains his property in a world without the initial wrong is entitled to all (or even any) of it in that world. A world in which that particular wrong is rectified may still be morally deficient in other respects. Because of this, the real question is not how much property the victim *does* have in the rectified world, but rather how much he *should* have in it. Moreover, to avoid arbitrariness, we must say something similar about persons whose losses do not involve property as well. If this is not generally recognized, it is probably because deleting the initial wrong act, which is properly only necessary for establishing what the victim should have had, is easily taken to be sufficient for it. But whatever the source of the oversight, the fact that the operative judgments about rectified worlds are themselves normative is a major complication in the theory of compensation; for normative judgments do not always transfer smoothly to the actual world. By spelling out the conditions under which they do not, we may hope finally to clarify the status of ancient wrongs.

Let us begin by considering a normative judgment that plainly does not carry over from a rectified world to our own. Suppose that X, a very promising student, has been discriminatorily barred from entering law school; and suppose further that although X knows he will be able to gain entry in another year, he becomes discouraged and so does not reapply. In a rectified world W_r which lacks the initial discrimination, X studies diligently and eventually becomes a prominent lawyer who enjoys great prestige and a high salary. In that world, we may suppose, X is fully entitled to these goods. However, in the actual world, W_a, the compensation to which X is entitled appears to fall far short of them or their equivalent. Hence, our normative judgment does not fully carry over from W_r to W_a.

Why does our normative judgment about W_r not fully carry over? In part, the answer to this question seems to lie in X's own contribution to the actual course of events. Given more perseverance, X could have avoided most of the effects of the initial wrong act; and this certainly seems relevant to what he should now have. However, quite apart from what X does or does not do in W_a, there is another factor to consider here. Insofar as X's entitlements in W_r stem from what X does in law school and thereafter, they arise through a sequence of actions that X does not perform in W_r until well after the original wrong and that he does not perform in W_a at all. These entitlements are not merely inherited by X in W_r, but rather are created anew by his actions in that world. But if X's actions in W_r are themselves the source of some of his entitlements in that world, then it will make little sense to suppose that those entitlements can exist in an alternative world (that is, the actual one) which lacks the generating actions. To say this would be to hold

that what a person should have may be determined by certain actions
that neither he nor anyone else has actually performed.[8] We are plainly
unwilling to say things like this in other contexts (nobody would say
that a person deserves to be punished simply because he would have
committed a crime if given the opportunity),[9] and they seem to be no
more supportable here.

In view of these considerations, it seems that the transferability of a
person's entitlements from a rectified world to the actual one is limited
by two distinct factors. It is limited, first, by the degree to which one's
actual entitlements have been diminished by one's own omissions in
this world and, second, by the degree to which one's entitlements in a
rectified world are generated anew by one's own actions there. In the
case of X, this means that what transfers is not all of his entitlements
in W_r, but at best his entitlement to the basic opportunity to *acquire*
these entitlements—in this instance, the entitlement to (the value of)
the lost opportunity to attend law school. Of course, the value of this
opportunity is itself determined by the value of the further goods
whose acquisition it makes possible. But the opportunity is clearly not
worth as much as the goods themselves.

This reasoning, if sound, sheds considerable light on the general
concept of compensation. But because the reasoning applies equally to
compensation for ancient *and* recent wrongs, its connection with our
special problem about ancient wrongs is not yet clear. To bring out this
connection, we must explore its implications over time. So let us now
suppose that not just X, but also X's son Z, has benefited from X's
admission to law school in W_r. As a result of X's wealth and status, Z
enjoys certain advantages in W_r that he does not enjoy in W_a. Assuming
that X is fully entitled to his advantages in W_r, and assuming also that
X only confers advantages upon Z in morally legitimate ways (whatever these are), it follows that Z too is fully entitled to his advantages
in W_r. Under these circumstances, Z may well deserve some compensation in W_a. However, because Z's entitlement to his advantages in W_r
stems directly from X's exercise of his own entitlements in that world,
it would be anomalous to suppose that the former entitlements could
transfer in greater proportion than the latter. Moreover, and crucially,
given the principles already adduced, it seems that Z's entitlements in
W_r will have to transfer to W_a in even *smaller* proportion than X's.

The reason for this diminution in transferability is easy to see. Just
as the transferability of X's entitlements is limited by certain facts
about X's omissions in W_a and X's actions in W_r, so too is the transferability of Z's entitlements limited by similar facts about Z's omissions
in W_a and Z's actions in W_r. More specifically, the transferability of Z's
entitlements is also limited by Z's own failure to make the most of his

opportunities in W_a, and by the degree to which Z's entitlements in W_r have arisen through his use of his own special opportunities there. Of course, the opportunities available to Z in W_r and W_a may be very different from the opportunity to attend law school; but this difference is hardly a relevant one. Whether Z's advantages in W_r and W_a take the form of wealth, political power, special skills or abilities, or simply self-confidence, the fact remains that they are, inter alia, potential opportunities for him to acquire further entitlements. Because of this, the way they contribute to his total entitlements in these worlds must continue to affect the degree to which his entitlements in W_r can transfer to W_a.

Once all of this is made clear, the outline of a general solution to our problem about ancient wrongs should begin to emerge. Because the transferability of Z's entitlements is diminished twice over by the contribution of actions performed in W_r and omitted in W_a, while that of X's entitlements is diminished only once by this contribution, it follows that Z is likely to deserve proportionately less compensation for the effects of the original wrong than X; and Z's offspring, if any, will deserve proportionately less compensation still. Moreover, since few original entitlements are preserved intact over succeeding generations (quite apart from any instability of property rights, the consumption of goods and the natural non-inheritability of many entitlements must each take a large toll), the progressive diminution in the transferability of entitlements from W_r to W_a must be absolute, not just proportional. But if the transferability of entitlements from rectified worlds does decrease with every generation, then over the course of very many generations, any such transferability can be expected to become vanishingly small. Where the initial wrong was done many hundreds of years ago, almost all of the difference between the victim's entitlements in the actual world and his entitlements in the rectified world can be expected to stem from the actions of various intervening agents in the two alternative worlds. Little or none of it will be the automatic effect of the initial wrong act itself. Since compensation is warranted only for disparities in entitlements that *are* the automatic effect of the initial wrong act, this means that there will be little or nothing left to compensate for.

V

This approach to the problem posed by ancient wrongs is not dissimilar to the one extracted from Lyons's discussion. Like Lyons, I have argued that a proper appreciation of the entitlements upon which claims to compensation are based suggests that these claims must fade with time. However, whereas Lyons argued that the entitlement to property itself fades with time, I have held instead that it is the transferability of that and other entitlements from rectified worlds to the actual one that becomes progressively weaker. By thus relocating the basic instability, we avoid the objections that the analysis of property rights is controversial, that some claims to compensation do not view the right to the lost property as continually held in a rectified world, and that other claims to compensation do not involve property at all. But although our account is not open to these objections, it may seem to invite others just as serious. More specifically, it may seem that our presupposition that entitlements are historically transmitted is itself controversial, that our distinction between newly generated and continuing entitlements is problematical, and that we have failed to account satisfactorily for the status of wrongs that are neither recent nor ancient. In this final section, I shall consider each of these objections in its turn.

The first objection, that the historical transmission of entitlements is as controversial as any analysis of property, is easily answered. Put briefly, the answer is that this presupposition *is* controversial, but that unlike any special view of property rights, it is internal to the very notion of compensation that generates our problem. If entitlements were never historically transmitted—if a person's entitlements at a given time were never derived from the prior entitlements of others— then someone like Z would not be entitled to any special advantages in W_r and so would not deserve any compensation in W_a. Moreover, although it is less obvious, the same point holds even if Z is only minimally well off in W_r, but is extremely disadvantaged in W_a. It may seem, in that case, that Z's entitlements in W_r are independent of X's—that Z, like everyone else in W_r, is entitled to a certain decent minimum no matter what X was entitled to or did in the past. But even if this is so, it cannot form the basis for compensating Z for the effects of the initial wrong act; for if Z *is* absolutely entitled to such a minimum in W_r, then he will also be absolutely entitled to it in W_a, and so the original wrong act will drop out as irrelevant.

Given these considerations, some form of historical transmission of entitlements is plainly presupposed by any view permitting compensation for a variety of prenatal (and so a fortiori ancient) wrongs.[10] But just because of this, there may seem to be a problem with our central distinction between continuing and newly produced entitlements. This distinction appeared plausible enough when we first considered X's entitlements in W_r. However, once we take seriously the fact that people can transmit, confer, and waive their entitlements, the distinction seems to blur. When a parent confers advantages upon his children by educating or bequeathing wealth to them, the entitlements acquired are both related to earlier ones *and* the product of new generating actions. Moreover, something similar may be said to hold even when someone merely retains his own entitlement to property; for he too is acting at least in the sense that he is refraining from transferring or waiving that entitlement. Because human actions and omissions are thus crucial in perpetuating so many entitlements, our premise that this role cancels transferability from rectified worlds may well appear too strong. Given this premise, it seems to follow that not only ancient wrongs, but also recent ones, such as systematic racial discrimination, and perhaps even fresh property crimes, are largely non-compensable.

These worries are serious ones and would require careful consideration in any full account of compensation. Here, however, I shall only outline what I take to be the correct response to them. Put briefly, my response is that the transferability of entitlements from rectified worlds should be viewed as disrupted not by *all* intervening acts or omissions in those worlds, but rather only by those acts or omissions that alter previously established structures of entitlements. When an entitlement is already established in a rectified world and is naturally stable over a period of time, its retention during that period is totally explainable in terms of its initial acquisition. In this case, the entitlement need not be attributed to any further doings of the agent; and so those doings seem irrelevant to the entitlement's transferability to the actual world. Moreover, assuming the legitimacy of inheritance, something similar may well hold for advantages that are transmitted to one's offspring; for here again, the resulting entitlements can be viewed as natural continuations of initial ancestral acts of acquisition. Of course, the principle of the conservation of entitlements that underlies these remarks would require considerable elaboration to be fully convincing. But something like it does seem initially plausible, and anything along these lines will nicely preserve the conclusion that desert of compensation is not entirely momentary and evanescent.

A final difficulty remains. Our argument has been that desert of compensation fades gradually over time and that ancient wrongs therefore call for no significant amounts of compensation. But even if this is correct, it does not dispose of the vast intermediate class of wrongs that are not ancient, but were still done one or more generations ago. Since the process we have described is gradual, our account suggests that such wrongs do call for some compensation, although not as much as comparable recent ones. But if this is so, then our account may seem at once too strong and too weak. The account may seem too strong because it will classify as intermediate even the wrongs done to blacks and Indians—wrongs that appear to be among our paradigms of full compensability. However, the account may also seem too weak, since it implies that very many partially compensable wrongs remain undiscovered and that our problem of how to act justly in the face of incurable ignorance is therefore unresolved. Because any response to one aspect of this objection will only aggravate the other, the difficulty seems intractable.

But this dilemma is surely overdrawn. On the side of the claims of blacks and Indians, it may first be said that even if the initial wrongs to these persons do go back several centuries, the real source of their claims to compensation may lie elsewhere. As Lyons notes, the truly compensable wrong done to the Indians may be not the initial appropriation of their land, but rather the more recent acts of discrimination and neglect that grew out of this; and the same may hold, mutatis mutandis, for the truly compensable wrongs done to blacks.[11] Moreover, even if the compensable wrongs to blacks and Indians do go back a number of generations, they may be highly atypical of other wrongs of that period. We have seen that one reason that compensability fades over time is that victims neglect reasonable opportunities to acquire equivalent entitlements; and so if slavery or the appropriation of Indian lands have made it specially difficult for their victims to recoup their lost entitlements, then these wrongs may call for far more compensation than others of similar vintage. Here our earlier results provide a natural framework for further inquiry. Finally, even if these suggestions do not establish full compensability for blacks and Indians, they do at least promise very substantial compensation for them; and this is perhaps all that is needed to satisfy our intuitions on the matter.

The other horn of our dilemma—that this account leaves untouched our incurable ignorance about past compensable wrongs—is also overstated. The account does leave us unable to diagnose more than a small fraction of the past wrongs requiring compensation; but by itself, this only implies that we cannot right all of history's wrongs. The deeper worry, that in rectifying one injustice we may only be reverting to another, is at least mitigated by the fact that the most significant period of history from the standpoint of compensation is also the best known. Given this fact, the likelihood that our compensatory efforts will make things better rather than worse is greatly increased. If this solution is less precise than we might wish, it is perhaps the best that we have a right to expect.

Notes

1. Robert Nozick, *Anarchy, State, and Utopia* (New York: Basic Books, 1974), 231.

2. For development of this charge as it pertains to entitlement, see Nozick, *Anarchy, State, and Utopia*, chap. 7. For discussion involving desert, see George Sher, "Effort, Ability, and Personal Desert," *Philosophy and Public Affairs* 8, no. 4 (Summer 1979): 361–76. A modified version of that essay appears as chapter 5 of this volume.

3. Lawrence Davis, "Comments on Nozick's Entitlement Theory," *Journal of Philosophy* 73, no. 21 (December 2, 1976): 842.

4. Michael Levin, "Reverse Discrimination, Shackled Runners, and Personal Identity," *Philosophical Studies* 37, no. 2 (February 1980): 139–49.

5. George Sher, "Compensation and Transworld Personal Identity," *Monist* 62, no. 3 (July 1979): 378–91; chapter 2 of this volume.

6. Although I have presented them as alternatives, the two suggestions need not be viewed as mutually exclusive. Indeed, the most promising approach appears to be to combine them. The first suggestion appears the more natural in those cases where there are many close alternative worlds that lack the initial wrong act but contain the victim himself, while the second appears indispensable in those instances where the initial wrong is so intimately associated with the victim's existence that there is no such world.

7. David Lyons, "The New Indian Claims and the Original Rights to Land," *Social Theory and Practice* 4, no. 3 (Fall 1977): 249–72.

8. This point is discussed in a more limited context in George Sher, "Justifying Reverse Discrimination in Employment," *Philosophy and Public Affairs* 4, no. 2 (Winter 1975): 166ff. That essay is reprinted as chapter 3 of this volume.

9. For discussion, see Thomas Nagel, "Moral Luck," in his *Mortal Questions* (Cambridge: Cambridge University Press, 1979), 24–38.

10. Thus, compensation is in one sense a strongly conservative notion. One can consistently advocate redistributive measures on compensatory grounds or on non-historical consequentialist grounds, but not, I think, on both grounds together.

11. Lyons, "The New Indian Claims," see esp. 268–71. See also Boris Bittker, *The Case for Black Reparations* (New York: Random House, 1973), chap. 2.

2

Compensation and Transworld Personal Identity

A natural way of viewing compensation is to see it as the restoration of a good or level of well-being that someone would have enjoyed if he had not been adversely affected by the act of another. This view underlies Nozick's assertion that "something fully compensates . . . person X for Y's action A if X is no worse off receiving it, Y having done A, than X would have been without receiving it if Y had not done A";[1] and it has been held by many others as well. Because the notion that compensation is the restoration of a good that a person would have had but for the act of another is so pervasive, I shall refer to it as the *official view* of compensation. One noteworthy feature of the official view is the ease with which it allows compensation to be justified in particular cases. If compensation is just the restoration of a good that one would have had if the ordinary course of things had not been disrupted, then to provide a prima facie justification of it, one need only argue that the natural course of things should not have been disrupted in the first place.

   Although it is both plausible and extremely pervasive, the official view of compensation raises a difficulty that has so far gone largely unnoticed.[2] According to the official view, a necessary condition for X's deserving compensation for Y's doing A is that X would have been better off if A had not been done. The statement that X would have been better off if A had not been done is a counterfactual which compares X's level of well-being in the actual world with his level of well-being in some alternative possible world. Such a comparison can only be made if X himself exists in both alternative worlds. However, if X has been harmed in a way that affects him physically or psychologically—if he has been rendered bitter by unjust imprisonment, dull-witted by poisoning, or paraplegic by assault—then the X who exists

29

in the actual world may be very dissimilar to any person who exists in the alternative world in which the harmful act has not been performed. When such harm is at issue, the preservation of X's identity across possible worlds surely cannot be taken for granted.

It is intuitively clear that a person who has been changed by unjust imprisonment, poisoning, or paralysis can still deserve compensation for the harm he has undergone. Because our intuitions about these and related cases are so firm, it seems safe to assume that no theory of compensation that conflicts with them can possibly be correct. More specifically, if the official view of compensation systematically requires impossible identifications in cases where our intuitions tell us that compensation is deserved, it is the official view rather than the intuitions that will have to go. In the present paper, I shall attempt to decide whether or not this is so. In the initial section, I will examine the identifications required by the official view in light of the existing literature on modality and its metaphysics. In the second section, I will raise a number of questions about the one substantive criterion of transworld personal identity that seems to offer the official view a fighting chance of success. In the final section, I will attempt to draw some conclusions from the official view's ultimate failure.

I

The recent literature on the metaphysics of modality contains little explicit discussion of the identities of persons across possible worlds. However, many philosophers have discussed the more general problem of the identities of *objects* across possible worlds, and it is reasonable to expect their accounts to apply to the transworld identity of persons inter alia. Generally speaking, the philosophers who have tried to make sense of transworld identity claims have taken three main approaches. One position, held by Saul Kripke and Alvin Plantinga, is that transworld identity claims assert a genuine identity relation and that this identity relation is established by stipulation and not by any criterion.[3] A second approach, elaborated by David Lewis, attempts to replace the strict identity relation with a different relation, the "counterpart" relation, which is defined in terms of similarity.[4] A third suggestion, implicit in some of Kripke's remarks and discussed by J. L. Mackie, is that transworld identity depends on joint continuity with single earlier objects.[5] Prima facie, each of these accounts appears to offer a reasonable prospect for the identifications required by the official view of compensation.[6] However, a closer inspection reveals that the situation is a good deal less hopeful than this.

To see the problem more clearly, let us first consider the account of transworld identity proposed by Kripke and Plantinga. In independent discussions, both of these philosophers have argued that when we say an object O might have had a property P which it lacks in the actual world, we do not first find a possible world in which something has P and then establish that this something is O. Instead, as long as P is compatible with all of O's essential properties, we simply stipulate a world in which O *itself* has P. Since this possible world is initially speci-fied as containing O, its very specification guarantees the identity of the appropriate object in it with the O of the actual world. Because of this, no questions about identity criteria need even arise. The idea that we establish transworld identity by scrutinizing pre-existing possible worlds through a kind of imaginary telescope is incorrect in principle.

There is clearly something right about the suggestion that trans-world identity is established stipulatively. When we say that Y might not have done A, or that certain consequences would have ensued if Y hadn't done A, our assertion can indeed be viewed as immediately determining a world in which Y himself does not do A. In such con-texts, questions about identity criteria do not even seem to arise. How-ever, it may be wondered whether such questions can also be avoided when the relevant world is determined by a counterfactual with a name or definition description in its *consequent* as well as, or instead of, its antecedent. To see why such counterfactuals pose a special problem, consider again the statement that X would have been better off if Y had not done A. If the stipulative approach is to succeed, this counterfac-tual will have to stipulate a world in which Y himself refrains from doing A, and also in which X himself is better off than he is in the actual world. Furthermore, if the counterfactual is to be non-trivial, the stipulated world must be reasonably close to the actual world—the actual world's causal laws, or laws close to them, must continue to hold in it. However, the combination of Y himself refraining from doing A and the actual world's causal laws continuing to hold may ensure that the only persons who can exist in the stipulated world are ones who differ radically from the actual X in physical makeup, beliefs, desires, moral character, etc. If these differences are drastic enough, then the attempt to stipulate a world in which X himself is better off than he is in the actual world may simply fail.[7] Given this possibility, our initial question of what determines personal identity across possible worlds will reappear as the question of which conditions must prevail in order for the desired stipulation to succeed. Kripke and Plantinga would un-doubtedly insist that we often know this intuitively; but even so, our intuitive beliefs will hardly count as knowledge if they do not them-selves reflect some consistent underlying principle or principles. Since these principles may or may not permit all the identifications that are required by the official view of compensation, the Kripke-Plantinga stipulative approach does not resolve, but only postpones, the question of the official view's viability.

These considerations show that we cannot easily avoid the need to specify a substantive set of conditions under which possible entities are identical to actual ones. These conditions must presumably be couched in terms of one or another relationship between the entities to be identified. Because the relations that hold most straightforwardly between possible and actual entities are similarity relations, it is extremely tempting to suppose that a possible entity's identity to an actual one is determined by the two entities' degree of similarity. However, this temptation is a dangerous one; for, as David Lewis has pointed out, the logic of similarity is decisively different from that of identity. For one thing, identity is transitive while similarity is not; for another, an entity in w_1 can be equally similar to each of two different entities in w_2, but can be identical to only one of them.[8] For these and other reasons, Lewis has argued that what appear to be transworld identity statements are not really identity statements at all. Instead, they are best interpreted as ascribing only a different relation, the 'counterpart' relation, to the alternative entities in question.

Although Lewis's dismissal of strict identity across possible worlds is obviously controversial, we need not here discuss the controversy it has engendered. Instead, our more immediate problem is that, as it is stated, Lewis's account is not detailed enough to allow us to assess the identifications that the official view requires. To permit an evaluation of those identifications, Lewis's account would have to specify precisely the kind of similarity that constitutes the counterpart relation for persons; and yet Lewis's remarks about that relation have a studied vagueness which precludes this. He characterizes the relevant similarities only as ones that pertain to "personhood and personal traits";[9] and of two competing transworld identity claims, he remarks that "I want to say either—though perhaps not both in the same breath—depending on which respects of comparison are foremost in my mind."[10] From the perspective of his own objectives, Lewis's above-the-fray attitude towards the details of the personal counterpart relation is entirely legitimate; but from the more parochial perspective of someone interested in the official view of compensation, a permanent refusal to take sides on this issue would be disastrous. If the personal counterpart relation were tied to no single determinate respect of similarity, then there would be no single determinate answer to the question of whether any given person is better off in any alternative world, and so also no single determinate answer to the question of whether any particular person deserves compensation.

In light of these considerations, it is clear that Lewis's account can help the official view only if it is supplemented by a single and well-motivated interpretation of the personal counterpart relation. Prima facie, the most obvious way of interpreting that relation is in terms of some combination of similarities of physical structure, beliefs, desires, and character traits. These are the characteristics that are most often thought pertinent to personal identity through time, and so they may naturally seem to be the ones that are pertinent to transworld personal identity as well. However, as natural as this suggestion appears, it does not support, but rather undercuts, the official view of compensation. We have already noted that acts that lead to imprisonment, poisoning, or trauma can render their victims physically or psychologically dissimilar to any persons in the relevant alternative world, and this consequence will be even more pronounced when the acts in question have still more drastic and global effects. If the truth-conditions of the counterfactuals required for desert of compensation did include the existence of physically or psychologically similar alternative persons, then the relevant counterfactuals would be false whenever the victim had undergone a drastic harm of this sort. Because of this, the official view would entail that such a victim could never deserve compensation. Since this consequence is so counterintuitive, it would simply be a reductio of the views that led to it. Thus, failing a plausible alternative interpretation of the personal counterpart relation, Lewis's approach will not be compatible with the official view of compensation.

One further approach to transworld personal identity remains to be examined. We have already noted that any possible world that is relevant to the counterfactual "X would have been better off if Y had not done A" must be one whose causal laws after the time of A (call this time m) coincide with those of the actual world. To this we may now add that the relevant world must also be one whose *history* coincides with that of the actual world *prior* to m. What the counterfactual in question asserts is plainly that X would have been better off if Y had not done A, *given the world as it was until m*. When this implication is brought to light, it becomes clear that we are talking about an alternative world w which coincides with the actual world prior to m, diverges from it with respect to A's absence at m, and thereafter diverges from it in other ways as well as the effects of A's absence progressively make themselves felt. Because w's causal laws are just those of the actual world, its post-m inhabitants must include many persons who have developed from pre-m persons through just the sort of process— whatever it is—that establishes personal identity through time. In particular, the post-*m* *w* may well contain someone who has developed in this way from the pre-*m* X. If someone in *w* has so developed from the pre-*m* X, he will stand in a uniquely close, if indirect, relation to the current actual X; for the latter will ex hypothesi also have developed in this way from the pre-*m* X, and so both persons will be transtemporally identical to a single earlier one. Once we look at the situation in this way, we are led quite naturally to a new way of understanding personal identity across possible worlds. Put in general form, the suggestion is that a person in one possible world is identical to a person in another whenever the two possible worlds are alternative developments, or "branches," of what was initially a single world, and both persons are transtemporally identical to one who existed in the single world before the branching. This branching approach to transworld personal identity is suggested by some of Kripke's remarks about the essentiality of a thing's origins and has been developed further by Mackie.[11]

The branching approach appears to offer us a number of considerable advantages. For one thing, although it has been introduced as a third possible approach to transworld personal identity, it can be viewed not as a competitor, but rather as a natural complement, to the accounts considered above. The branching account can be read as telling us what we stipulate when we stipulate transworld personal identity, or as explicating the kind of similarity that goes to make up the personal counterpart relation. When considered as an explication of the personal counterpart relation, it offers a clear alternative to the "personal characteristics" reading considered above. When considered independently, it offers a way of understanding transworld identity claims without invoking any relation weaker than strict identity. On either reading, it has considerable intuitive appeal. In light of this, its connection with the official view of compensation is a matter of more than incidental interest.

Prima facie, the branching criterion appears made to order to handle the identifications the official view requires. Even when it is applied to cases in which persons have been drastically changed by physical or mental harm—the sorts of cases that have seemed to pose the greatest difficulty for the official view—the branching account can accommodate the required identifications without any strain. According to it, the embittered victim of an unjust prison sentence will be identical to a happier unimprisoned person in the relevant alternative world if and only if the two persons are transtemporally identical to a single pre-branching person; and so too, mutatis mutandis, for persons who have been rendered dull-witted by poisoning, paraplegic by assault, etc. In no case will the required identification be ruled out by the dissimilarity of the alternative persons to be identified; for the branching criterion can tolerate *any* amount of post-branching dissimilarity as long as it is the result of diverging paths of development from a single pre-branching person.

Of all the approaches to transworld personal identity that we have considered, only the branching account is both independently plausible and prima facie compatible with the official view of compensation. Because of this, it is plainly the branching account that offers the official view its greatest chance of survival. Nevertheless, on closer inspection, it is far from clear that even adoption of the branching account can save the official view. Despite its success in accounting for the most obvious identifications required by the official view, the branching account runs into trouble when we cast our nets a bit more widely.

II

The official view of compensation says that X deserves compensation for A only if X is better off in an alternative world in which A is not performed. The branching account of transworld personal identity says that X is better off in a world in which A is not performed if and only if the actual X and a better-off inhabitant of the A-less world are both transtemporally identical to a single earlier person. Letting "branching relation" stand for the relation of joint transtemporal identity to a single earlier person, we can sum this up by saying that, on the combined account now under consideration, X deserves compensation for A only if he stands in the branching relation to some better-off inhabitant of the relevant A-less world.

This combined account works well enough as long as A is performed after X has begun to exist as a person. However, suppose now that A is performed *before* X begins to exist as a person. In such a case, any A-less world will have to diverge from the actual world before X begins to exist as a person as well. Because of this, the X who subsequently begins to exist in the actual world will be unable to stand in the branching relation to any inhabitant of the relevant A-less world. A fortiori, X will be unable to stand in the branching relation to any *better-off* inhabitant of the relevant A-less world. Since X's standing in the branching relation to such a person is ex hypothesi necessary for his deserving compensation, it follows that X will here be unable to deserve compensation for any harm that is done to him by A.

Our intuitions tell us that some acts which are performed before their victims begin to exist as persons may clearly call for compensation nevertheless. Although nothing turns on our acceptance of any particular instance of this, three cases that many people would accept as examples are: (a) the European annexation of the North American continent which eventually led to the plight of the American Indians; (b) the careless polluting of the environment which eventually leads to illness and financial loss; and (c) the administration of untested drugs to women whose offspring later become ill as a result.[12] Because the intuition that the timing of a harmful act is irrelevant to its victim's desert of compensation is so firm, that intuition will again simply override any account of compensation that conflicts with it. In light of this, our combined account will only be acceptable if its apparent conflict with the intuition can somehow be resolved. To resolve the conflict, one might pursue either of two strategies. One strategy is to argue that, despite appearances, the moment of branching does not precede the victim's existence in any relevant case. Another is to recast the branching relation so that it permits transworld identifications even when the moment of branching *does* precede the victim's existence. Let us now examine each of these strategies in some detail.

The branching account was introduced as an interpretation of the transworld identity claims implicit in the counterfactuals that the official view sees as necessary for compensation. Because of this, it is apparently these counterfactuals that determine when the relevant alternative worlds may begin. As long as the counterfactual that is appropriate to X's desert of compensation is one that asserts that X would have been better off if Y had not done A, there will always be cases in which the moment of branching precedes the victim's existence. However, the appropriateness of this sort of counterfactual to X's desert of compensation may itself be called into question. Strictly speaking, it is not A itself, but rather the harm that Y's doing A has caused to X, that compensation for X is aimed at setting right. Because of this, the genuinely appropriate counterfactual may be thought to be not "X would have been better off if Y had not done A," but rather "X would have been better off if he had not been *harmed* by Y's doing A." If it is the latter counterfactual that is appropriate to X's desert, then the moment of branching will be determined not by the time of A, but rather by the time of A's harmful effect on X. Since X cannot be harmed by A until he exists, this adjustment will ensure that the moment of branching can never precede the moment at which the victim begins to exist.

The suggestion that we might resolve our difficulty by pitching the moment of branching to the time of the harm rather than the time of the harmful act is an intuitively attractive one. However, a closer look reveals a serious difficulty. Put briefly, the problem is that even if the suggestion does ensure that the victim exists in *some* form when the branching occurs, it does *not* ensure that he then exists *as a person*. This problem emerges clearly when we consider a case in which someone is permanently harmed while still *in utero*. In such a case, the harm may be irreversibly done a number of months before the victim's birth. If it is, the moment of branching will occur when the victim is still a fetus in an early stage of development. Such a fetus is highly unlikely to have a coherent set of beliefs, desires, or memories, and so is also unlikely to be capable of the degree of psychological continuity with later person-stages that is commonly thought necessary for transtemporal personal identity. Because the fetus is thus incapable of transtemporal personal identity to any later person, the person into whom it subsequently develops will not stand in the branching relation to anyone in the relevant alternative world. On the combination of accounts we are considering, he will therefore be unable to deserve compensation. Since in fact a person *may* deserve compensation for a permanent injury inflicted before his birth, the proposed adjustment will remain unable to capture our intuitions in at least one important class of cases.

Although this objection is a formidable one, it may seem somewhat less than decisive. One might try to avoid it by arguing either that transtemporal personal identity depends entirely on bodily continuity through time, or else that fetuses have enough psychological structure to permit at least an attenuated form of psychological continuity with later person-stages. However, even if one or another of these arguments were correct, there would remain a further and more conclusive objection to the claim that the crucial counterfactual is one whose antecedent mentions the victim's injury rather than one that mentions the act that led to it. Put simply, the objection is that, in the current context, the former counterfactual is every bit as problematical as the latter.

To bring this objection into focus, let us consider a particular case in which a harmful act precedes its victim's existence. Suppose that Y introduces a toxic substance into the food supply at t_0, that X comes into existence at t_1, and that X consumes the toxic substance and is paralyzed by it at t_2. In this case, the two counterfactuals whose relevance to X's desert of compensation is at issue are

C1: X would have been better off if Y had not poisoned the food supply at t_0; and

C2: X would have been better off if he had not been paralyzed by poison at t_2.

Of these counterfactuals, C2 is plainly unthreatening to the official view of compensation. Let us therefore grant that it, or something like it, must be true in order for X to deserve compensation. However, even so, it will hardly be possible for C2 to be the *only* statement that must be true in order for X to deserve compensation. It is uncontroversial that not every sequence of events that leads to X's being paralyzed will call for his subsequent compensation. He would plainly *not* deserve to be compensated if the poison that paralyzed him had entered the food supply through some unavoidable natural process rather than through any human act or omission. Because this is so, C2 will only support X's desert of compensation if it is supplemented by the statement that X's paralysis at t_2 is caused by (something like) Y's poisoning the food supply at t_0. However, the latter causal statement—that X's paralysis is caused by Y's poisoning the food supply—is itself one that commits us to a further counterfactual, namely that X would *not* have been paralyzed if Y had *not* poisoned the food supply. Once this further counterfactual is brought into the open, our initial assumption that C2 determines a separate branching world is called into question; for the point of conjoining the new counterfactual with C2 is plainly not to describe events in two distinct possible worlds, but rather to describe a single alternative world in which Y does not poison the food supply, X is not paralyzed, and X is consequently better off than he is in the actual world. Since any such alternative world must diverge from the actual world no later than Y's act, it follows that in the current context, the world relevant to C2 does not diverge from the actual world at t_2, but rather diverges from it at the earlier moment t_0. Because this is so, the appeal to C2 appears merely to re-raise in altered form all the difficulties originally associated with C1.

These considerations show that we are unlikely to gain any ground by denying that the moment of branching can precede the victim's existence. But what, now, of the alternative strategy of recasting the branching relation in a way that makes the moment of branching insignificant? To see what such a strategy would involve, let us again consider the case in which Y poisons the food supply and thus paralyzes X. Our problem in this case is that the relevant alternative world diverges from the actual world before X begins to exist. Because this is so, the identity of the actual X and a better-off person in the alternative world cannot be determined by the two persons' joint transtemporal identity to a single earlier person. If any branching relation is to hold between them, it must consist rather of the fact that both persons are offspring of parents who are *themselves* jointly identical to single pre-branching persons. However, while this sort of relationship may indeed be necessary for identity when branching precedes conception, it clearly cannot be sufficient for it; for some offspring of parents who are identical across possible worlds are not themselves identical, but rather are brothers or sisters. To eliminate this possibility, we need to require that the persons to be identified be the *same* offspring of the same parents—a requirement that obviously calls for a further criterion of sameness in the offspring of identical parents. Because the most basic feature of these offspring is their genetic makeup, the most plausible way to explain their sameness is to say that they are identical if and only if they share a common genotype. If this suggestion is correct, then we will be able to broaden the branching account by saying that persons are identical across possible worlds that diverged before they existed as persons if and only if they share the same genotypes at conception, their parents shared the same genotypes at their conception, and those parents were in turn produced by . . . parents with identical pre-branching stages.

Although something like this expanded version of the branching account represents the last best hope of the official view of compensation, I do not think it is ultimately any more successful in saving that view than its simpler predecessor. Once again, the essential problem is that it remains possible to envision cases in which our intuitions dictate compensation, but where the proposed criterion does not allow us to make sense of the required identifications. One kind of troublesome case involves the phenomenon of identical twins: offspring of the same parents who share the same genetic structure. Suppose, for example, that a woman is given a drug that causes both of the twins that she subsequently conceives to suffer a measure of brain damage; and suppose further that if she had *not* been given the drug, then only *one* of her twins would have suffered the damage. In such a case, our intuitions tell us that as least one twin deserves to be compensated; but we run into trouble when we try to make sense of the claim that either twin is better off in an alternative world in which the drug is not administered. Because that alternative world has diverged from the actual world before the twins were conceived, any attempt to identify either twin with a better-off person in it will have to turn on the fact that the persons to be identified share a common genotype. However, since the alternative world contains *two* persons with the relevant genotype, any attempt to identify either actual twin with any single inhabitant of it will fail. Even if we adopt Lewis's strategy of replacing identity with a looser counterpart relation, each actual twin will have one counterpart who *is* better off than he is, but another who is not. Because of this, our combined account will not be capable of yielding any decisive reading as to whether either twin deserves compensation.

This case undoubtedly poses an embarrassment for the combination of views under consideration. However, it may be suspected that the difficulty is merely a special instance of a more general problem about qualitatively similar individuals, and so should not be held against any one particular combination of views. To forestall this objection, let us consider one further counterexample, this one involving the different phenomenon of genetic drift over a number of generations. Imagine that a development corporation has concealed the fact that one of its houses is built on a dump for nuclear waste and that residual radiation from the waste induces a progressive series of mutations in a family living in the house. If the guilty corporation still exists when a congenitally deformed child is born in the family's fourth generation, our intuition is surely that the child may deserve compensation from it. However, the official view of compensation asserts that the child can only deserve to be compensated if it is identical to a better-off person in the alternative world in which the initial deception is absent; and the expanded branching criterion asserts that the child is identical to a better-off person in that world only if the two persons share a common genotype and set of ancestral genotypes. The child's sharing a common genotype and set of ancestral genotypes with a better-off person in the alternative world is ruled out by the fact that the exposure responsible for the child's genotype and ancestral genotypes (and thus also for its low level of well-being) is absent from the alternative world. Because this is so, the views under consideration will again leave us unable to make the required identification, and so also unable to account for the intuition that compensation is deserved.

III

The foregoing arguments do not constitute a knock-down refutation of the official view of compensation. Despite what has been said, it remains conceivable that someone might rescue the official view by further amending one of the familiar approaches to transworld identity, by developing some new approach, or by interpreting the relevant counterfactuals in a way that avoids the possible worlds framework altogether. Nevertheless, the systematic and recurrent nature of the difficulty raises the strong suspicion that any such maneuver would merely re-raise the same problem in yet another guise. In light of this, we may well wonder what alternative views of compensation are possible.

To clarify the range of possible answers to this question, we may begin by reconsidering the genetic damage case just discussed. In that case, the defective child was felt to deserve compensation despite the fact that he could not have existed if the initial wrong had been absent. What determined his desert of compensation was evidently not the fact that he would have been better off in the wrong's absence, but rather the simpler fact that the wrong caused him to exist at a level of well-being that falls below some crucial minimum. Prima facie, the crucial level may appear to be simply that of the average person or the average member of the child's society. However, I think we would be inclined to say that the child was less deserving of compensation if defects of the sort with which he was born occurred naturally and regularly in his family—or even if they *would* occur regularly among the alternative persons who might have existed in his place. This suggests that the collection of persons whose levels of well-being are pertinent to the child's desert of compensation is wider in one direction, but narrower in another, than it first appears to be. It is wider because it evidently includes some persons who do not actually exist, but would exist under other circumstances. It is narrower because it does not include all members of the victim's society, but only the members of some more circumscribed familial group. One possibility here is that the crucial group consists of all the descendants of the victim's antecedents who would have existed if the act that harmed him had not been performed; but other, still more sensitive ways of narrowing the circle are undoubtedly possible.

However we decide which collection of actual or possible persons should determine the level of well-being that is pertinent to the defective child's desert of compensation, two more general questions about compensation will remain. The first question concerns the scope of the "averaging" approach just sketched. We seem forced to take this approach in some instances; but it is much less clear that we should take it in every instance. It seems counterintuitive to consider how well off *other* persons would have been under alternative circumstances in cases where we can say how well off the victim himself would have been; and yet to restrict our attention to the victim's own alternative level of well-being in such cases would be to allow a deep ambiguity to infect the notion of compensation. The second question concerns the justification of compensation in cases where the averaging approach is in effect. As I remarked at the outset, it is easy to see why we should compensate as long as compensation is viewed as the restoration of a level of well-being that the victim should have had in the first place. However, it is far less easy to see why we should compensate someone when doing so would only elevate him to the level that certain *other* persons would (or should) have had. These questions go well beyond the questions raised by the official view of compensation. To the extent that they do, the notion of compensation is both more difficult and more interesting than has generally been supposed.

Notes

1. Robert Nozick, *Anarchy, State, and Utopia* (New York: Basic Books, 1974), 57.

2. To my knowledge, the only philosopher who has raised this question at all is Michael Levin. I was originally led to think about the problem by reading an unpublished draft of his paper "Reverse Discrimination, Shackled Runners, and Personal Identity," *Philosophical Studies* 37, no. 2 (February 1980): 139–49. In his more recent work, Levin has independently pursued a number of the lines suggested here.

3. Saul Kripke, "Naming and Necessity," in *Semantics of Natural Languages*, eds. Donald Davidson and Gilbert Harman (Dordrecht, Holland: Reidel, 1972), 253–355; and Alvin Plantinga, *The Nature of Necessity* (London: Oxford, 1974).

4. Lewis's general approach to transworld personal identity is set forth in "Counterpart Theory and Quantified Modal Logic," *Journal of Philosophy* 65, no. 5 (March 7, 1968): 113–26; and *Counterfactuals* (Cambridge: Harvard University Press, 1973). The application of this approach to persons is discussed in his "Counterparts of Persons and Their Bodies," *Journal of Philosophy* 68, no. 7 (April 8, 1971): 203–11.

5. Kripke, "Naming and Necessity"; and J. L. Mackie, "*De* What *Re* Is *De Re* Modality?" *Journal of Philosophy* 71, no. 16 (September 19, 1974): 551–61.

6. On the face of it, it may appear that a fourth approach to transworld identity is possible. Such identity, it may be said, can be established by appealing to whichever properties belong to an object, and only to it, in every possible world—that is, by appealing to those properties that Plantinga has called the object's *essence*. This seems to be what Leonard Linsky has in mind when he suggests that "perhaps . . . objects can be identified across possible worlds by some of their essential properties" (Leonard Linsky, "Reference, Essentialism, and Modality," *Journal of Philosophy* 66, no. 20 [October 16, 1969]: 698). However, it seems to me that there is less to this suggestion than meets the eye; for any questions that we have about when a possible entity is identical to an actual one will merely reappear as questions about which properties comprise the actual entity's essence.

7. Levin, "Reverse Discrimination," makes a similar point.

8. Lewis, "Counterpart Theory," 115–16.

9. Lewis, "Counterparts of Persons and Their Bodies," 208.

10. Lewis, *Counterfactuals*, 41.

11. Although Mackie agrees that the branching approach is the one we actually take, he does not agree that it reflects any ultimate truth about the entities under consideration. Instead, Mackie views our acceptance of the branching approach as itself explainable in terms of our "libertarian view of causal possibilities, conjoined with our view of the past as fixed" (Mackie, "*De Re* Modality," 558–59). We need not consider this part of Mackie's discussion here.

12. In a recent discussion, Joel Feinberg has noted similar cases in which the law recognizes the victim's desert of compensation. One of these is "the case where a blood transfusion to a mother gives her syphilis. One year later she

conceives, and her child is subsequently born syphilitic. In an actual German case of a few years ago, the infant was able to recover damages from the hospital for its negligence in administering the blood transfusion almost two years before *he* was even born." Joel Feinberg, "Is There a Right to Be Born?" in *Understanding Moral Philosophy*, ed. James Rachels (Encino, Calif.: Dickinson, 1976), 350.

3

Justifying Reverse Discrimination in Employment

A currently favored way of compensating for past discrimination is to afford preferential treatment to the members of those groups that have been discriminated against in the past. I propose to examine the rationale behind this practice when it is applied in the area of employment. I want to ask whether, and if so under what conditions, past acts of discrimination against members of a particular group justify the current hiring of a member of that group who is less than the best qualified applicant for a given job. Since I am mainly concerned about exploring the relations between past discrimination and present claims to employment, I shall make the assumption that each applicant is at least minimally competent to perform the job he seeks; this will eliminate the need to consider the claims of those who are to receive the services in question. Whether it is ever justifiable to discriminate in favor of an incompetent applicant, or a less than best-qualified applicant for a job such as teaching, in which almost any increase in employee competence brings a real increase in services rendered, will be left to be decided elsewhere. Such questions, which turn on balancing the claim of the less than best-qualified applicant against the competing claims of those who are to receive his services, are not as basic as the question of whether the less than best-qualified applicant ever *has* a claim to employment.[1]

I

It is sometimes argued, when members of a particular group have been barred from employment of a certain kind, that because this group has in the past received *less* than its fair share of the employment in question, it now deserves to receive *more* by way of compensation.[2] This argument, if sound, has the virtue of showing clearly why preferential treatment should be extended even to those current group members who have not themselves been denied employment: if the point of reverse discrimination is to compensate a wronged *group*, it will presumably hardly matter if those who are preferentially hired were not among the original victims of discrimination. However, the argument's basic presumption, that groups as opposed to their individual members are the sorts of entities that can be wronged and deserve redress, is itself problematic.[3] Thus the defense of reverse discrimination would only be convincing if it were backed by a further argument showing that groups can indeed be wronged and have deserts of the relevant sort. No one, as far as I know, has yet produced a powerful argument to this effect, and I am not hopeful about the possibilities. Therefore I shall try not to develop a defense of reverse discrimination along those lines.

Another possible way of connecting past acts of discrimination in hiring with the claims of current group members is to argue that even if these current group members have not (yet) been denied *employment*, their membership in the group makes it very likely that they have been discriminatorily deprived of *other* sorts of goods. It is a commonplace, after all, that people who are forced to do menial and low-paying jobs must often endure corresponding privations in housing, diet, and other areas. These privations are apt to be distributed among young and old alike, and so to afflict even those group members who are still too young to have had their qualifications for employment bypassed. It is, moreover, generally acknowledged by both common sense and law that a person who has been deprived of a certain amount of one sort of good may sometimes reasonably be compensated by an equivalent amount of a good of another sort. (It is this principle, surely, that underlies the legal practice of awarding sums of money to compensate for pain incurred in accidents, damaged reputations, etc.) Given these facts and this principle, it appears that the preferential hiring of current members of discriminated-against groups may be justified as compensation for the *other* sorts of discrimination these individuals are apt to have suffered.[4]

But, although this argument seems more promising than one presupposing group deserts, it surely cannot be accepted as it stands. For one thing, insofar as the point is simply to compensate individuals for the various sorts of privations they have suffered, there is no special reason to use reverse discrimination rather than some other mechanism to effect compensation. There are, moreover, certain other mechanisms of redress that seem prima facie preferable. It seems, for instance, that it would be more appropriate to compensate for past privations simply by making preferentially available to the discriminated-against individuals equivalent amounts of the very same sorts of goods of which they have been deprived; simple cash settlements would allow a far greater precision in the adjustment of compensation to privation than reverse discriminatory hiring ever could. Insofar as it does not provide any reason to adopt reverse discrimination rather than these prima facie preferable mechanisms of redress, the suggested defense of reverse discrimination is at least incomplete.

Moreover, and even more important, if reverse discrimination is viewed simply as a form of compensation for past privations, there are serious questions about its fairness. Certainly the privations to be compensated for are not the sole responsibility of those individuals whose superior qualifications will have to be bypassed in the reverse discriminatory process. These individuals, if responsible for those privations at all, will at least be no more responsible than others with relevantly similar histories. Yet reverse discrimination will compensate for the privations in question at the expense of these individuals alone. It will have no effect at all upon these other, equally responsible persons whose qualifications are inferior to begin with, who are already entrenched in their jobs, or whose vocations are noncompetitive in nature. Surely it is unfair to distribute the burden of compensation so unequally.[5]

These considerations show, I think, that reverse discriminatory hiring of members of groups that have been denied jobs in the past cannot be justified simply by the fact that each group member has been discriminated against in other areas. If this fact is to enter into the justification of reverse discrimination at all, it must be in some more complicated way.

II

Consider again the sorts of privations that are apt to be distributed among the members of those groups restricted in large part to menial and low-paying jobs. These individuals, we said, are apt to live in substandard homes, to subsist on improper and imbalanced diets, and to receive inadequate education. Now, it is certainly true that adequate housing, food, and education are goods in and of themselves; a life without them is certainly less pleasant and less full than one with them. But, and crucially, they are also goods in a different sense entirely. It is an obvious and well-documented fact that (at least) the sorts of nourishment and education a person receives as a child will causally affect the sorts of skills and capacities he will have as an adult—including, of course, the very skills needed to compete on equal terms for jobs and other goods. Since this is so, a child who is deprived of adequate food and education may lose not only the immediate enjoyments that a comfortable and stimulating environment brings but also the subsequent ability to compete equally for other things of intrinsic value. But to lose this ability to compete is, in essence, to lose one's access to the goods that are being competed for; and this, surely, is itself a privation to be compensated for if possible. It is, I think, the key to an adequate justification of reverse discrimination to see that practice, not as the redressing of *past* privations, but rather as a way of neutralizing the *present* competitive disadvantage *caused* by those past privations and thus as a way of restoring equal access to those goods that society distributes competitively.[6] When reverse discrimination is justified in this way, many of the difficulties besetting the simpler justification of it disappear.

For whenever someone has been irrevocably deprived of a certain good and there are several alternative ways of providing him with an equivalent amount of another good, it will ceteris paribus be preferable to choose whichever substitute comes closest to actually replacing the lost good. It is this principle that makes preferential access to decent housing, food, and education especially desirable as a way of compensating for the experiential impoverishment of a deprived childhood. If, however, we are concerned to compensate not for the experiential poverty, but for the effects of childhood deprivations, then this principle tells just as heavily for reverse discrimination as the proper form of compensation. If the lost good is just the *ability* to compete on equal terms for first-level goods like desirable jobs, then surely the most appropriate (and so preferable) way of substituting for what has been lost is just to remove the *necessity* of competing on equal terms for these goods—which, of course, is precisely what reverse discrimination does.

When reverse discrimination is viewed as compensation for lost ability to compete on equal terms, a reasonable case can also be made for its fairness. Our doubts about its fairness arose because it seemed to place the entire burden of redress upon those individuals whose superior qualifications are bypassed in the reverse discriminatory process. This seemed wrong because these individuals are, of course, not apt to be any more responsible for past discrimination than others with relevantly similar histories. But, as we are now in a position to see, this objection misses the point. The crucial fact about these individuals is not that they are more *responsible* for past discrimination than others with relevantly similar histories (in fact, the dirty work may well have been done before any of their generation attained the age of responsibility), but rather that unless reverse discrimination is practiced, they will *benefit* more than the others from its effects on their competitors. They will benefit more because unless they are restrained, they, but not the others, will use their competitive edge to claim jobs that their competitors would otherwise have gotten. Thus, it is only because they stand to *gain* the most from the relevant effects of the *original* discrimination that the bypassed individuals stand to *lose* the most from *reverse* discrimination.[7] This is surely a valid reply to the charge that reverse discrimination does not distribute the burden of compensation equally.

III

So far, the argument has been that reverse discrimination is justified insofar as it neutralizes competitive disadvantages caused by past privations. This may be correct, but it is also oversimplified. In actuality, there are many ways in which a person's environment may affect his ability to compete; and there may well be logical differences among these ways that affect the degree to which reverse discrimination is called for. Consider, for example, the following cases:

1. An inadequate education prevents someone from acquiring the degree of a certain skill that he would have been able to acquire with a better education.
2. An inadequate diet, lack of early intellectual stimulation, etc., lower an individual's ability, and thus prevent him from acquiring the degree of competence in a skill that he would otherwise have been able to acquire.
3. The likelihood that he will not be able to use a certain skill because he belongs to a group that has been discriminated against in the past leads a person to decide, rationally, not even to try developing that skill.
4. Some aspect of his childhood environment renders an individual incapable of putting forth the sustained effort needed to improve his skills.

These are four different ways in which past privations might adversely affect a person's skills. Ignoring for analytical purposes the fact that privation often works in more than one of these ways at a time, shall we say that reverse discrimination is equally called for in each case?

It might seem that we should say it is, since in each case a difference in the individual's environment would have been accompanied by an increase in his mastery of a certain skill (and, hence, by an improvement in his competitive position with respect to jobs requiring that skill). But this blanket counterfactual formulation conceals several important distinctions. For one thing, it suggests (and our justification of reverse discrimination seems to require) the possibility of giving *just enough* preferential treatment to the disadvantaged individual in each case to restore to him the competitive position that he would have had, had he not suffered his initial disadvantage. But in fact, this does not seem to be equally possible in all cases. We can roughly calculate the difference that a certain improvement in education or intellectual stimulation would have made in the development of a person's skills if his efforts had been held constant (cases 1 and 2), for achievement is known to be a relatively straightforward compositional function of ability, environmental factors, and effort. We cannot, however, calculate in the same way the difference that improved prospects or environment would have made in the degree of *effort* expended; for although effort is affected by environmental factors, it is not a known compositional function of them (or of anything else). Because of this, there would be no way for us to decide how much preferential treatment is just enough to make up for the efforts that a particular disadvantaged individual would have made under happier circumstances.

There is another problem with cases 3 and 4. Even if there were a way to afford a disadvantaged person just enough preferential treatment to make up for the efforts he was prevented from making by his environment, it is not clear that he *ought* to be afforded that much preferential treatment. To allow this, after all, would be to concede that the effort he *would* have made under other conditions is worth just as much as the effort that his rival actually *did* make; and this, I think, is implausible. Surely a person who *actually has* labored long and hard to achieve a given degree of a certain skill is more deserving of a job requiring that skill than another who is equal in all other relevant respects, but who merely *would* have worked and achieved the same amount under different conditions. Because actual effort creates desert in a way that merely possible effort does not, reverse discrimination to restore precisely the competitive position that a person would have had if he had not been prevented from working harder would not be desirable even if it were possible.

There is perhaps also a further distinction to be made here. A person who is rationally persuaded by an absence of opportunities not to develop a certain skill (case 3) will typically not undergo any sort of character transformation in the process of making this decision. He will be the same person after his decision as before it and, most often, the same person without his skill as with it. In cases such as 4, however, this is less clear. A person who is rendered incapable of effort by his environment does in a sense undergo a character transformation; to become truly incapable of sustained effort is to become a different (and less meritorious) person from the person one would otherwise have been. Because of this (and somewhat paradoxically, since his character change is itself apt to stem from factors beyond his control), such an individual may have less of a claim to reverse discrimination than one whose lack of effort does not flow from even an environmentally induced character fault, but rather from a justified rational decision.[8]

IV

When reverse discrimination is discussed in a non-theoretical context, it is usually assumed that the people most deserving of such treatment are blacks, members of other ethnic minorities, and women. In this last section, I shall bring the results of the foregoing discussion to bear on this assumption. Doubts will be raised both about the analogy between the claims of blacks and women to reverse discrimination and about the propriety, in absolute terms, of singling out either group as the proper recipient of such treatment.

For many people, the analogy between the claims of blacks and the claims of women to reverse discrimination rests simply upon the undoubted fact that both groups have been discriminatorily denied jobs in the past. But on the account just proposed, past discrimination justifies reverse discrimination only insofar as it has adversely affected the competitive position of present group members. When this standard is invoked, the analogy between the claims of blacks and those of women seems immediately to break down. The exclusion of blacks from good jobs in the past has been only one element in an interlocking pattern of exclusions and often has resulted in a poverty issuing in (and in turn reinforced by) such other privations as inadequate nourishment, housing, and health care, lack of time to provide adequate guidance and intellectual stimulation for the young, dependence on (often inadequate) public education, etc. It is this whole complex of privations that undermines the ability of the young to compete; and it is largely because of its central causal role in this complex that the past unavailability of good jobs for blacks justifies reverse discrimination in their favor now. In the case of women, past discrimination in employment simply has not played the same role. Because children commonly come equipped with both male *and* female parents, the inability of the female parent to get a good job need not, and usually does not, result in a poverty detracting from the quality of the nourishment, education, housing, health, or intellectual stimulation of the female child (and, of course, when such poverty does result, it affects male and female children indifferently). For this reason, the past inaccessibility of jobs for women does not seem to create for them the same sort of claim on reverse discrimination that its counterpart does for blacks.

Many defenders of reverse discrimination in favor of women would reply at this point that although past discrimination in employment has of course not played the *same* causal role in the case of women that it has in the case of blacks, it has nevertheless played *a* causal role in both cases. In the case of women, the argument runs, that role has been mainly psychological: past discrimination in hiring has led to a scarcity of female "role models" of suitably high achievement. This lack, together with a culture that in many other ways subtly inculcates the idea that women should not or cannot do the jobs that men do, has in turn made women psychologically less able to do these jobs. This argument is hard to assess fully, since it obviously rests on a complex and problematic psychological claim.[9] The following objections, however, are surely relevant. First, even if it is granted without question that cultural bias and absence of suitable role models do have some direct and pervasive effect upon women, it is not clear that this effect must take the form of a reduction in women's *abilities* to do the jobs men do. A more likely outcome would seem to be a reduction in women's *inclinations* to do these jobs—a result whose proper compensation is not preferential treatment of those women who have sought the jobs in question, but rather the encouragement of others to seek those jobs as well. Of course, this disinclination to do these jobs may in turn lead some women not to develop the relevant skills. To the extent that this occurs, the competitive position of these women will indeed be affected, albeit indirectly, by the scarcity of female role models. Even here, however, the resulting disadvantage will not be comparable to those commonly produced by the poverty syndrome. It will flow solely from lack of effort, and so will be of the sort (cases 3 and 4) that neither calls for nor admits of full equalization by reverse discrimination. Moreover, and conclusively, because there is surely the same dearth of role-models, etc., for blacks as for women, whatever psychological disadvantages accrue to women because of this will beset blacks as well. Because blacks, but not women, must also suffer the privations associated with poverty, it follows that they are the group more deserving of reverse discrimination.

Strictly speaking, however, the account offered here does not allow us to speak this way of *either* group. If the point of reverse discrimination is to compensate for competitive disadvantages caused by past discrimination, it will be justified in favor of only those group members whose abilities have actually been reduced; and it would be most implausible to suppose that *every* black (or *every* woman) has been affected in this way. Blacks from middle-class or affluent backgrounds will surely have escaped many, if not all, of the competitive handicaps besetting those raised under less fortunate circumstances; and if they have, this account provides no reason to practice reverse discrimination in their favor. Again, whites from impoverished backgrounds may suffer many, if not all, of the competitive handicaps besetting their black counterparts; and if they do, the account provides no reason *not* to practice reverse discrimination in their favor. Generally, the proposed account allows us to view racial (and sexual) boundaries only as roughly suggesting which individuals are likely to have been disadvantaged by past discrimination. Anyone who construes these boundaries as playing a different and more decisive role must show us that a different defense of reverse discrimination is plausible.

Notes

1. In what follows I will have nothing to say about the utilitarian justifications of reverse discrimination. There are two reasons for this. First, the winds of utilitarian argumentation blow in too many directions. It is certainly socially beneficial to avoid the desperate actions to which festering resentments may lead—but so too is it socially useful to confirm the validity of qualifications of the traditional sort, to assure those who have amassed such qualifications that "the rules of the game have not been changed in the middle," that accomplishment has not been downgraded in society's eyes. How could these conflicting utilities possibly be measured against one another?

Second and even more importantly, to rest a defense of reverse discrimination upon utilitarian considerations would be to ignore what is surely the guiding intuition of its proponents, that this treatment is *deserved* where discrimination has been practiced in the past. It is the intuition that reverse discrimination is a matter not (only) of social good but of right that I want to try to elucidate.

2. This argument, as well as the others I shall consider, presupposes that jobs are (among other things) *goods*, and so ought to be distributed as fairly as possible. This presupposition seems to be amply supported by the sheer economic necessity of earning a living, as well as by the fact that some jobs carry more prestige, are more interesting, and pay better than others.

3. As Robert Simon has pointed out in "Preferential Hiring: A Reply to Judith Jarvis Thomson," *Philosophy and Public Affairs* 3, no. 3 (Spring 1974): 312–20, it is also far from clear that the preferential hiring of its individual members could be a proper form of compensation for any wronged group that *did* exist.

4. A version of this argument is advanced by Judith Jarvis Thomson in

"Preferential Hiring," *Philosophy and Public Affairs* 2, no. 4 (Summer 1973): 364–84.

5. Simon, "Preferential Hiring," sec. III.

6. A similar justification of reverse discrimination is suggested, but not ultimately endorsed, by Thomas Nagel in "Equal Treatment and Compensatory Discrimination," *Philosophy and Public Affairs* 2, no. 4 (Summer 1973): 348–63. Nagel rejects this justification on the grounds that a system distributing goods solely on the basis of performance determined by native ability would itself be unjust, even if not *as* unjust as one distributing goods on a gender or sexual basis. I shall not comment on this, except to remark that our moral intuitions surely run the other way: the average person would certainly find the latter system of distribution *far* more unjust than the former if, indeed, he found the former unjust at all. Because of this, the burden is on Nagel to show exactly why a purely meritocratic system of distribution would be unjust.

7. It is tempting, but I think largely irrelevant, to object here that many who are now entrenched in their jobs (tenured professors, for example) have already benefited from the effects of past discrimination at least as much as the currently best-qualified applicant will if reverse discrimination is not practiced. While many such individuals have undoubtedly benefited from the effects of discrimination upon *their original* competitors, few if any are likely to have benefited from a reduction in the abilities of the *currently best-qualified applicant's* competitor. As long as none of them have so benefited, the best-qualified applicant in question will still stand to gain the most from that *particular* effect of past discrimination, and so reverse discrimination against him will remain fair. Of course, there will also be cases in which an entrenched person *has* previously benefited from the reduced abilities of the currently best-qualified applicant's competitor. In these cases, the best-qualified applicant will *not* be the single main beneficiary of his rival's handicap, and so reverse discrimination against him will *not* be entirely fair. I am inclined to think that there may be a case for reverse discrimination even here, however; for if it is truly impossible to dislodge the entrenched previous beneficiary of his rival's handicap, reverse discrimination against the best-qualified applicant may at least be the fairest (or least unfair) of the practical alternatives.

8. A somewhat similar difference might seem to obtain between cases 1 and 2. One's ability to learn is more intimately a part of him than his actual degree of education; hence, someone whose ability to learn is lowered by his environment (case 2) is a changed person in a way in which a person who is merely denied education (case 1) is not. However, one's ability to learn is not a feature of *moral* character in the way ability to exert effort is, and so this difference between cases 1 and 2 will have little bearing on the degree to which reverse discrimination is called for in these cases.

9. The feminist movement has convincingly documented the ways in which sexual bias is built into the information received by the young; but it is one thing to show that such information is received and quite another to show how, and to what extent, its reception is causally efficacious.

4

Groups and Justice

The practice of extending preferential treatment to current members of groups whose past members have suffered discrimination has recently been defended in a number of different ways. Some have argued that this practice is justified on utilitarian grounds,[1] others that it serves to compensate for injustices suffered by the affected individuals,[2] and still others that it serves to compensate for injustices suffered by the affected *groups*.[3] In this paper, I want to raise some general objections against the possibility of a defense of the last sort. Because discrimination typically involves the withholding of goods from deserving parties (and because the withholding of goods is just the sort of wrong most clearly calling for compensation), I shall begin by considering an appeal to that principle of justice that is most appropriate to the distribution of goods, that is, to the principle of distributive justice. Against the claim that past inequities in the distribution of goods among groups could justify reverse discrimination now, I shall argue that, first, the racial and sexual groups usually mentioned in this context are simply not enough like persons to fall under the principle of distributive justice and, second, even if such groups did fall under it, that principle could not possibly justify preferential treatment for their current, undeprived members. Finally, I shall argue more briefly against the view that reverse discrimination in favor of discriminated-against groups can be justified by an appeal to the principle of retributive justice.

I

There is an initial appeal to the claim that discriminated-against groups have received "less than their fair share" of good jobs, educational opportunities, and other benefits in the past, and so deserve

55

more of those benefits than they ordinarily would by way of compensation now. We have a fairly firm grasp of what constitutes fair sharing among individuals, and it is not unnatural to think that this notion might be extended to groups as well. However, there are pitfalls here. What constitutes an individual's fair share is determined by a principle of distributive justice dictating that goods should be distributed equally except when the persons involved differ in need or merit; and so a person's fair share is inextricably bound up with, and cannot be determined without a knowledge of, his merits and needs. If our notion of fair sharing is to be extended to groups, this connection will have to carry over: what constitutes a group's fair share will have to be bound up with that group's needs and merits in a manner at least strongly analogous to that in which an individual's fair share is bound up with his needs and merits. It seems to me, however, and I shall argue in this section, that a number of obvious considerations militate against racial and sexual groups having needs and merits of the appropriate sorts at all. If this is so, the seemingly natural claim that discriminated-against groups have been denied their fair share will actually be quite ill formed.

Consider, first, the sense of "need" that is relevant to the principle of distributive justice. To say that X needs G in this sense is just to say that G is necessary for X's well-being; and so only those entities that are in principle capable of attaining states of well-being can possibly entertain needs of the appropriate sorts. For human beings, this restriction poses no problem: they are equipped, physiologically and psychologically, to benefit in an indefinitely large number of ways, and so the only problem about determining their needs is to decide which levels of well-being should be considered minimally acceptable to them. For racial and sexual groups, however, the situation is dramatically different. Such groups, unlike their members, do not satisfy the presuppositions for attaining any of the states of well-being with which we are familiar. They do not have single organized bodies and so can neither sustain good bodily health nor suffer illness. They do not have nervous systems and so cannot experience the various states of comfort and discomfort that these systems make possible. They do not have consciousness and so cannot entertain either states of amusement, happiness, interest, or self-esteem, or the less pleasant, opposite states. They do not even have the degree of legal or conventional organization shared by corporations, clubs, and other composite entities and so cannot increase or decrease their wealth or holdings as these others can. Because they lack the sorts of organization that alone confer the capacity to attain states of well-being, racial and sexual groups can hardly have the sorts of needs that presuppose this capacity. Any statements that appear to attribute such needs to these groups must therefore either be elliptical ways of attributing the relevant needs to some of their members (in which case no additional properties will be attributed to the groups as wholes), or else must be ways of speaking about *average* degrees of need within the groups (in which case additional properties will in a sense be attributed to the groups as wholes, but those properties will not be relevant to the distribution of goods: average needs are no more genuine needs than average citizens are citizens).

It is also difficult to see how racial or sexual groups could satisfy any of the criteria for *merit* relevant to the principle of distributive justice. Our criteria for merit are notoriously diverse: we sometimes tie merit to pure ability (however measured), but at other times we consider also, or instead, efforts expended, degrees of skill acquired, and goods produced. Despite this diversity, however, and whatever the logical and historical relations among them actually are, our criteria for merit are at least unified by one common presupposition: to satisfy any of them, an entity must in some sense be capable of *acting*. Skills and abilities are exercised only through actions, and so it would be senseless to speak of either the abilities or the skills of a nonagent; and much the same is true of the exertion of effort and the production of goods. Once again, this presupposition hardly restricts our application of the criteria of merit among human beings: persons are the source of our concept of action, and so of course it applies par excellence to them. The presupposition does, however, seem to rule out our application of those criteria to racial and sexual groups, which do not have the organization required for action and so a fortiori cannot perform the sorts of actions through which alone efforts are made, skills exercised, abilities demonstrated, and goods produced. Once again, therefore, it seems that any statements that appear to be about racial or sexual groups' merits must really be about either the merits of individual group members or average degrees of merit within groups.

These considerations show that racial and sexual groups cannot have the sorts of needs and merits that justify deviations from strict equality of distribution of goods among them. However, even if no racial or sexual group can deserve more of any good than any other, it may still seem that each such group can deserve the *same* amount of goods as each other, so that questions of fair sharing among them can still arise. To suppose this, though, would be to overlook the common roots of the different elements of our concept of distributive justice. As Gregory Vlastos has made clear,[4] equal distribution under ordinary circumstances and unequal distribution when needs differ are both ways of achieving the single goal of *equalizing benefits*: the first is appropriate when each recipient would benefit equally from the good in question, the second when some would benefit more than others. If equal treatment and special treatment under special circumstances do share the single goal of equalizing benefits, however, then the desert of each must alike presuppose the capacity to benefit. Hence, the proper conclusion to our discussion must be not merely that racial and sexual groups do not qualify for exemptions from equal treatment, but rather, and more radically, that such groups do not fall under the principle of distributive justice at all.[5] There may indeed be circumstances in which considerations of distributive justice dictate preferential treatment for each member of a given group; but if there are, this will have to be because each group member has suffered deprivation in the past. In any such case, it will be the affected individuals, and not the group itself, to whom the principle of distributive justice applies.

II

So far, the argument has been that racial and sexual groups lack the sorts of organization they would have to have to deserve goods and that consequently all talk of unjust distribution of goods among them is out of place. In this section I want to make the further point that even if it were possible to distribute goods unjustly among these groups, a policy of preferential treatment that extended to their undeprived members could not possibly be a proper form of compensation for such injustices.

It seems obvious enough that it cannot be only racial and sexual groups to which the principle of distributive justice applies. If it is to apply to groups of these sorts, it will have to apply also to cultural, religious, and geographic ones. But, having widened our horizons this far, why should we stop here? There are really as many groups as there are combinations of people; and if we are going to ascribe claims to equal treatment to racial, sexual, and other groups with high visibility, it will be mere favoritism not to ascribe similar claims to all these other groups as well. Moreover, if all groups do have the same claim to equal treatment, then all groups must also have the same claim to compensation for unequal treatment: any compensation that is deserved by a deprived racial or sexual group must also and equally be deserved by any other similarly deprived group. Once these natural assumptions are granted, however, it is easily shown that any case for the preferential treatment of undeprived members of deprived racial or sexual groups would be precisely matched, and so destroyed, by similar cases for the preferential treatment of all other undeprived individuals.

For suppose C is a group composed of all the individuals with racial or sexual characteristic C and that most, but not all, of these individuals have suffered privations in the past. Let U, V, and W be the *non*deprived members of C, and let X, Y, and Z be a similar number of arbitrarily chosen nondeprived members of non-C. If deprived groups do deserve compensation, and if preferential treatment of their undeprived members is a proper way of effecting such compensation, the past deprivation of C will justify preferential treatment for U, V, and W now. However, since all deprived groups must be deserving of compensation if any are, and since the "mixed" group consisting of the deprived members of C plus X, Y, and Z (call this group M) must have been precisely as deprived as C itself, the case for preferential treatment of U, V, and W will be precisely matched by a similar case for the preferential treatment of X, Y, and Z. Moreover, because the same reasoning must also justify preferential treatment for the undeprived members of all other similar mixed groups—and because everyone belongs to one or another of these—the ultimate conclusion must be that all undeprived individuals (as well, of course, as all deprived ones) deserve preferential treatment now. But this is plainly absurd: if everyone deserved preference, there would be no one left to whom anyone deserved to be preferred.

It might seem possible to avoid these difficulties by showing that U, V, and W deserve preference over X, Y, and Z in a slightly different way. It seems no less reasonable to suppose that groups that have been overprivileged in the past deserve less than what would ordinarily be their fair share than it does to suppose that groups that have been underprivileged deserve more; and because non-C has been precisely as overprivileged in the past as C has been underprivileged, it might seem that non-C's members, X, Y, and Z, deserve less than equal treatment now, and so, indirectly, that U, V, and W deserve preference over them. However, this argument is just as vulnerable to refutation by generalization as its twin. If discrimination is called for against the current members of any overprivileged groups, it must be equally called for against the current members of all such groups; and because M has been precisely as underprivileged as C in the past, its complement, non-M, must have been precisely as overprivileged as C's complement, non-C. Hence, any case for discrimination against X, Y, and Z because of their membership in non-C will again be precisely matched by a parallel case for discrimination against U, V, and W because of their membership in non-M.

If this line of argument is correct, it will decisively block the move from the premise, granted *arguendo*, that deprived racial and sexual groups have been denied distributive justice, to the conclusion that the current, undeprived members of such groups ought to be afforded preferential treatment now. However, there may appear to be a problem with the argument's pivotal claim that artificially constructed groups like *M* are as deserving of compensation as deprived racial or sexual groups like *C*. Even though *M* has undoubtedly suffered the same amount of deprivation as *C*, the fact remains that it was prejudice focused upon the relevant racial or sexual characteristic, but not prejudice focused upon the arbitrary characteristic of *M*-ness, that was responsible for the deprivation of the two groups. In light of this difference, it may appear that despite the two groups' equal deprivation it is *C* that is the more deserving of compensation, so that there is after all a reason to afford *U*, *V*, and *W* preference over *X*, *Y*, and *Z*.

However, I do not think this objection can be sustained. To see the difficulties it involves, we may first consider its underlying presupposition—that certain intentions on the part of discriminatory agents can increase their victims' degrees of desert. The most plausible version of this presupposition is that desert of compensation increases when discriminatory acts are performed with the intention of harming their victims; and yet there are at least two reasons why the presupposition, thus interpreted, is not likely to support the conclusion that *C* deserves compensation more than *M*. First, many of those who have discriminated in the past have held stereotyped views of their victims: blacks have been perceived as possessing criminal tendencies and lacking industry, women as being unable to do a full day's work, etc. In light of these stereotypes, it seems reasonable to suppose that much discrimination has been practiced not with the intention of harming blacks or women, but rather only with the intention of denying goods to anyone with those legitimately desert-canceling characteristics that blacks and women were mistakenly thought to possess. To the extent that this has been so, it is hard to see how the rationale behind the discrimination could increase the desert of these groups now. Moreover, second, even when discrimination has been guided by the intent to do harm, the intention is hardly likely to have been to harm any racial or sexual *group*. Only a very sophisticated bigot could intend to harm a group as opposed to its members; and yet in the absence of any intention to harm *C* itself, the principle that the discriminators' intentions to harm their victims increase those victims' degrees of desert will not serve to distinguish *C*'s desert from *M*'s.

There is also a deeper difficulty with the claim that the rationale behind past discrimination has made *C* more deserving of compensation than *M*. This difficulty emerges when we recall the point of making compensation for breaches of distributive justice. To compensate someone for receiving less than his proper share of a given good is simply to restore to him, as far as possible, the good of which he has been unjustly deprived, or which he has been unjustly prevented from attaining. Since this is so, his desert of compensation must depend on precisely the same consideration as those that determined his initial desert of that good. But, except perhaps in some freakish and irrelevant cases, initial desert of goods is never a function of the (future) intentions of disruptive agents. Hence, subsequent desert of compensation for unjust distribution can hardly be affected by those intentions either.[6] Because desert of compensation for unjust distribution is independent of the intentions of those who have acted unjustly, the fact that the common members of C and M were deprived because they were C but not because they were M cannot possibly bear on the degrees to which the two groups deserve compensation. Thus our conclusion, that no breach of distributive justice involving a group could call for a preferential policy extending to that group's current undeprived members, remains intact. If past violations of distributive justice are to license preferential treatment for all the current members of any given group, this can only be because each of these individuals has himself or herself been treated unjustly.[7]

III

It has been argued above that reverse discrimination cannot be defended as the restoration of distributive justice to groups that have been discriminatorily denied goods in the past. This takes us part of the way toward the conclusion that only considerations of justice involving individuals can enter into its justification; but it is not the whole story. Justice is often thought to have a retributive as well as a distributive aspect, and it might seem that the former could apply to groups even if the latter does not. As far as I know, no one has explicitly taken this line in a published defense of reverse discrimination. However, those who claim that discriminated-against groups have suffered injustice have not been entirely clear as to which sort of injustice they were discussing, and I suspect that this lack of clarity may reflect a tension between distributive and retributive elements in their position.[8] It will be worthwhile, therefore, to end this discussion by showing how some of the same considerations that tell against distributive justice for discriminated-against groups also tell against a retributive defense of reverse discrimination in their favor.

One who urged that reverse discrimination in favor of deprived groups can be justified retributively could mean either one of two things. He might, on the one hand, be appealing to the principle that anyone responsible for another's injury or loss is under a special obligation to make reparations for what he has done; on the other hand, he might be appealing rather to the principle that one who intentionally causes (certain sorts of) injuries or losses ought to be *punished* for what he has done. We need not linger over the first of these appeals, because the claim that discrimination involves injury or loss to racial or sexual groups has already been shown to be implausible. If these groups do not have the sorts of organization that the capacity to benefit presupposes, they can hardly be capable of suffering loss or injury either; so there can be no question of anyone's being specially obligated to compensate them for any injuries or losses he has inflicted upon them. However, the second claim, that reverse discrimination in favor of such groups can be justified as punishment for those who have discriminated, may appear to escape this criticism. Even if they cannot suffer harm or loss, we have seen that racial and sexual groups have entered, at least indirectly, into the intentions with which losses have been inflicted upon their members. Given this fact, together with the retributivist principle that any punishment should "fit the crime," it may seem possible to justify reverse discrimination in favor of such groups as a specially appropriate way of punishing those who have discriminated.

However, this suggestion will surely not do either; for reverse discrimination, conceived as punishment for those who have discriminated in the past, must violate the retributivist's fundamental tenet that punishment should be visited on the guilty, but not the innocent. Many of those who have discriminated most, after all, are either no longer alive or else not in a position to be harmed by reverse discrimination; while many others who would be bypassed in the reverse discriminatory process are likely not to have discriminated at all. (Many or all of these may have *benefited* from past discrimination; but in a society in which such benefit can hardly be avoided, this is surely not a punishable offense.) Given these facts, even a policy of preference for the individual victims of past discrimination is apt to harm many who are innocent while leaving untouched many who are guilty; and a fortiori this will happen also when preference is extended to the other members of the victims' racial or sexual groups as well. Since this is so, no such preferential policy could be an appropriate form of punishment for those who have discriminated.

Of course, this difficulty would not arise if the retributivist's argument could be backed by a theory of group responsibility. If it were the group of non-Cs that bore the responsibility for the privations undergone by the past victims of discrimination, then even that reverse discrimination that harmed nondiscriminating non-Cs might be justified as punishment for the guilty group. However, and finally, any such theory of group responsibility would once again be vulnerable to the sorts of arguments we have deployed against distributive justice for racial and sexual groups. Just as an entity must be capable of benefiting and acting meritoriously in order to qualify for distributive justice, so too must it be capable of entertaining intentions and acting upon them in order to be morally responsible. Hence, the same lack of organization that disqualifies the groups in question from deserving distributive justice must also disqualify them from moral responsibility, and so too from desert of punishment. And, again, just as the existence of mixed groups like *M* leads to the conclusion that all persons must belong to deprived groups if any do, so too does the existence of mixed groups like non-*M* lead to the conclusion that all persons must belong to blameworthy groups if any do. (Since groups like non-*C* cannot themselves entertain intentions or perform actions, a blameworthy group must be one a majority of whose members have acted blameworthily; and by this standard, non-*M* must be precisely as blameworthy as non-*C*.) In light of these difficulties, no theory of group responsibility for past discrimination is tenable. Since this is so, we may conclusively reject the claim that reverse discrimination in favor of discriminated-against groups (or individuals) can be justified as punishment for those who have discriminated in the past.

Notes

1. Thomas Nagel, "Equal Treatment and Compensatory Discrimination," *Philosophy and Public Affairs* 2, no. 4 (Summer 1973): 348–63.

2. Judith Jarvis Thomson, "Preferential Hiring," *Philosophy and Public Affairs* 2, no. 4 (Summer 1973): 364–84; and my "Justifying Reverse Discrimination in Employment," *Philosophy and Public Affairs* 4, no. 2 (Winter 1975): 159–70 (chapter 3 of this volume).

3. Paul W. Taylor, "Reverse Discrimination and Compensatory Justice," *Analysis* 33, no. 6 (June 1973): 177–82; and Michael D. Bayles, "Reparations to Wronged Groups," *Analysis* 33, no. 6 (June 1973): 182–84.

4. Gregory Vlastos, "Justice and Equality," in *Social Justice*, ed. Richard B. Brandt (Englewood Cliffs, N.J.: Prentice-Hall, Inc., 1962), 31–72.

5. Vlastos actually argues that *all* justified exceptions to equal distribution, those based on differences in merit as well as those based on differences in need, have a common egalitarian ground. If true, this claim would provide an even stronger reason to reject the view that racial and sexual groups can qualify for distributive justice than what has been said so far. However, because Vlastos's argument concerning merit is rather intricate, and because the considerations already raised seem quite sufficient to disqualify those groups from deserving distributive justice, I will not pursue the point further.

6. This conclusion is borne out by our intuitions in simple cases. If *A* is

deprived of a month's Social Security benefits by a malicious clerk while *B* is deprived of a similar amount by a merely careless clerk, our reaction is surely that despite the clear difference in the clerks' intentions both *A* and *B* deserve precisely what has been withheld from them, perhaps including interest, and nothing more.

7. The argument of this section is related to, yet distinct from, an argument advanced by Robert Simon in his "Preferential Hiring: A Reply to Judith Jarvis Thomson," *Philosophy and Public Affairs* 3, no. 3 (Fall 1974): 312–20. Simon contends that (a) it is not *obvious* that the preferential treatment of group members could serve to compensate a wronged group, and (b) at least in the case of preferential hiring, this is unlikely because "preferential hiring policies award compensation to an arbitrarily selected segment of the group; namely those who have the ability and qualifications to be seriously considered for the jobs available" ("Preferential Hiring," 315). My contention, by contrast, is that even if all members of a particular disadvantaged group were compensated, the procedure would still be arbitrary in that it would stop short of compensating the equally deserving members of *other* disadvantaged groups.

8. Bayles is altogether silent as to the sort of justice involved; and while Taylor does say that "the principles of *distributive* justice were transgressed by the past treatment of C-persons" ("Reverse Discrimination," 197, emphasis his), his reference to "C-persons" (as opposed to the C group) at the crucial juncture renders problematical his view concerning the wrong done to the discriminated-against *group.*

5

Effort, Ability, and Personal Desert

A familiar argument in recent social theory is that because no one deserves either his native talents or his ability to exert effort, no one can be said to deserve any advantages made possible by his talents or abilities. The premises of this argument are perhaps most clearly stated in the following well-known passage from Rawls's *A Theory of Justice*:

> It seems to be one of the fixed points of our considered moral judgments that no one deserves his place in the distribution of natural endowments, any more than one deserves one's initial starting place in society. The assertion that a man deserves the superior character that enables him to make the effort to cultivate his abilities is equally problematical; for his character depends in large measure upon fortunate family and social circumstances for which he can claim no credit. The notion of desert seems not to apply in these cases.[1]

If these contentions are correct, and if Rawls is also correct in concluding that nobody deserves "the greater advantages he could achieve with [his natural endowments],"[2] then personal desert will play no role at all in determining which system of distributing goods is just. At best, the connection will work the other way around: a social system that is just for other reasons may itself determine a (logically secondary) sense in which people deserve things. But, as Rawls insists, personal desert will not be among the *fundamental* facts of morality at all.[3]

In this essay, I want to argue against this way of showing that people never deserve things for reasons prior to or independent of social conventions. My attempt to rebut the anti-desert argument will proceed in three stages. In the first stage (sections I and II), I shall try to interpret Rawls's influential formulation of the argument as sympathetically as possible. In the second stage (sections III and IV), I shall contend that even when the argument *is* interpreted sympathetically, its normative premises do not support the conclusion that people rarely or never deserve things. In the third stage (section V), I shall raise some questions about those normative premises themselves. As this essay's thrust is primarily defensive, I shall not offer a detailed defense of any positive theory of personal desert, nor even try to decide whether such desert attaches primarily to effort or to achievement. My aim is merely to secure the moral import of personal desert against the Rawlsian attack, and so indirectly to cast doubt upon those theories of justice that are insensitive to it.

I

Before we can begin any evaluation of Rawls's argument against personal desert, we must get somewhat clearer about what that argument says. We have seen that Rawls wants to move from the premise that people do not deserve their character or abilities to the conclusion that people do not deserve the advantages these "natural assets" make possible. But why, exactly, does Rawls believe that people do not deserve their character and abilities in the first place?

Because Rawls mentions the social causes of our effort-making abilities, and because our other talents and abilities seem obviously to be caused as well, it may be tempting to interpret him as claiming that our natural assets are undeserved simply because they are caused. However, this claim is nowhere explicitly made by Rawls and would, in any event, be no less controversial than the related claim that an agent is not responsible if his *act* is caused. For these reasons, I shall not attribute it to Rawls here. Instead, I shall take him to hold the more reasonable view that our natural assets are undeserved because they are brought into existence by events independent of anything we ourselves have done. A person may indeed take steps to develop his talents and increase his effort-making capacity; but his ability to take such steps must itself depend on some earlier complement of talents and effort-making abilities which are not the result of any such actions. Because of this, he may indeed be held unable to "claim credit" for any of these earlier talents or abilities.

If an agent's possession of an ability is not the result of anything he has done, I shall refer to that ability as a *basic* ability of the agent. When it is formulated in terms of basic abilities, the complete anti-desert argument looks something like this:

1. Each person has some basic set of abilities, including an ability to exert effort, which does not belong to him as a result of anything he has done.

2. If a person's having X is not a result of anything he has done, then he does not deserve to have X.

Therefore,

3. No person deserves to have his basic abilities.

Moreover,

4. Each action a person performs is made possible, directly or indirectly, by some subset of his basic abilities.
5. If a person does not deserve to have X, and X makes Y possible, then that person does not deserve Y.

Therefore,

6. No person deserves to perform his actions, and neither does anyone deserve to enjoy any of the benefits that his actions make possible in their turn.

I do not know if Rawls would endorse this version of the argument as his own. However, whether or not he would, it is the version that initially seems most likely to yield his conclusion, and in any event it is worthy of consideration in its own right. For these reasons, I shall confine my discussion to it in what follows. Is this argument, or some further refinement of it, sound?

II

Although each step has some intuitive appeal, the argument surely cannot be accepted as it stands, for premise 5, at least, is implausibly strong. If deserving the benefits of our actions did require that we deserve everything that makes our actions possible, then all such desert would immediately be cancelled by the fact that no one has done anything to deserve to be born or to live in a life-sustaining environment.[4] If this were the case, then Rawls's insistence that people do not deserve their natural assets would be quite superfluous. Moreover, as Alan Zaitchik has pointed out, anyone who accepts both premise 5 and "the truism that all deserving is deserving in virtue of some ground or other" will immediately be led to a vicious regress: in order to deserve Z, a person must deserve Z's ground Y; in order to deserve Y, he must deserve Y's ground X; and so on.[5] This regress shows again that premise 5 rules out the possibility of personal desert for reasons quite independent of the (alleged) fact that we do not deserve our natural talents or abilities.

According to Zaitchik, the fact that premise 5 rules out the possibility of personal desert, and so contradicts many people's "pre-theoretical certainty that at least some people deserve something,"[6] is itself a reductio of 5. It seems to me, however, that this particular way of dismissing premise 5 proceeds too quickly. If Zaitchik has correctly represented Rawls as intending to produce "a completely general argument which alleges that *no* desert theory could be true for the simple reason that no one ever deserves things,"[7] then we cannot appeal to our intuitive conviction that people *do* deserve things without begging the question against Rawls. What we can ask, however, is that Rawls's premises about personal desert should themselves not be question-begging in turn. Although they must of course be strong enough to yield the desired conclusion, Rawls's premises should also be uncontroversial enough to be acceptable even to persons initially sympathetic to personal desert. As we have stated it, premise 5 fails to satisfy this requirement. Can any alternative premise do better?

Perhaps one can. The basic problem with 5 is that it promiscuously allows a person's desert of Y to be cancelled by *all* undeserved necessary conditions for his having Y. Intuitively, this seems excessive because many such conditions are satisfied not only by the person in question, but also by everyone else. *All* claimants to goods must satisfy such conditions as having been born and existing in life-sustaining environments; and so these conditions, though undeserved by the possessor of Y, have not given him an unfair advantage over anyone. In light of this, the obvious way to amend premise 5 is to construe it as requiring not that a person deserve *all* the conditions necessary for his having Y, but rather only that he deserve any of those conditions that are not shared by all rival claimants. This modification will in effect transform premise 5 from a statement of the conditions necessary for a person's deserving Y simpliciter into a statement of the conditions necessary for his deserving to have Y while someone else does not. When desert is consistently interpreted as involving a relation of this sort, 5 becomes

5a. If one person does not deserve to have X while another does not, and if having X enables the first person to have or do Y while the second does not, then the first person does not deserve to have or do Y while the second does not.

By shifting from premise 5 to 5a, we can avoid both the charge that this premise is violated by universally satisfied necessary conditions for having Y and the charge that it leads to a vicious regress. Yet despite these gains, the shift to 5a brings costs of its own. For one thing, since 5a's antecedent is now cast in comparative terms, the anti-desert argument's earlier premises will also have to be recast if they are to mesh with 5a. More seriously, the shift to a comparative conception of desert will also require us to make new distinctions among the elements of a person's basic abilities. As long as personal desert was construed non-comparatively, it was quite permissible to speak of one's whole basic package of abilities as either deserved or undeserved. However, once we shift to a comparative conception of desert, we must go beyond this. If a person M has a set of basic abilities $a_1 \ldots a_5$, while another person N has the smaller set $a_1 \ldots a_4$, then only special ability a_5 will give M an advantage over N. Because of this, the argument's earlier premises must be reformulated to factor out such shared basic abilities as $a_1 \ldots a_4$.

When both of the required alterations are made, the anti-desert argument emerges looking like this:

1a. Each person has some basic set of abilities, including an ability to exert effort, which does not belong to him as a result of anything he does. Suppose M's basic abilities include $a_1 \ldots a_5$ while N's include only $a_1 \ldots a_4$.
2a. If a person's having X is not a result of anything he has done, then he does not deserve to have X while another does not.

Therefore,

3a. M does not deserve to have a_5 while N does not.
4a. Let A be an action that a_5 enables M, but not N, to perform.
5a. If one person does not deserve to have X while another does not, and if having X enables the first person to have or do Y while the second does not, then the first person does not deserve to have or do Y while the second does not.

Therefore,

6a. M does not deserve to perform A while N does not, and neither does M deserve to enjoy the benefits of A while N does not.

There may be problems with the assumption that abilities are goods that people can deserve relative to other people; for abilities, unlike other goods, are not transferable among persons. But instead of pursuing these problems further, I want to raise a different sort of question.

Assuming that its treatment of abilities can be made intelligible, what, if anything, will this version of the argument tell us about desert in particular cases?

III

By demonstrating that the Rawlsian argument must be reformulated in comparative terms, we have already compelled a measure of retreat from its initial unqualified conclusion that nobody ever deserves anything. In its current form, the argument does leave room for desert in cases in which all the relevant parties have equivalent sets of basic abilities. However, if basic abilities are in fact generally *unequally* distributed, then this concession will leave essentially intact Rawls's central conclusion that personal desert counts for little or nothing. If we are to challenge this conclusion, we must examine more closely the claim that people's basic abilities vary systematically in significant ways. Since this claim is most controversial as it applies to the ability to exert effort, we may begin by considering this aspect of it. On what basis, exactly, can people be said to differ in effort-making ability?

Although Rawls is plainly committed to an environmental explanation of *how* people come to differ in effort-making ability, he offers no explicit defense of the prior claim that they *do* differ in this ability. Thus, any discussion of the rationale for this claim must be quite speculative. As a first attempt at reconstructing that rationale, let us consider the argument that people are shown to differ in effort-making ability by the great differences in the efforts they actually make. If M applies himself assiduously to whatever task is at hand while N's efforts are interspersed with evasion and procrastination, the argument might run, then M must have some effort-making ability that N lacks. N must indeed have *some* effort-making ability because he does try sporadically; but whatever such ability N has, M must have that much ability plus some additional ability. For how else are we going to account for M's additional industry?

Although this argument may have some initial plausibility, a closer look reveals its weakness. If we are going to infer directly from M's additional industry to his superior effort–making ability, then we will have to do so on the basis of the more general principle that people are not capable of making any more effort than they actually do make. But this principle seems simply to be false. Even persons who would be acknowledged to have superior effort-making abilities are often inclined not to make the effort necessary to accomplish their goals. Many goals, though desirable, are not worth the effort it would take to attain them; and others, though worth the effort, are blocked by conflicting goals. In light of this, there is obviously room for a distinction between the *possession* of an ability to exert effort and the *exercise* of that ability; and given this distinction, it is easy to understand the difference between M's and N's efforts without supposing that they differ in effort-making ability. To do so, we need only view the difference between their efforts as stemming from the different degrees to which they have exercised their common effort-making ability.

Given these considerations, we clearly cannot infer directly from the fact that people differ in their efforts to the conclusion that they also differ in effort-making abilities. However, it remains possible to defend the different-ability thesis in another way. While persons who exert different amounts of effort always *can* be viewed as drawing differently upon similar effort-making abilities, this suggestion may seem implausible when the difference between their efforts is pronounced, systematic, and obviously disadvantageous to the less industrious. In such a case, there is simply no good reason for N to refrain from exercising his effort-making ability; and so it may seem most reasonable to suppose that he does not have a full measure of that ability to begin with. If we defend "the unequal–ability thesis" in this way, we will in effect be deriving it not as a logical consequence of the difference between M's and N's efforts, but rather via an inference to the best explanation of that difference.

This second way of defending the different-ability thesis is considerably more sophisticated than the first. It is not, however, notably more successful; for even when N's failure to try as hard as M is clearly disadvantageous to him, there remain plausible ways of accounting for it that do not commit us to anything as momentous as a difference in effort-making ability. For one thing, N's comparative lack of effort may simply reflect the fact that he is not as consistently attentive to his interests as M. For another, it may reflect the fact that he is (sometimes or always) less concerned than M to further those interests—that, at least at some moments, he has other priorities. Given these (and no doubt other) alternatives, the different-ability thesis will only provide the best explanation of N's comparative lack of effort in cases in which M and N are equally attentive to their own interests and in which they are equally concerned to further those interests. But why, in any given case, should we say that M and N *are* equally attentive to, and consistently concerned to further, their respective interests? We surely cannot infer this from the different amounts of effort they make; neither does it seem to be supported by any other easily imaginable fact about them. Moreover, simply to assume it would be to beg the question against the equal-ability thesis. Thus, the proposed explanatory inference seems problematical at best.[8]

There is a further difficulty here. Even if we grant the contention that people commonly differ in effort-making abilities, its conjunction with the other Rawlsian premises still will not entail that M does not deserve the benefits of his superior efforts. According to premise 5a, a difference in M's and N's effort-making ability will rule out M's desert relative to N only if the difference in their abilities makes it *impossible* for M and N to exert equal amounts of effort. But not every difference in effort-making ability need have this effect. It is easy to see how M and N might differ in effort-making ability, but N might still take steps to match M's superior efforts. For one thing, N can maintain a special vigilance against those distractions that he but not M finds attractive; for another, if N foresees difficulty in avoiding these temptations, he can always take action to avoid them or to increase his ability to resist them. Of course, Rawls could always maintain that these steps, as well as N's efforts themselves, are blocked by N's lesser effort-making ability; but this contention becomes progressively more difficult to maintain as the range of N's inability is said to increase. Whatever it is that N cannot do, there are surely many things that he *can* do; and since there is no theoretical limit to the steps one can take to increase one's effort-making ability, the number of cases in which differences in such ability render differences in effort inevitable seems minimal at best. In light of this, even genuine differences in effort-making ability, should they exist, would seem unlikely to have the moral significance attributed to them by Rawls.[9]

IV

So far, we have seen that Rawls's anti-desert argument is plausible only if desert is understood comparatively; that the argument under this interpretation implies that desert is threatened only by unequal basic abilities; and that it is doubtful whether people's abilities to exert effort are unequal in the relevant way. The Rawlsian argument has thus evidently failed to discredit the thesis that personal desert may be established by conscientious effort. However, people manifestly *do* differ in abilities like physical strength and intelligence, and so a parallel defense does not seem available for the further thesis that personal desert is established by superior achievement. Thus, it is tempting to view Rawls's argument as showing, in effect, that personal desert is properly associated with effort rather than with achievement. Although Zait-chik's approach to the Rawlsian argument differs substantially from mine, he has drawn from it a qualified version of this conclusion. It seems to me, however, that the truth lies elsewhere.

Let us again consider the argument advanced at the end of the preceding section. It was contended there that even if people *did* differ in effort-making abilities, those differences would not inevitably lead to differences in efforts actually expended. By suitably compensating for his lesser effort-making abilities, N might have put himself in a position to exert the same amount of effort that M made; and if N could have done this, then his lesser effort-making ability was not a violation of premise 5a at all. But surely something similar can be said for other differences in initial ability as well. Even if M is initially stronger or more intelligent than N, this difference will only entail that M does not deserve what he has achieved relative to N if the difference between them has made it impossible for N to achieve as much as M. However, differences in strength, intelligence, and other native gifts are rarely so pronounced as to have this effect. The far more common effect of such differences is merely to make it more *difficult* for the less talented person to reach a given level of attainment. He must work harder, husband his resources more carefully, plan more shrewdly, and so on. Because the latter differences do *not* combine with 5a to yield any conclusions about desert, the Rawlsian premises are evidently compatible with desert for achievement in at least a large number of cases.

The conclusion is reinforced, moreover, by a careful reconsideration of premise 5a itself. We were initially led to accept the premise because intuitively it seemed unfair for one person to enjoy benefits from which another has been barred through no act or omission of his own. However, on second glance, this unfairness may be largely mitigated if there is another, comparable benefit that the second person can enjoy instead. It is merely perverse for someone to remain deeply upset over his inability to become a professional athlete when he is perfectly capable of making a successful career in education or business. Because this is so, premise 5a is actually *im*plausible when it is applied to particular benefits without regard to alternatives available. To make 5a generally plausible, we must insist that it range not over particular benefits, but rather over general levels of well-being. Properly understood, 5a should assert only that if M does not deserve to have X while N does not and X makes it possible for M to achieve a particular level of well-being that N does not share, then M does not deserve to exist at *that level of well-being* while N does not. Since this alteration will permit even persons with very superior talents to deserve the benefits of their achievements as long as others are capable of attaining equivalent levels of well-being in other areas, its result will be to relax still further the constraints that the Rawlsian premises place upon desert for achievement.

But despite this loosening, some constraints clearly do remain. Even after we have allowed both for the greater efforts of the less talented and for the possibility of equivalent achievement in alternative areas, there will remain many cases in which one person has achieved a level of well-being that another could not possibly have achieved. This may be because the first person's talents were great, because the second person's talents were minimal, or because the first person was just lucky enough to be in the right place at the right time. Moreover, there will remain many other cases in which a person of meager attainments could indeed have achieved more, but only through efforts that it would have been unreasonable to expect of him. In the former cases, and perhaps even in the latter, premises like Rawls's will indeed suggest that the person who has achieved more does not deserve the full benefit of his achievement relative to the other, but rather deserves only the proportion of it that the other could reasonably have been expected to match. Since every high achiever can be paired with some low achiever in this way, it seems to follow that few people can lay absolutely full claim to all the benefits they have achieved.

These considerations suggest that if the Rawlsian premises are correct, we cannot allow people to enjoy the full benefits of their achievements without permitting many persons to be better off than they deserve to be with respect to at least some others. Assuming that undeserved inequalities that do not bring appropriate compensating benefits are unjust, this concession may seem to tell heavily against allowing people to enjoy whatever they have achieved. In fact, however, the situation is more complicated than this; for even if allowing people to enjoy the benefits of their achievements does permit some undeserved inequalities, it may still come closer to giving everyone what he deserves relative to everyone else than any alternative. To see why, consider a simplified situation in which M has much talent and has achieved much, while N has much talent but has achieved little, and O has little talent and has achieved little. In this situation, N and O may well deserve the same amount relative to each other; but M will deserve more relative to N than he does relative to O. Because of this, M's getting precisely what he deserves relative to N will require that he *not* get precisely what he deserves relative to O, and vice versa. Such cases show that it is almost certainly impossible to allow everyone to get exactly what he deserves relative to everyone else. At best, we can try to design a system in which as few people as possible get more or less than they deserve relative to others. Nothing in Rawls's argument suggests either that such a system will not allow most or all people to enjoy most or all of the benefits they have achieved, or that its remaining undeserved inequalities will be so weighty as to render it unjust. Hence, there remains at least one version of the claim that people deserve what they have achieved which the Rawlsian argument leaves quite untouched.

V

Up to now, my criticism of the Rawlsian argument has been mainly internal. I have contended that even if we grant that people only deserve things relative to others when having those things is of their own doing (2a), and when it is not the result of further undeserved differences (5a), we are still not forced to deny that people commonly do deserve things. To conclude, I will abandon this internal perspective and examine premises 2a and 5a themselves. Despite their surface plausibility, I will argue that both are questionable.

Of the two premises, 2a has the more immediate appeal. There is clearly something attractive about the idea that the ways people fare should not be determined by factors beyond their control—by factors that are "arbitrary from a moral perspective."[10] Yet upon further inspection, this suggestion is neither consistent with Rawls's own reasoning nor clearly defensible on its merits. It is not consistent with Rawls's own reasoning because after dismissing all particular facts about persons, he goes on to derive his own principles of justice from abstract and hypothetical facts that are even further removed from anything persons have done or can control. In particular, his own principles are grounded in choices that *would* be dictated by the abstract features of free and rational agency if persons were placed in a certain constrained choice situation. Because these choices are merely hypothetical and not choices anyone has actually made, they are plainly not within the control of actual agents. Thus, if Rawls's criterion of moral arbitrariness is correct, these choices must be no less morally arbitrary than a person's actual abilities or character traits. Conversely, if his criterion is incorrect, then there is no reason to say that a person's lack of control over his abilities and traits renders *them* morally arbitrary.

Because this rejoinder is merely ad hominem, it does not settle the question of whether characteristics not involving action really are morally arbitrary. At most, it shows that saying that they are arbitrary cuts deeper than many have thought. But there are also other reasons to view Rawls's criterion of arbitrariness with suspicion. If we accepted it, we would in effect be saying that how a person fares may legitimately depend on what he *does*, but never on what he *is*. Yet even if it is an overstatement to say, with R. E. Hobart, that one's actions are morally significant only insofar as they reveal one's character,[11] it certainly is plausible to say that one's character and other traits may have a moral significance that does not *reduce to* the significance of one's acts. In defense of this statement, we may note both that an agent's character and other traits are more stable and enduring than his acts, and that they are, in a familiar sense, more central to his identity. In addition, we may cite our common practice of evaluating character as well as acts. Given all of this, our intuitions and practices do not unqualifiedly support Rawls's claim that all traits beyond one's control are "arbitrary from a moral point of view." To be defensible, that claim would require far more discussion than Rawls provides.

As tenuous as the case for premise 2a is, the case for 5a seems weaker yet. As we have seen, the intuitive reason for accepting 5a—for saying that *M* does not deserve to have something *N* lacks if *M* has acquired it through the use of an ability *N* lacks—is that *M*'s greater ability seems to have given him an unfair advantage. But an advantage is only unfair when it prevents one person from competing on equal terms with another. Once this is made clear, the defense of 5a is seen to presuppose a single (and overly simple) view of the way desert is acquired. Properly understood, it presupposes a wholly competitive model of desert-acquisition. Yet while competition is certainly *one* important context that gives rise to desert, it is clearly not the *only* such context. Instead, anyone initially sympathetic to desert will hold that people may also come to deserve things in many other ways. They may acquire desert by working hard, acting wrongly, behaving virtuously, performing heroic acts, and so on. There is, of course, much room for disagreement over this list; but the basic point is beyond dispute. Extending effort, acting wrongly, and exhibiting virtue are not variant forms of winning. Hence, where they are concerned, the notion of unfair advantage is hopelessly out of place.

Thus the only plausible general defense of 5a collapses. If that premise is ever to be acceptable, it will be only in those comparatively few contexts in which desert does arise through victory in competition. Some such contexts—for example, those in which the best qualified are said to deserve jobs and other opportunities, and entrepreneurs to deserve profits made in competitive markets—are extremely important. However, even in these contexts, the truth of 5a is hardly obvious; for although some undeserved competitive advantages are plainly unfair, it is far from clear that all of them are. Indeed, if we follow Rawls in construing anything that leads to victory, including superior effort-making ability, as a competitive advantage, then all competitive advantages cannot be unfair. To say that they are would be to preclude the possibility of anyone winning, and so would rule out the idea of competition itself.

All in all, Rawls has not succeeded in showing that people rarely or never deserve things. There may be other routes to that conclusion, and there may be independent reasons for systematically ignoring or overriding personal desert; but pending the advancement of some further argument, no satisfactory theory of justice can afford to ignore personal desert.

Notes

1. John Rawls, *A Theory of Justice* (Cambridge: Harvard University Press, 1971), 104; see also pp. 15, 75–76, 310–15, and passim.

2. Rawls, *Theory of Justice*, 104.

3. Although Rawls has presented the most developed version of the anti-desert argument, an abbreviated version of it also appears in Richard Wasserstrom, "The University and the Case for Preferential Treatment," *American Philosophical Quarterly* 13, no. 2 (April 1976): 167. For related discussion, see also Thomas Nagel, "Equal Treatment and Compensatory Discrimination," *Philosophy and Public Affairs* 2, no. 4 (Summer 1973): 348–63; John Schaar, "Equal Opportunity and Beyond," in *Equality: Nomos IX*, eds. J. Roland Pennock and John W. Chapman (New York: Atherton Press, 1967), 228–49; and John Hospers, "What Means This Freedom?" in *Determinism and Freedom in the Age of Modern Science*, ed. Sidney Hook (New York: Collier, 1961), 126–42.

4. I owe this point to Wendy Lotz.

5. Alan Zaitchik, "On Deserving to Deserve," *Philosophy and Public Affairs* 6, no. 4 (Summer 1977): 373.

6. Zaitchik, "Deserving to Deserve," 373.

7. Zaitchik, "Deserving to Deserve," 371.

8. Although I have argued against Rawls's uncritical assumption that people differ in effort-making abilities, I do not wish to suggest that Rawls has been the only philosopher to fall into this error. For another example of it, see my own earlier paper, "Justifying Reverse Discrimination in Employment," *Philosophy and Public Affairs* 4, no. 2 (Winter 1975): 165–67. That paper appears as chapter 3 of this volume.

9. For the argument of this paragraph, I owe an obvious debt to Stuart Hampshire, *Thought and Action* (New York: Viking, 1959), ch. 3.

10. Rawls, *Theory of Justice*, 74.

11. R. E. Hobart, "Free Will as Involving Determination and Inconceivable Without It," *Mind* 43, no. 169 (January 1934): 1–27.

Preferential Treatment, the Future, and the Past

According to many, the current members of groups that suffered discrimination in the past should be given preference when they compete for jobs and educational opportunities. Of those who favor such preference, some regard it as compensation for disadvantages caused by past discrimination, while others argue that it does not matter how the disadvantages arose—that the important thing is simply to eliminate them. Here I shall examine several arguments of the second, purely forward-looking sort. These arguments, I shall contend, cannot succeed in justifying a policy of preference that extends to all members of the relevant groups unless they are backed by assumptions that few of their own proponents would accept. Because most preferential programs *do* strictly follow group lines, my conclusion will be that each apparently forward-looking defense of preferential treatment is best reconstructed as compensatory.

I

The groups most often mentioned in connection with preferential treatment are blacks and women, but affirmative action guidelines have also listed American Indians and Alaskan natives, certain Asians and Pacific Islanders, and persons of Hispanic descent. Although defenders of preferential treatment do not always specify its scope, many seem to favor extending it to all of these groups. Thus, for simplicity, I shall use the term "minority" to encompass all the groups mentioned above except women. For simplicity, too, I shall assume that every affirmative action program involves some form of preferential treatment. While some take affirmative action to require no more than aggressive efforts to broaden applicant pools,[1] its most controversial and interesting feature is precisely its preferential element.

The main areas in which preference is urged are education and employment—just the areas in which much earlier discrimination took place. Thus, one natural way to defend preferential treatment is as compensation for the lingering effects of past discrimination. On this account, its point is not merely to benefit present or future group members, but to do so in ways that nullify or offset harms done by injustice. However, to this common argument, there are two equally common objections: first, that many women and some minority group members have not been harmed by discrimination and, second, that today's young white males are not the ones who discriminated. If preferential treatment both benefits and burdens the wrong persons, its use as compensation will be neither effective nor fair.

By themselves, of course, these objections are far from conclusive. Indeed, to meet them, proponents of the compensatory approach can make any of three replies. They can maintain that: (1) every woman and minority group member has indeed suffered, and every nonminority male has at least indirectly benefited, from the effects of discrimination;[2] that (2) the entities to be compensated are not past or present individuals but the groups to which the initial victims belonged;[3] or that (3) we should extend preference not to every woman or minority group member, but only to those who actually *were* harmed by discrimination.[4] However, responses 1 and 2 raise obvious and well-known difficulties in their turn,[5] while response 3 represents what many regard as an intolerable weakening of the original thesis.

Perhaps for these reasons, many defenders of preferential treatment do not see it as a form of compensation at all. Instead of construing it as a way of righting past wrongs, they defend it simply as a means of promoting certain desirable effects. In the earlier days of affirmative action, these desirable effects were said to consist mainly of benefits to women and members of minority groups. By giving members of these groups access to desirable positions and thus bringing them into the socioeconomic mainstream, preferential treatment was said to disrupt otherwise self-perpetuating cycles of poverty and subservience.[6] However in recent years, the emphasis has shifted to the claim that preferential treatment promotes "diversity" in educational institutions and the workplace. Such diversity, in turn, is said to be valuable because it fosters racial harmony, because it combats racist and sexist stereotypes, because it brings fresh perspectives to academic subjects, or because it realizes some sort of independent ideal.

I suspect that many who now emphasize diversity do so because they consider it an easier sell. Anticipating continued resistance to a policy that helps disadvantaged groups at the expense of others, they seek to show that preferential treatment also benefits many members of more advantaged groups. However, my topic is not the motives of those who advance this (or any other) forward-looking argument, but rather the content and merits of the arguments themselves. To prepare for an assessment of their strength, let us look more closely at their normative underpinnings.

Where the older forward-looking arguments are concerned, the crucial normative question is "Why is it important to bring women and minority groups into the social and economic mainstream?" To this question, the two most common answers are, first, that including these groups will increase their members' well-being without comparably decreasing the well-being of others, and, second, that it will make our society more equal. Thus, any forward-looking defense of preferential treatment that stresses its effects on the disadvantaged groups is apt to be grounded either in the principle of utility or in some variant of the principle of equality. Moreover, at least initially, one or the other of these principles may also appear to undergird each sort of argument from diversity; for any appeal to the generalized benefits of diversity is really an appeal to utility, while one ideal that diversity might satisfy is precisely that of equality.

However, while there is no harm in adding the benefits of diversity to the other benefits associated with preferential treatment, we would beg important questions if we assumed that all non-utilitarian appeals to diversity had to be egalitarian. Quite apart from the difficulty of identifying the relevant principle of equality, this would foreclose the possibility of arguing either that diversity has value in itself or that it promotes some further outcome, such as knowledge, whose value is independent of utility. To leave these possibilities open, I shall not restrict my discussion to appeals to utility and equality, but will also consider the prospects for appealing to some distinct but as-yet-unspecified normative claim about diversity.

II

So far, I have only gestured at a utilitarian defense of preferential treatment; I have briefly mentioned the claim that bringing women and members of minority groups into the socioeconomic mainstream will promote overall utility, but have not said much about how that might occur. To flesh this claim out, I would have to discuss such topics as the diminishing marginal utility of wealth, the effects of its diffusion through minority communities, and the influence of exemplars or "role models" on other group members. Similarly, to flesh out the claim that preferential treatment promotes diversity which in turn promotes useful knowledge, I would have to specify how and when diversity expands our cognitive horizons. Furthermore, to do full justice to the utilitarian approach, I would have to mention many additional benefits of preferential treatment, such as improved access to medical and legal resources within minority communities.

But with the exception of the links between diversity and knowledge, to which I shall return, I do not propose to explore any of these topics. Instead, I shall simply assume that the benefits associated with preferential treatment are reasonably well understood, that preferential treatment does in fact bring at least some of them, and that no fairer way of realizing those benefits would be equally effective. Accepting these assumptions will allow us to move directly to the pivotal question of whether the benefits of preferential treatment can be said to outweigh its costs.

Those costs have also been widely discussed. They include not only the inevitable losses of efficiency that occur when less-than-best-qualified applicants are chosen, but also the devaluation of the real accomplishments of the members of the targeted groups. They include, as well, the promulgation of the destructive view that the members of these groups are less able than others and the hostility and suspicion of the bypassed candidates who believe—rightly or wrongly—that their efforts and accomplishments have been ignored. Most of all, they include what I take to be the extremely damaging balkanization of public life that flows from policies centered on group membership.

My reason for mentioning these costs should not be misunderstood. My point is certainly not that they definitively tip the balance *against* a policy of preference. To draw that conclusion would be as rash as concluding that the costs definitively *fail* to tip the balance. Instead, I mean only that the issue is uncertain enough to make mysterious the common conviction that the balance has definitively been tipped. Thus, when utilitarians portray the case for preferential treatment as urgent and pressing, it is hard to avoid the impression that they are assuming a suppressed premise that has little to do with utility.

That impression is confirmed, moreover, by a dialectic that is initiated by the familiar observation that if we may discriminate in *favor* of minorities and women whenever doing so will maximize utility, then it should also be acceptable to discriminate *against* minorities and women whenever doing *that* would maximize utility. This observation is troublesome because most defenders of preferential treatment deny that racial or sexual discrimination can ever be legitimate. Thus, to reconcile the utilitarian argument for preferential treatment with their other commitments, they must somehow block the implication that it can be reversed.

One way to do this would be to discredit the possibility that racial and sexual discrimination could ever maximize utility. Along these lines, Thomas Nagel has suggested that unlike preferential treatment, racial and sexual discrimination "has no social advantages . . . and attaches a sense of reduced worth to a feature with which people are born."[7] But Nagel's suggestion seems too quick; for as Amy Gutmann and Dennis Thompson have rightly noted,

> In a sexist or racist environment, evidence may very well show that being white and male will help one do a job more effectively. A white male supervisor . . . , for example, may command more respect from racist and sexist co-workers who do not want to work for blacks or women, or who believe that only white males should be in positions of authority.[8]

A utilitarian could of course reply that these benefits are merely short-term, and that in the longer run, utility is best served by instituting color- and gender-blind or preferential policies that will eventually *alter* racist or sexist preferences. But even if this rejoinder is correct, it does not follow that we can always maximize utility by implementing neutral or preferential policies *immediately*. If the conditions that prevail at time *t* would make such policies impractical or self-defeating, then what utility requires may be straightforward racial or sexual discrimination at *t* plus an alteration of that policy later.

A second response to the reversal objection goes deeper. In a well-known discussion, Ronald Dworkin tried to defeat the possibility that racial or sexual discrimination could maximize utility by introducing a distinction between two kinds of preference. He wrote that

> the preferences of an individual for the consequences of a particular policy may be seen to reflect, on further analysis, either a *personal* preference for his own enjoyment of some goods or opportunities, or an *external* preference for the assignment of goods and opportunities to others, or both.[9]

According to Dworkin, this distinction is significant because when utilitarians take account of external preferences, they tie each person's chances of satisfaction to "the respect or affection [others] have for him or for his way of life."[10] If someone is liked or held in high esteem, his preferences count once because he has them and again because others prefer their satisfaction, while if someone is disliked or disdained, he is correspondingly disadvantaged. To avoid such "double counting," Dworkin argued that utilitarians should seek to maximize only the satisfaction of *personal* preferences. He argued, further, that although any utilitarian argument for racial (or, we may add, ethnic or sexual) discrimination will inevitably appeal to external preferences, various plausible utilitarian arguments for preferential treatment appeal only to personal preferences. On these grounds, Dworkin concluded that utilitarians can safely advocate preferential treatment without running the risk of endorsing racial or sexual discrimination.

A preference that positions of authority be held exclusively by white males is obviously external, and so, at least arguably, is a preference that one's own supervisor not be black or female. Thus, Dworkin's strictures may indeed rule out the kind of utilitarian argument for racial or sexual discrimination that Gutmann and Thompson envision. However, despite Dworkin's bare assertion that racial or sexual discrimination can never maximize the satisfaction of purely personal preferences, it is far from clear that this is so. Also, even if it is, there remain extremely serious—indeed, in my view, insuperable—objections to Dworkin's argument against counting external preferences. Because I have developed these objections elsewhere,[11] I shall only briefly summarize them here.

Their point of departure is a question posed by H. L. A. Hart: namely, *which* preferences are counted twice when utilitarians count external as well as personal preferences?[12] As Hart pointed out, the preferences of the person who is liked or disliked and those of the person who likes or dislikes him both seem to be counted exactly once. Moreover, Dworkin subsequently conceded that Hart might be right about this "if votes rather than preferences were in issue, because if someone wished to vote for [another's] success rather than his own, his role in the calculation would be exhausted by this gift."[13] But Dworkin went on to argue that preferences are *not* relevantly like votes because

> someone who reports more preferences to the utilitarian computer does not (except trivially) diminish the impact of the other preferences he also reports; he rather increases the role of his preferences overall, compared with the role of other people's preferences, in the giant calculation.[14]

As this rejoinder makes clear, Dworkin's considered reason for refusing to count external preferences is not that this would count any particular preferences twice, but rather that it would allow some persons to have *more preferences that count than do others*.

But would it? To reach Dworkin's conclusion, we would have to assume, at a minimum, that different people have different numbers of external preferences. If everyone had the *same* number of external preferences, we could avoid any inequity simply by counting all the external preferences that each person has. But if we do grant that different people have different numbers of external preferences—if we stipulate that indifference about the activities of others is not itself a preference—then Dworkin must grant in return that different people also have different numbers of *personal* preferences. Yet if they do, then even discounting all external preferences will not guarantee that we count the same number of preferences for each person. Indeed, in the absence of further information, discounting all external preferences seems just as likely to increase as to decrease any disparities in the numbers of preferences that we count. Also, of course, even if discounting all external preferences were an effective way of counting the same number of preferences for each, it would hardly be the *only* way: we could also do this by discounting an appropriate number of the *personal* preferences of any person who had more overall preferences than others.

All in all, neither Dworkin nor Nagel has succeeded in showing that utility can never be maximized by racial or sexual discrimination. Thus, pending some further argument, utilitarians must regard the wrongness of such discrimination as fundamentally an empirical accident. To whatever extent a forward-looking defender of preferential treatment would find this unacceptable, his position must have some basis other than the principle of utility.

III

Might it rest, instead, on some principle of equality? Could preferential treatment be defended on the grounds that disrupting the existing cycles of disadvantage, and thus bringing women and members of minority groups into the economic mainstream, will make our society significantly more equal?[15] Although this argument, too, might theoretically be reversed to support outright racial or sexual discrimination, it could only be used in that way if women or minorities had already become *more* advantaged than white males—a development that would draw much of the reversal's sting.

Still, before we can evaluate the prospects for an egalitarian defense of preferential treatment, we must clarify the sense in which preferential treatment *is* egalitarian. This requires clarification because what is at issue is precisely the allocation of jobs and opportunities that are *more desirable than others*. Although preferential treatment does channel these jobs and opportunities to members of less-well-off groups, it does not contest the unequal reward schedule that *makes* them especially desirable. Indeed, if anything, it actually presupposes an unequal reward schedule; for preferential treatment would have little point if all jobs paid the same and all opportunities provided identical access to goods. Thus, properly understood, such a policy does not abolish, but merely rearranges, the economic inequalities that prevail among individuals.

This does not mean that preferential treatment cannot be defended on egalitarian grounds, but it does mean that any egalitarian defense must make essential reference to groups. The argument must be that because, say, whites are on average wealthier than blacks, giving blacks preference when they compete for well-paying jobs will narrow the economic gap between these groups. Although this reasoning would not be promising if it assumed that racial and sexual groups have independent moral standing—that assumption is no more plausible in a forward-looking context than it is in a backward-looking one—we can easily preserve the argument's essential reference to groups *without* attributing independent standing to them. To do so, we need only add that the reason it is important to narrow the economic gaps between racial and sexual groups is that doing so will reduce certain collateral inequalities among their members.

These collateral inequalities arise because both the way someone regards himself and the way others regard him are closely bound up with the fortunes of persons *like* him. As Owen Fiss has put the point,

> members of the group identify themselves—explain who they are—by reference to their membership in the group; and their well-being or status is in part determined by the well-being or status of the group.[16]

Given the widespread tendency to identify with others like oneself, even a white who is poor and uneducated is unlikely to despise himself for belonging to an inferior group, while even an affluent and well-educated black may think badly of himself because so many other blacks occupy inferior positions. Also, of course, economic inequalities between groups are notoriously linked to inequalities of status among their members—inequalities of status that influence everything from a person's prospects for friendship and marriage to the treatment he receives from store clerks and the police.

Because the scarcity of blacks in well-paying, prestigious positions reduces the self-respect and status of so many blacks, equalizing the proportions of these positions among the races should *raise* the self-esteem and status of many blacks. Mutatis mutandis, something similar may hold for members of other minorities and women. Moreover, because preferential treatment does not deprive any currently ascendant group of *its* proportionate share of desirable positions—because the groups that are now ascendant and subordinate will not simply change places—the net effect should be to make individuals more equal in self-respect and status. Thus, even if preferential treatment does no more than reshuffle the economic inequalities that prevail among individuals, it may be far more effective in reducing *other* inequalities among them.

Although I shall not argue the point, I think any coherent egalitarian defense of preferential treatment will have to take roughly this form. But is it really consistent to condemn inequalities so selectively? If an egalitarian opposes the inequalities of self-respect and status that are sustained by economic inequalities among racial and sexual groups, mustn't he also oppose the inequalities of self-respect and status that are sustained by economic inequalities simpliciter? Why take race- and sex-based inequalities of self-respect and status more seriously than simple income-based (or class-based) inequalities? For that matter, why take any of these more seriously than the low self-respect and/or status of, say, the disabled, the unintelligent, the physically unattractive, and the uneducated? And what about inequalities of wealth themselves? If someone really favors equality among persons, mustn't he object to economic arrangements under which two persons who try equally hard can end up with very different amounts of wealth and income? And, hence, mustn't he also oppose the unequal reward schedules upon which preferential treatment was seen to depend?[17]

We must of course distinguish between the claim that an inequality is unimportant and the claim that a given remedy for it is ineffective. Thus, to the objection that he cannot consistently oppose race- and gender-related inequalities of self-respect and status without also opposing many other inequalities, a defender of preferential treatment could reply that his attitude reflects not a belief that the other inequalities are unobjectionable, but only a conviction that they must be dealt with in other ways. Moreover, to the more pointed objection that preferential treatment actually *presupposes* a framework of unequal rewards, he could similarly reply that his support of preferential treatment is merely conditional—that it is predicated on the assumption that unequal rewards are a regrettable but unalterable fact of contemporary life, and that no more extensive equality is currently attainable.

But although these positions are there to be occupied, they are very seldom actually taken. Indeed, despite the occasional attempt to include homosexuals or the handicapped among the recipients of preference, what is most striking is precisely how few defenders of preferential treatment have represented it either as part of a comprehensive egalitarian package or as a second-best strategy acceptable only in light of our inability to implement more sweeping egalitarian reforms.[18] Instead, preferential treatment is usually proffered as a free-standing remedy for a single, well-defined set of social evils—a stance that implies that the condition to be remedied is objectionable for reasons independent of the demands of equality.

Like my earlier objections to the utilitarian defense, this objection to the egalitarian defense is in a sense ad hominem. Its thrust is not that no egalitarian principle could be paired with defensible supplementary premises to yield a plausible defense of preferential treatment, but only that no such combination underlies the arguments of most supporters of preferential treatment. But because my topic is just the arguments as they are actually advanced—because my central point is precisely that few who favor affirmative action really do so on purely forward-looking grounds—this implication can simply be accepted. For the record, I also doubt that preferential treatment *is* any part of the best available egalitarian package: we have, after all, now had twenty years of affirmative action, and despite the emergence of a sizeable black middle class, the differences in self-image and status between the races seem if anything to have widened.[19] I am skeptical, too, of the tenability of any suitably robust egalitarian principle. However, because any discussion of these claims would quickly take us far afield, we must dismiss them as beyond our scope.

IV

Let us therefore turn instead to the last of our forward-looking defenses, the argument from diversity—an argument more beloved of college administrators than philosophers. As we saw, some versions of this argument, including the one that claims that diversity fosters racial understanding and harmony, are in effect appeals to utility and as such have already been dealt with. However, others, such as the arguments that diversity advances the aims of intellectual inquiry and that it is valuable just in itself, raise new issues which require separate treatment.

The claim that diversity contributes to intellectual inquiry is very familiar. Neil Rudenstine, the president of Harvard, recently expressed what has become the conventional wisdom this way:

> A diverse educational environment challenges [students] to explore ideas
> and arguments at a deeper level—to see issues from various sides, to
> rethink their own premises, to achieve the kind of understanding that

comes only from testing their own hypotheses against those of people with other views.[20]

Although this argument obviously does not support all forms of preferential treatment—it is, for example, irrelevant both to non-academic hiring and to contractual "set-asides"—it does purport to justify, through an appeal to values internal to the academy's own mission, both preferential admission to many educational institutions and preferential hiring across the curricular spectrum.

Its reasoning can itself be fleshed out in various ways. Some of its proponents, including Rudenstine, stress the value *to students* of exposure to different perspectives, while others stress the value of diversity in research. Of those who focus on research, some argue that including hitherto excluded groups will open up new areas of investigation, while others emphasize the value of diverse challenges to all hypotheses, including, or especially, hypotheses in traditional, well-worked areas. Of those who emphasize challenges to hypotheses, some stress the importance of confronting all hypotheses with the broadest possible range of potentially falsifying tests, while others focus on exposing the hidden biases of investigators.[21] Because the argument is so protean, I shall not work systematically through its variants, but will pose only a single question that applies to each (and applies, as well, to the related claim that diversity is valuable just in itself). Predictably enough, the question is why we should focus on just the groups that affirmative action singles out.

For even if diversity yields every one of the benefits that are claimed for it, why should we assume that these benefits are greatest when the scholarly community contains substantial numbers of blacks, women, Hispanics, American Indians, Aleuts, and Chinese-Americans? Why not focus instead, or in addition, on Americans of Eastern European, Arabic, or Asian Indian extraction? For that matter, can't we achieve even greater diversity by extending preference to *native* Africans, Asians, Arabs, and Europeans? And why understand diversity only in terms of gender, ethnicity, and national origin? Why should a population that is diverse in this dimension provide any more educational or scholarly benefit than one that is ethnically homogeneous but includes suitable numbers of gays, religious fundamentalists, the young, the old, the handicapped, ex-military officers, conservatives, Marxists, Mormons, and blue-collar workers? These groups, too, have characteristic concerns, types of experience, and outlooks on the world. Thus, why not also give *them* preference whenever they are not represented in proportion to their numbers?[22] And why, to realize the benefits of the female perspective, must we further increase the number of women in the academy when it already contains far more women than members of many other non-preferred groups?

The most salient feature of the groups on the official list is of course the discrimination they have suffered. While this may not entirely explain the composition of the list—that may, in part, reflect the play of political forces—it does explain the prominence of such core groups as blacks and women. Thus, the most promising way to complete the argument without smuggling in non-academic values is to add that beliefs and attitudes shaped by oppression are better suited than others to advance educational or scholarly aims.

Although we obviously cannot assume that all the members of any group think alike, a history of discrimination may indeed have an effect on the way many of a group's members tend to view the world. In addition to the already-noted high degree of collective identification, the perspective of the oppressed is often said to include a keen awareness of the motives, prejudices, and hidden agendas of others, a heightened sense of the oppressive effects of even seemingly benign social structures, and a strong commitment to social change. As a corollary, this perspective may include a degree of antagonism toward received opinion and a certain impatience with abstraction. Thus, to complete this part of our discussion, we must ask whether, and if so how, any of these beliefs, attitudes, or traits might make a special contribution to education or research.

Here it is important to distinguish between the educational or scholarly value of *learning about* the perspective of the oppressed and the educational or scholarly value of *actually taking* that perspective. This distinction is important because some who urge wide exposure to the relevant beliefs, attitudes, etc., do appear to believe that what matters is simply learning about them. This, at any rate, is one natural interpretation of the common claim that diversity is important because it acquaints non-minority students with the hardships and obstacles that many members of minority groups confront daily, and because it teaches non-minority students that many members of these groups consider themselves disenfranchised and do not trust social institutions whose necessity and justice others take for granted. Yet while such knowledge may contribute significantly to mutual understanding and social harmony, the beliefs, attitudes, traits, and experiences that are characteristic of oppressed groups are in the end only one class of facts among innumerable others. Considered simply as objects of study—and this is how we must consider them if the diversity argument is not to be just another tributary of the great utilitarian river—the beliefs, attitudes, traits, and experiences of the oppressed are no more important than those of the non-oppressed, which in turn are no more important than indefinitely many other possible objects of inquiry.

Thus, to give their variant of the diversity argument a fighting chance, those who attach special educational and scholarly value to the perspective of the oppressed must take the other path. They must locate its special educational or scholarly value not in anyone's *coming to know* that oppressed groups hold certain beliefs, attitudes, etc., but rather in the contribution of those beliefs and attitudes to the acquisition of *other* knowledge. Their argument must be that this perspective uniquely enhances our collective ability to pose or resolve questions across much of the intellectual spectrum. To show that the perspective of the oppressed generates new lines of inquiry, friends of diversity often cite the tendency of women to pursue scientific research with humanitarian rather than militaristic applications and the contributions that various minorities have made to history and other fields by studying their own past and present. To show that this perspective contributes to the investigation of established topics, they point out that black and female investigators tend to be specially attuned to the inclusion of blacks and women in experimental control groups, that black students bring to the study of law a well-founded mistrust of the police, and that enhanced sensitivity to power relations has opened up fruitful new ways of interpreting literary texts.

We certainly must agree that the beliefs, attitudes, and traits of oppressed groups have made important contributions to the way academic questions are now formulated and addressed. However, what friends of diversity must show is not merely that these beliefs, attitudes, and traits make *some* significant contribution to effective inquiry, but that they are *more* conducive to it, all things considered, than any of the alternative mixtures that would emerge if there were no affirmative action or if preference were given to other sorts of groups. To see what is wrong with this stronger conclusion, we need only revisit the argument's two main branches.

First, oppressed groups are hardly the only ones whose concerns and interests can be expected to channel research in some directions rather than others. Just as the recent influx of blacks, Hispanics, and women has led to a variety of new scientific, historical, and literary projects, and to various new interpretive strategies, so would any comparable influx of, say, Baptists, Muslims, Marxists, or vegetarians. More subtly, any admissions policy that self-consciously sought out persons with certain traits of intellect or character would also greatly influence what people study and how they study it. The academic agenda would evolve very differently if students and faculty were selected primarily for, say, altruism than if they were selected for intellectual honesty, literary imagination and a flair for language, or dogged persistence. Indeed, even without any attempt to depart from traditional merit-based selection criteria, the endless play of human creativity can be expected to ensure continuing novelty in the projects and approaches that find adherents. The history of inquiry prior to affirmative action is hardly a chronicle of stagnation.

Nor, second, are the beliefs, attitudes, and traits of the oppressed any more likely to be helpful in *answering* intellectual questions than any number of others. There are, to be sure, many contexts in which antagonism toward received opinion, impatience with useless abstraction, and a desire to unearth or vindicate the contributions of a particular group do make important contributions to the solution of a problem—but there are also many contexts in which these traits and attitudes are highly counterproductive. They are, for example, more likely to be distorting than helpful when one is trying to construct a mathematical proof, evaluate the properties of a new chemical compound, understand how neurotransmitters work, or write a computer program. Where such tasks are concerned, the biases of others are irrelevant unless they issue in bad inferences or dishonesty in handling data—flaws that the standard techniques of review and replication seem well suited to discover. Neither skepticism about others' motives nor deep commitment to social change seems likely to generate many potentially falsifying hypotheses.

My own view is that we will make the most progress if we simply stock the academy with persons who display the traditional academic excellences to the highest degree. The students and faculty members who are most likely to help us progress toward true beliefs, powerful explanations, deep understanding, and a synoptic world view are just the ones with the greatest analytical ability, the most imagination, the best memory, and the strongest desire to pursue the truth wherever it leads. However, while these are things that I deeply believe, my argument does not require any premise this strong. Instead, it requires only the much weaker premise that indefinitely many traits of intellect or character are sometimes useful in advancing cognitive or pedagogical aims, and that we have no reason to expect the beliefs and attitudes of the oppressed to be preeminent among these.

This reasoning, of course, presupposes that the aims of the academy *are* to be understood in terms of truth, understanding, explanation, and the rest. If they are not—if, for example, the basic aim is instead to promote social change—then the case for favoring the beliefs and attitudes of the oppressed may well be stronger. However, if someone does take the basic aim to be social change, and if he urges that we hire or admit more members of oppressed groups to expedite such change, then he will no longer be appealing to the very academic values that even his opponents share. This, again, is an implication that few who advance the proposed argument would welcome.

V

We have now examined the three most prominent forward-looking defenses of preferential treatment. Although much more could obviously be said, we have seen enough to show that all three are vulnerable to what is at bottom the same objection.

For when we examined the utilitarian defense, we asked why it is legitimate to promote utility by giving preference to women and members of minority groups but not to white males; when we examined the egalitarian defense, we asked why mitigating inequalities of self-respect and status that track membership in racial and sexual groups is more important than mitigating other inequalities; and when we examined the diversity defense, we asked why increasing the number of women and members of minority groups in the academy is more academically valuable than promoting diversity of other sorts. In each case, the central question was "Why focus on just these groups?" In each case, too, we found no forward-looking answer that was consistent with the other commitments of most who propose the argument.

In view of this, it seems reasonable to take those proponents to be appealing to a premise of some different sort. Moreover, given the broader context in which the discussion has taken place, their further premise is not hard to find. Because the most salient fact about blacks, women, American Indians, Hispanics, etc., is just that they *were* so often discriminated against, the suppressed reason for focusing attention on them can hardly fail to be that they, unlike the others, now have claims to compensation.[23]

If this suggestion is correct, then even the defenses of preferential treatment that at first seem purely forward-looking will have an ineliminable backward-looking component. They will indeed justify preferential treatment for women and members of minority groups on the grounds that this will promote desirable future outcomes; but their concentration on these groups will in turn be rooted in wrongs done to their members in the past. They will indeed shift the emphasis from harms already done to harms or benefits that have yet to occur; but their selection among these future harms and benefits will depend on what they see as the ongoing effects of injustice.

Because this reasoning reconnects preferential treatment to past wrongdoing, it also reestablishes the claim that the only persons who ought to receive preference are those who were (or are in danger of being) *affected* by wrongdoing. These persons will undoubtedly include many blacks and members of other official minorities, but there is little reason to believe they will include them all. Moreover, they are also likely to include many members of other discriminated-against groups, such as Italians, Jews, Slavs, and the Irish, which are not on the official list. Because so many groups have been treated unjustly, any attempt to single out the endangered future members of some few of them is likely to be quite arbitrary. Thus, the proposed arguments do not avoid, but if anything actually extend, the crucial question of who should be compensated for the effects of past wrongdoing.

Notes

1. See, for example, Amy Gutmann and Dennis Thompson, *Democracy and Disagreement* (Cambridge: Harvard University Press, 1996), chap. 9.

2. Judith Jarvis Thomson, "Preferential Hiring," *Philosophy and Public Affairs* 2, no. 4 (Summer 1973): 381; and Allison Jaggar, "Relaxing the Limits on Preferential Hiring," *Social Theory and Practice* 4, no. 2 (Spring 1977): 231.

3. Paul W. Taylor, "Reverse Discrimination and Compensatory Justice," *Analysis* 33, no. 6 (June 1973): 177–82; and Michael D. Bayles, "Reparations to Wronged Groups," *Analysis* 33, no. 6 (June 1973): 182–84.

4. George Sher, "Justifying Reverse Discrimination in Employment," *Philosophy and Public Affairs* 4, no. 2 (Winter 1975): 159–70 (chapter 3 of this volume); and Alan H. Goldman, "Limits to the Justification of Reverse Discrimination," *Social Theory and Practice* 3, no. 3 (Spring 1975): 289–306.

5. For discussion of these difficulties, see George Sher, "Groups and Justice," *Ethics* 87, no. 2 (January 1977): 174–81 (chapter 4 of this volume); and Robert Simon, "Preferential Hiring: A Reply to Judith Jarvis Thomson," *Philosophy and Public Affairs* 3, no. 3 (Spring 1974): 312–20.

6. For versions of the forward-looking approach, see Ronald Dworkin, *Taking Rights Seriously* (Cambridge: Harvard University Press, 1977), 223–39; Thomas Nagel, "Equal Treatment and Compensatory Discrimination," *Philosophy and Public Affairs* 2, no. 4 (Summer 1973): 348–63; Irving Thalberg, "Reverse Discrimination and the Future," *Philosophical Forum* 5, nos. 1 and 2 (Fall-Winter 1973–74): 294–308; and Richard Wasserstrom, "The University and the Case for Preferential Treatment," *American Philosophical Quarterly* 13, no. 2 (April 1976): 165–70. For additional discussion, see Richard Wasserstrom, "Racism, Sexism, and Preferential Treatment: An Approach to the Topics," *UCLA Law Review* 24, no. 3 (February 1977): 581–622.

7. Nagel, "Equal Treatment and Compensatory Discrimination," 360.

8. Gutmann and Thompson, *Democracy and Disagreement*, 325–26.

9. Dworkin, *Taking Rights Seriously*, 234.

10. Dworkin, *Taking Rights Seriously*, 235.

11. See George Sher, *Beyond Neutrality: Perfectionism and Politics* (New York: Cambridge University Press, 1997), 97–100.

12. H. L. A. Hart, "Utility and Rights," *Columbia Law Review* 79 (1979): 842.

13. Ronald Dworkin, *A Matter of Principle* (Cambridge: Harvard University Press, 1985), 365.

14. Dworkin, *A Matter of Principle*, 366.

15. For such an approach, see Thalberg, "Reverse Discrimination and the Future," and Dworkin, *Taking Rights Seriously*.

16. Owen Fiss, "Groups and the Equal Protection Clause," *Philosophy and Public Affairs* 5, no. 2 (Winter 1976): 148.

17. Because there are many possible egalitarian principles, the exact significance of the cited inequalities of self-respect and status can be expected to vary. There is no reason to expect them to have the same significance to an advocate of, say, equality of resources as to someone who advocates equality of welfare, of opportunity, of opportunity *for* welfare, or of capacity for functioning. However, for our purposes, what matters is only that *no* major egalitarian theory takes these inequalities to eclipse all others. Even welfare-egalitarians, whom we might expect to pay more attention to them than do (some) others, have no reason to ignore such additional determinants of inequality of welfare as inequalities of wealth and income.

18. An important exception is Nagel, who writes, "If we were to act on the principle that different abilities do not merit different rewards, it would result in much more equality than is demanded by proponents of compensatory discrimination" ("Equal Treatment and Compensatory Discrimination," 352–53). However, Nagel does not defend the principle that he takes to require this much equality.

19. At the very least, the gap between the best-off whites and the worst-off blacks seems pretty clearly to have widened. For resourceful discussion of the different ways in which we can think about inequality between groups, see Larry Temkin, *Inequality* (New York: Oxford University Press, 1993).

20. Neil L. Rudenstine, "Why a Diverse Student Body Is So Important," *Chronicle of Higher Education*, April 19, 1996: B1.

21. For discussion that touches on both positions, see Elizabeth Anderson, "The Democratic University: The Role of Justice in the Production of Knowledge," *Social Philosophy and Policy* 12, no. 2 (Summer 1995): 186–219.

22. For related discussion, see Robert Simon, "Affirmative Action and the University: Faculty Appointment and Preferential Treatment," in *Affirmative Action and the University: A Philosophical Inquiry*, ed. Steven M. Cahn (Philadelphia: Temple University Press, 1993), 74–82.

23. Here I assume that any backward-looking defense of preferential treatment is in effect compensatory. As Alan Wertheimer has pointed out to me, this assumption may require defense: it is possible that "in choosing among the social problems that we want to remedy, we should give a higher priority to those that arise from wrongdoing even though our goal is not to compensate groups or even members of those groups" (unpublished letter). I agree that this possibility is worth investigating, but I doubt that it would figure in the best reconstruction of what proponents of ostensibly forward-looking defenses of preferential treatment have in mind.

7

Right Violations and Injustices: Can We Always Avoid Trade-Offs?

A unifying theme in recent social philosophy is that considerations of rights or justice place significant constraints on action. On one strong interpretation, these constraints are said to imply that, if an action would violate X's rights or do X an injustice, then we can never justify it by saying that it would prevent violations of the rights or claims of justice of Y and Z. This position is taken, for example, by Robert Nozick:

> A theory may include in a primary way the nonviolation of rights, yet include it in the wrong place and the wrong manner. For suppose some condition about minimizing the total (weighted) amount of violations of rights is built into the desirable end state to be achieved. We then would have something like a "utilitarianism of rights"; violations of rights (to be *minimized*) merely would replace the total happiness as the relevant end state in the utilitarian structure.[1]

In this essay, I will argue that this view is mistaken and that we must acknowledge a need for trade-offs among right violations or injustices if we wish to accept the framework of rights or justice at all. First, I will adduce several problems of social policy that suggest this result. Next, I will argue against some possible ways of avoiding the force of the examples. Finally, I will make some more positive observations about the extent of the required trade-offs and their relation to utilitarianism.

I

To see why we must sometimes accept trade-offs among right violations or injustices, consider the following three examples.

1. Any system of criminal justice aims to convict and punish all and only those who are guilty of crimes. Hence, within such a system, an injustice is done either when an innocent person is punished or when a guilty one is not. To minimize injustices of the first sort, many criminal justice systems incorporate strict procedural safeguards, stringent rules of evidence, and the like. Unfortunately, in so guarding against the punishment of the innocent, such rules also increase the number of guilty persons who will be acquitted. Rules of due process protect the innocent and guilty alike. More generally, it seems that most, if not all, attempts to reduce injustice in one direction will also increase it in the other. Because no actual system can avoid both acquitting some guilty persons and punishing some innocent ones, we cannot simply refuse to adopt any system that will yield some unjust decisions. Instead, if we are to base our selection upon justice at all, it must be in some more complicated way.[2]

2. Discrimination on the basis of race or sex is widely held either to be unjust or to violate a right. When past discrimination has reduced a person's ability to qualify for a good job that he otherwise would have gotten, a natural way of compensating him is to hire him instead of the better-qualified applicant. Because preferential hiring rectifies (part of) the effect of discrimination without depriving the better-qualified applicant of anything he would have had in a totally just society, it may itself be called for by rights or justice. However, if preference is extended to someone who would not have been best qualified in the absence of discrimination, then better-qualified applicants are themselves treated unjustly or in a way that violates their rights. In view of this, rights or justice may well dictate preference for all and only those who would have been best qualified in the absence of discrimination. However, given the imperfection of our causal knowledge, we cannot accurately single out those persons whose abilities were reduced by past discrimination; and still less can we specify the precise degree to which anyone's abilities were reduced. Thus, here again, any policy we choose may involve some injustice or violate some people's rights.[3]

3. Some people cannot earn enough to purchase everything they need. When such persons live in an affluent society and when their poverty is not the result of their own responsible choice, they are plausibly said to have a right to have their needs met. If someone whose poverty stems from an inability to act responsibly is simply given the money to buy what he needs, he is apt to squander it instead of using it to purchase necessities. Hence, providing such persons with stipends rather than services will not satisfy their right to have their needs met. However, if someone is capable of acting responsibly and is poor for some other reason beyond his control, then providing aid in a restric-

tive manner will violate what many consider his right not to be treated paternalistically. In the absence of a reliable test for the ability to choose responsibly, any actual welfare policy is sure to involve many violations of at least one of these rights. Thus, here again, we seem unable to reject every policy that violates someone's rights.[4]

The rights and principles of justice just postulated are obviously controversial. However, for our purposes, any controversy they engender may be ignored. The point of the examples is not to resolve any substantive issues but only to illustrate the variety of contexts in which we seem forced to choose among policies, all of which involve some injustice or violate some people's rights. That this dilemma crosses political lines is shown by the fact that "positive" or welfare rights are favored mainly by liberals, while the need for a just system of punishment is granted by liberals and conservatives alike, and the propriety of compensating for the effects of past wrongs is acknowledged even by entitlement theories such as Nozick's.[5] Given this diversity, the dilemma is plainly not the exclusive possession of any single ideology. Indeed, I suspect it must arise within any plausible account of what people have a right to or what justice requires.[6]

II

Our examples seem to cast serious doubt upon Nozick's blanket prohibition against trade-offs involving right violations or injustices. However, philosophical examples are rarely self-explanatory, and these will not be conclusive until their theoretical import is clarified. To do this, we must now consider a number of objections.

Perhaps the most familiar response to the contention that we cannot satisfy everyone's rights or claims of justice is that this contention trades on an incomplete specification of the relevant rights or claims. To see what is meant by this, consider a simple case in which X's medical needs cannot be met without the use of something Y owns, while Y refuses to allow X the use of that thing. If there are exceptionless rights both to have one's medical needs met and to control the use of one's property, then X's right will indeed conflict with Y's. However, if the right to have one's medical needs met does not extend to the use of private property without permission, or if property rights do not include the right to dictate the use of one's property under all circumstances, there will be no conflict. Thus, by building exceptions into rights, we appear able to avoid the need to choose among alternative right violations.[7]

There are obvious questions here. Without further argument, it cannot be assumed that the exceptions to any right are finite in number; nor is it clear why we should prefer a scheme in which absolute rights are hedged with complicated exceptions to one in which simple rights differ in weight. However, for our purposes, these questions can be set aside; for even if they can be answered, no redrawing of the boundaries of rights or justice can dispose of our original examples. At best, such redistricting may succeed in cases like that of X and Y, where, given prevailing conditions, the same act that is required by one party's rights or claims is forbidden by the other's. However, in our earlier examples, the problem was very different. The difficulty there was not that any circumstance rendered all rights or claims incapable of joint satisfaction but rather that we simply could not learn enough about each party's characteristics and history to determine what his rights or claims of justice were. We were unable to ascertain with accuracy who had committed which crime, who had been harmed to what degree by past discrimination, and which of the poor were incapable of managing their own lives. These inabilities would not be affected by any more elaborate specification of the characteristics that determine rights or claims of justice. Instead, because such specification would increase the gap between what we can know and what we must know to satisfy all rights or claims, it would actually make the problem worse.

III

These considerations show that we cannot avoid all trade-offs by building exceptions into rights or principles of justice. They also show that we cannot describe every right or claim of justice that we cannot satisfy as overridden or cancelled rather than violated. Such locutions may be appropriate when the unsatisfied right or claim conflicts with another, but not when the problem lies in simple factual ignorance. Yet just because our problem is generated by ignorance, a second response may look more promising. There is some reason to believe that a prohibition against trade-offs should apply only to violations of the rights or claims of identifiable persons or only to violations that are intentional. Because our examples all involve unintended violations of the rights or claims of unidentifiable persons, either restriction would undercut their force.

The suggestion that trade-offs are only forbidden when they violate the rights or claims of identifiable persons may appear to reflect a common attitude toward "statistical lives." Many people attach more weight to the interests (and, by extension, to the rights and claims of justice) of identifiable persons than to those of persons known only as statistics. Yet even if this attitude can be justified (and the outlook here is not bright),[8] it actually supports a conclusion very different from the one Nozick needs. If correct, the popular view would imply a comparative weighting of the rights or claims of identifiable and unidentifiable persons. It would imply that, for some finite $N > 1$, violating the rights of N unidentifiable persons is equivalent to violating the rights of one identifiable person. However, if so, and if under conditions C it is permissible to violate the rights of one unidentifiable person to promote the rights of M unidentifiable others, then under C it must also be permissible to violate the rights of one unidentifiable person to promote the rights of M/N identifiable others or to violate the rights of one identifiable person to promote the rights of $N \times M$ unidentifiable others. But having come this far, we can hardly deny that under C it is permissible to violate the rights of one identifiable person to promote the rights of M identifiable others. Thus, properly understood, the popular view actually tells against the proposed qualification to Nozick's prohibition.

There is a further reason to reject the proposed qualification. Suppose that normally impermissible trade-offs were permissible as long as the affected parties could not be identified. Then it would be permissible to use such impersonal means as computers to select small numbers of persons whose rights would secretly be violated to promote the rights of many others. But nobody who held the Nozickean view would allow this sort of exception. Hence, the identifiability of the persons affected cannot be a relevant factor.

The other half of the current suggestion, that Nozick's prohibition applies only to intended violations, also has some initial appeal. The standard examples of intuitively impermissible trade-offs—cases in which an innocent person is executed to prevent the wrongful execution of others or one person's vital organs are forcibly redistributed to save several other lives—all involve violations of one person's rights or claims of justice as a means to satisfying the rights or claims of others. If intended results are defined to include results chosen as means, then these impermissible violations are indeed intended. Thus, it is a short step to the conclusion that their intentional nature is part of what makes them impermissible.

It is, however, far from clear that this step should be taken. If we took it, we would in effect imply that rights or claims of justice can only be violated by intentional deviations from the relevant norms. However, this view is accepted neither by Nozick nor his rivals. No defender of positive rights (to welfare aid, to a minimum standard of living, etc.) would deny that these rights can be violated by unintended as well as intended failures to provide the relevant goods. Moreover, no defender of Nozick's view that there are only rights to noninterference (and to compensation for interference) would deny that these rights can be violated by unintended interference. On Nozick's scheme, even the unintended destruction of someone's property may call for compensation. It may indeed be true that rights and justice always demand certain acts or omissions (as opposed to mere results) and that full compliance with this demand is always intentional. However, none of this implies that only intentional noncompliance counts as a violation.[9]

Confronted with this reply, one who denies the need for trade-offs may try a different tack. Instead of maintaining that the unintended consequences of acts never count as right violations or injustices, he may contend only that they lack this status when they are the unavoidable side effects of acts all of whose alternatives would involve intentional violations. To support this contention, he may invoke the well-known "doctrine of double effect." That doctrine says that, when a given act is required to avoid a significant harm (or to produce a significant good), the agent is allowed to bring about as an unintended but foreseen consequence of his act a result that he is not allowed to produce intentionally. In our examples, the unintentional production of some bad effects is indeed required to avoid even worse results. Hence, it may seem to follow that the former effects, when produced, do not count as right violations or injustices.

However, even if the doctrine of double effect is simply accepted without question,[10] this conclusion is doubly mistaken. First, even if the doctrine did apply to our examples, it would not imply that the permitted "punishment mistakes" or failures to compensate are not right violations or injustices. Instead, it would at most imply that these violations, being unintentional, are less serious than their intentional alternatives. But, second, the doctrine is clearly not applicable to our examples, because in them we are asked to choose not between acts with intended and unintended bad effects but rather among acts all of whose bad effects are equally unintended. We are asked to weigh the unintended conviction of some innocent persons against the equally unintended acquittal of some guilty ones, the unintended neglect of some claims to compensation against the equally unintended bypassing of some best-qualified job candidates who have not benefited from past discrimination, and so on. Where such choices are concerned, the doctrine of double effect offers no guidance at all. Because it does not, it leaves our dilemma intact.

IV

We have rejected attempts to disarm our examples by building restrictions into rights and principles of justice and by restricting the sphere of forbidden trade-offs. Given these results, any defensible prohibition against trade-offs must be backed by a more fundamental reorientation of our thinking. One familiar approach to rights and justice seems to embody just such a reorientation. Let us now consider it.

Much of the preceding discussion implies that rights or claims of justice exist prior to policy decisions—that they are moral facts whose degree of accommodation determines the acceptability of social arrangements. However, this implication has itself been questioned. As an alternative, it is sometimes held that rights or claims of justice are logically secondary and flow from the demands of whatever social system is preferable all in all. If someone believes this, he may deny that a right or claim of justice is violated every time an innocent person is convicted and punished, for he may believe that there is no right or claim to be acquitted if innocent. Instead, he may contend that there is only a weaker right to be accused and tried under a system that minimizes the likelihood of such "punishment mistakes." Of course, to decide which system is optimal, we must first establish the relative importance of not punishing the innocent and not acquitting the guilty; but precisely because this comparison is presystemic, it does not require us to weigh one sort of right violation or injustice against another. Because of this, the problem of weighing alternative sets of violations may be held not to arise.

This systemic approach to rights and justice is currently in vogue. It is suggested by the Rawlsian conceptions of primary goods, representative persons, and pure procedural justice, as well as by Rawls's more explicit remarks about macro and micro considerations.[11] Nevertheless, its introduction here is hardly decisive. Let us grant for argument's sake that the first task of social theory is to establish what the basic social framework should be like and that, prior to this, there are no rights or claims of justice and so a fortiori no need to choose among violations of them. Even so, the question of how to implement the rights and claims that are thus determined—of which policy arrangements will best accommodate them under actual social, economic, and epistemic conditions—is not necessarily resolved. It seems, prima facie, that such questions arise only after "punishment mistakes" and harms caused by discrimination are identified as incompatible with fundamental principles, and so as right violations or injustices. But if so, then, although there may be one sense in which the rights of an innocent person are not violated when he is convicted by an optimal system, there is another clear sense in which those rights are violated. Moreover, even if the latter assertion were somehow improper, the innocent person who is punished would still be treated unjustly. But if so, then the systemic approach does not eliminate all need for trade-offs among right violations or injustices.

We obviously cannot canvass all possible variations of the systemic approach. However, to appreciate just how unsuited it is to resolve our problem, we need only consider the details of Rawls's own version of it. Although Rawls abjures the policy questions of compensation and punishment that arise because people do not act justly, he does try to show how his machinery can determine the policies that a totally just society would adopt. To this end, he proposes a four-stage sequence in which the "veil of ignorance" is progressively lifted.[12] In that sequence, the parties in the original position are asked to make increasingly specific decisions under constraints imposed by their earlier decisions. In particular, they are asked in the third stage to choose laws (and, by extension, policies) that are appropriate to current conditions under constraints imposed by the structural and constitutional principles chosen in previous stages. Because the reasoning of the third stage is thus constrained, it presupposes that the most basic principles of justice are already established. Rawls in effect concedes this by acknowledging that laws chosen at this stage could be unjust. But if so, then the parties evaluating competing laws and policies *must* accept some injustice whenever (*a*) their previous decisions imply that all and only people who are *S* ought to be given treatment *T*, but (*b*) their information about current social conditions includes the fact that there is no reliable test for *S*. Statement *a* holds trivially, because it merely expresses the form of a moral principle, while *b*'s pervasive truth was the burden of section I. Thus, Rawls's own theory hardly dispenses with the need to balance injustices or right violations at the policy level. If anything, it actually provides a method of striking the needed balance.

V

Our examples appear to stand. Because they do, we cannot simultaneously satisfy all rights or claims of justice. Thus, we must accept some trade-offs among right violations or injustices. However, it is not yet clear what this comes to. For one thing, it is unclear whether our examples commit us, in any important sense, to a "utilitarianism of rights" (or justice). For another, it is not clear whether we should accept trade-offs only when we lack sufficient information to satisfy all rights or claims of justice or in other contexts as well.

Consider first the contention that our examples commit us to a "utilitarianism of rights" or justice. If this contention means only that we must base our trade-offs on a principle that dictates some form of maximization or minimization, then it follows immediately from what was said above. However, thus construed, the contention is uninteresting.

A more interesting interpretation, suggested by Nozick's assertion that the non-violation of rights may enter "in the wrong place and in the wrong manner," is that trade-offs among violations not only commit us to some form of minimizing principle but also obscure some fundamental difference between the framework of rights or justice and that of utility. If this were the case, then our examples would undermine the very coherence of rights and justice themselves.

Why should a principle governing trade-offs among violations be thought to have this implication? The answer, I think, is that any such principle may appear to embody two quite incompatible attitudes toward value and its maximization. When orthodox utilitarians tell us to maximize happiness or preference satisfaction, their rationale is that happiness or preference satisfaction has value and that we ought to maximize this value. When "ideal utilitarians" or teleologists urge the production of such noncommensurables as knowledge or aesthetic appreciation in addition to happiness, the value of these items serves both as their common measure and as the justification for their production. Thus, if any minimizing principle is to govern trade-offs among right violations or injustices, then it too is naturally viewed as dictating the minimization of some sort of negative value. This implies that what is wrong with right violations and injustices is precisely that they have negative value. Yet right violations and injustices, unlike other sorts of occurrences, may appear to resist this treatment. By their nature, rights and justice stand in opposition to mere interests and values. They place constraints or boundaries upon the ways in which values may be pursued. Thus, they may seem incapable of fulfilling their role if their satisfaction is itself construed as a special kind of value.

Given these considerations, the underlying worry appears to be that trade-offs commit us to regarding right violations and injustices as occurrences with negative value and so prevent us from regarding rights and justice as constraining the pursuit of value. To eliminate this worry, one might argue either that the principle governing trade-offs need not dictate the maximization or minimization of any kind of value or else that, even if it did, it would not prevent rights or justice from delimiting the pursuit of (other) values. In fact, I want to argue for both propositions. Consider first what is to be minimized or maximized. To see why this need not be any kind of value, we need only recall our reason for retreating to trade-offs when we lack sufficient information to avoid all right violations or injustices. Put simply, our reason is that, by accepting the right combination of violations, we can at least come as close as possible to treating all persons as their rights or claims of justice dictate. However, given this aim, we can naturally understand what we want to maximize as not a kind of value but rather simply the degree to which we fulfill our duties or treat people as they ought to be treated. Put in terms of minimization, our goal is to minimize not negative value but rather the degree to which we treat people wrongly.[13]

If right violations and injustices could not coherently be regarded as having negative value, then this interpretation, or something like it, would be required to make sense of the need to accept trade-offs among them. Yet even if the interpretation does fit some trade-offs, it may not seem to fit the trade-offs required by our own examples. As Nozick points out, it is often the case that "violating someone's rights might deflect others from *their* intended action of gravely violating rights, or might remove their motive for doing so, or might divert their attention, and so on."[14] If a principle acknowledges these possibilities and licenses trade-offs among violations inflicted by others as well as the agent himself, then it does not appear to tell the agent merely to minimize the degree to which he treats people wrongly. Instead, it seems to tell him to bring it about that there is as little wrong treatment as possible—an injunction that does seem to imply that wrong treatment has negative (moral) value which should be minimized. Moreover, when an agent must establish a large-scale policy under conditions of partial ignorance—as is the case in each of our examples—then he must expect that his policy will be implemented by others. Under these conditions, he cannot restrict his attention to violations that he himself will inflict. Thus, the principle governing his trade-offs apparently must imply that right violations or injustices are events with negative value.

However, upon closer inspection, this implication does not follow. Even if X's policies do have to be implemented by Y, X may still be responsible for any violations that ensue. In particular, X may well be responsible for any violations of Z's rights or claims of justice that Y inflicts in the course of implementing X's policies (without exceeding his authority, concealing his actions from X, etc.). Moreover, if X is responsible for the act through which Y treats Z unjustly or violates Z's rights, then X too may be said to treat Z unjustly or violate Z's rights. In view of this, the fact that decisions of large-scale policy must be implemented by intermediaries does not affect our basic point. Even so, the policy maker's trade-offs may still be governed by a principle that tells him to minimize the degree to which he treats others wrongly.

Thus far, I have argued that trade-offs among violations need not be aimed at minimizing or maximizing any sort of value. But even if this argument fails, the trade-offs still present few problems, for the other alleged source of difficulty—the claim that rights and justice cannot delimit the pursuit of (other) values if they themselves represent values—is also false. To see this, consider first the extreme view that rights and justice impose absolute limits on action and may never be sacrificed to promote mere happiness or preference satisfaction. This view can indeed be captured by the "side-constraint" interpretation of rights that Nozick favors. However, it can also be captured by an interpretation that does assign negative value to right violations or injustices but that regards minimizing such disvalue as lexically prior to maximizing the value associated with happiness or preference satisfaction. On the latter interpretation, the absolute priority of rights and justice over happiness is expressed not as a constraint upon a single value calculus but rather as a precedence relation between two such calculi. Moreover, a related interpretation can be supplied to capture the less extreme view that rights and claims of justice may indeed be violated, but only if the payoff in other sorts of value is extremely high. To capture this belief, we need only introduce a single value calculus that assigns a great, though not infinite, disvalue to right violations and injustices. In general, we seem able to reconcile the view that right violations and injustices are disvaluable occurrences with any interpretation of the stringency with which they constrain the pursuit of other values. Because we can, the framework of rights and justice seems entirely compatible with the view that right violations and injustices are themselves occurrences with negative value.

VI

Let us turn, finally, to the important question of how much our examples can be said to show. So far, the argument has been that a trade-off is warranted when it is unavoidable, that a trade-off is unavoidable when anything the agent does or abstains from doing can be expected to violate someone's rights or treat someone unjustly, and that ignorance frequently places agents in just this position. Yet even if all of this is true, it may not seem to warrant complete rejection of the no-trade-off thesis. For precisely because all our examples do turn on considerations of ignorance, it may seem possible to preserve the spirit, if not the letter, of Nozick's position by retreating to the claim that no trade-offs among violations would be permissible in a world of perfect information.

This amended version of the no-trade-off thesis is not easy to evaluate. On the one hand, the ignorance that generates our examples does appear to be merely contingent and so theoretically dispensable. However, on the other hand, the ignorance is not practically eliminable; and it is precisely such deep but contingent limitations that give rise to rights and justice in the first place. As Hume noted, the problem of distributive justice would not arise at all if various commodities and resources were not in short supply.[15] There is, moreover, little reason to treat information differently from any other resource. Because of this, protecting the no-trade-off thesis by retreating to a world of perfect information would appear to sever the connection between rights and justice and the conditions to which they are a response. If it does, then the resulting thesis is of no more interest than the claim that trade-offs are unnecessary in a world in which we can change the past or create food from air.

There is, moreover, a further objection to the claim that the no-trade-off thesis continues to hold in a world of perfect information. Even if all our examples do turn on epistemic limitations, several elements of our discussion strongly suggest that the problem is more general, and that the demands of rights and justice must also outrun such other resources as time, wealth, and energy. For one thing, as the preferential hiring example reminds us, even those who believe that all rights and claims of justice are negative, and require only that people not be treated in certain ways, are apt to hold that various positive actions are required to compensate for past violations. Moreover, and equally important, we have seen that abstentions may violate (even negative) rights when what one abstains from is the prevention of a right violation that one is responsible for preventing. In our examples, the responsibility was that of the policy maker for the acts of his subordinates; but other sources of responsibility clearly exist as well. In particular, once we have acknowledged the obligations that stem from the policy maker's role, there is little reason to deny that similar obligations may arise from one's position as parent, teacher, or friend and perhaps also in other ways.[16]

Given these considerations, it is easy to see how a shortage of resources other than knowledge may render us unable to avoid violating some people's rights or claims of justice. Whatever X's epistemic state, Z's rights or claims of justice, even if "negative," may well obligate X to compensate Z; and they may also obligate X to prevent Y from treating Z in various ways. If so, then X's failure to compensate Z or protect Z's rights will indeed violate Z's rights. However, if X does have to take active steps to avoid violating Z's rights, then taking these steps may exhaust X's time, energy, or wealth and so may prevent X from performing some act that is required by someone else's rights. It may be, for example, that X's obligations to compensate each of several persons whose rights he has violated outstrip X's earning capacity or that X's limited powers allow him to oversee the acts of some but not all of those persons for whose behavior he is responsible. Given these and related possibilities, even a fully informed agent must sometimes be unable to avoid violating all rights or claims of justice. However much a person knows, his limited access to resources other than knowledge must sometimes force him to treat one or another person in a way that rights or claims of justice (ordinarily) forbid.

In view of this, the need for trade-offs is evidently not an isolated phenomenon. Although our initial examples were indeed epistemic, many other trade-offs are required by the combination of limited material resources and the fact that rights and justice, however construed, at least require us to perform many positive acts of compensation and prevention. Of course, even these facts would not establish the need for trade-offs if people never violated rights or treated others unjustly in the first place. In that case, there would be no need for any positive acts of compensation or prevention. Because of this, the die-hard opponent of trade-offs can still insist that his thesis would apply within a world of perfect morality as well as perfect information. But while this further retreat into unreality might stave off outright defeat, it would do so at the cost of eliminating whatever remaining interest his thesis has for us. It is true that moral theory must always provide us with ideals toward which to strive. It is no less true that those ideals must be designed to govern our strivings in the actual, flawed world.

Notes

1. Robert Nozick, *Anarchy, State, and Utopia* (New York: Basic Books, 1974), 28. See also Alan H. Goldman, "The Paradox of Punishment," *Philosophy and Public Affairs* 9, no. 1 (Fall 1979): 42–58, esp. 51–54; and Judith Jarvis Thomson, "Some Ruminations on Rights," in *Reading Nozick*, ed. Jeffrey Paul (Totowa, N.J.: Rowman & Littlefield, 1981), 130–47, esp. 131–32.

2. These issues are explored in Alan Wertheimer, "Punishing the Innocent—Unintentionally," *Inquiry* 20, no. 1 (Spring 1977): 45–65.

3. See George Sher, "Preferential Hiring," in *Just Business: New Introductory Essays in Business Ethics*, ed. Tom Regan (New York: Random House, 1984), 32–59.

4. See George Sher, "Health Care and the 'Deserving Poor,'" *Hastings Center Report* 13, no. 1 (February 1983): 9–12.

5. At one point, Nozick himself comes close to acknowledging that the need to compensate raises problems of the type sketched here. At the end of his chapter on distributive justice, he writes that "an important question for every society will be the following: given *its* particular history, what operable rule of thumb best approximates the results of a detailed application in that society of the principle of rectification . . . Although to introduce socialism as

the punishment for our sins would be to go too far, past injustices might be so great as to make necessary in the short run a more extensive state in order to rectify them" (*Anarchy, State, and Utopia*, 231). Given Nozick's concession that rectification can only be approximate, he here seems to grant that any compensatory strategy will violate some people's rights.

6. Although the dilemma is pervasive, the problems it raises for the theory of rights and justice have seldom been noticed. Many philosophers have held that we cannot simultaneously satisfy all rights or claims of justice, but few have backed the claim with the sorts of examples cited here. One exception is James Fishkin, who does give such an example in "Moral Rights and Public Policy," *Daedalus* 108, no. 4 (Fall 1979): 55–67. Fishkin's example concerns a plague in a medieval city: if a quarantine is imposed, the right to liberty of the uninfected quarantined persons will be violated, while if no quarantine is imposed, then other persons' rights to protection will be violated.

7. This general strategy is considered, though not ultimately endorsed, by Thomson in "Some Ruminations on Rights," 134–35.

8. For a survey of problems and approaches, see Charles Fried, *An Anatomy of Values* (Cambridge: Harvard University Press, 1970), chap. 12, 207–36.

9. Charles Fried, in his *Right and Wrong* (Cambridge: Harvard University Press, 1978), chap. 3, 54–78, construes lying as essentially intentional. If correct, this implies that a right not to be lied to would proscribe only a type of intentional act. However, even so, it neither follows nor is plausible to believe that intention is similarly internal to all other rights.

10. For a critical discussion, see Philippa Foot, "The Problem of Abortion and the Doctrine of Double Effect," in *Killing and Letting Die*, ed. Bonnie Steinbock (Englewood Cliffs, N.J.: Prentice-Hall, 1980), 156–65.

11. John Rawls, *A Theory of Justice* (Cambridge: Harvard University Press, 1971).

12. Rawls, *Theory of Justice*, 31.

13. It may seem paradoxical to speak of minimizing one's wrong treatment of others, for if through no fault of his own an agent cannot avoid violating some people's rights or claims of justice, then his attempt to minimize violations is surely not wrong at all. However, just as we distinguish between obligations prima facie and on balance, so too can we distinguish between treating someone as he ought not be treated, other things being equal, and acting wrongly, all things considered. Given this distinction, it is perfectly consistent to describe an agent as acting rightly in treating someone wrongly.

14. Nozick, *Anarchy, State, and Utopia*, 28.

15. David Hume, *Treatise of Human Nature*, ed. L. A. Selby-Bigge (Oxford: Oxford University Press, 1967), book 3, part 2, sec. 2.

16. For illuminating discussion of the ways in which even "negative" rights may give rise to positive obligations, see Henry Shue, *Basic Rights: Subsistence, Affluence, and U.S. Foreign Policy* (Princeton: Princeton University Press, 1980), chap. 2, 35–64.

8

Our Preferences, Ourselves

Feminist social theorists make two main normative claims about women's preferences. They contend that, first, whatever their preferences happen to be, women should have as much opportunity to realize those preferences as men and, second, there is something badly wrong with women's traditional preferences (and certain associated traits), at least insofar as they are induced by sexual stereotypes and conditioning. Of these claims, the first is used to justify antidiscrimination laws and the provision of various supporting services. The second is used to justify "consciousness-raising"—revisions of language, alterations in the images of women (and men) in books and media, and the provision of "role models" to encourage preferences that would not otherwise develop. Although these claims occasionally seem to converge on the same policies (for example, affirmative action), they are conceptually quite distinct.

In recent years, philosophers have shed a good deal of light on the first claim. They have said much that is illuminating about equality of opportunity and the delicate balancing of interests that it requires. But discussion of the second has been much less useful. Although many have asserted that perpetuating women's traditional preferences is wrong, the reasoning behind this assertion has not been worked out in great detail. There have been ritual gestures toward utility, equality, and autonomy; but no appeal to one of these notions that does not itself presuppose the superiority of some preferences (or something equally problematical) has yet been produced. As a result, the arguments against the traditional preferences have been either inconclusive or question-begging. The main aim of the present essay is to demonstrate this in some detail. A secondary aim is to suggest a different and more promising approach to the problem.

It will be helpful to begin by delineating both the range of preferences and the range of arguments to be discussed. Although women's traditional preferences take a variety of forms, the central cases include preferences to devote one's time to one's tasks as housewife and mother, preferences to promote the career of one's husband and the well-being of one's children, and preferences for such traditionally female occupations as nurse and teacher. By extension, I shall also take them to include the personality traits apt to yield success in these roles such as gentleness, concern for others, and lack of (certain sorts of) aggressiveness. Of the popular arguments for altering these preferences or their manner of acquisition, one that is doing so would maximize overall utility by providing various new benefits. Another is that it would promote justice by equalizing the distribution of important goods, including the crucial good of self-respect. A third is that it would increase liberty and autonomy by allowing women the fullest possible range of life choices. In addition, each argument is sometimes supplemented by claims that the traditional preferences inhibit personal growth or are exploitative. Although the arguments all assume that the relevant preferences and traits are environmentally determined and that different environmental stimuli would produce different psychological characteristics, I shall not question this controversial assumption here. Instead, I shall simply accept it in order to assess its normative consequences.

To see the problem with such arguments, consider first the appeal to utility. Because the principle of utility says that we should always maximize value, and because utilitarians generally believe that only happiness has value, most versions of this argument maintain that perpetuating women's traditional preferences would bring less overall happiness than altering them. Although various reasons for believing this have been proposed, two of the most important are brought out by Jane English. According to English, within the traditional system "a woman who might lead a happy life as a pilot and a man who would find nursing rewarding are steered into professions they might not enjoy so much nor do so well. They lose happiness, and so do the rest of us in that we do not have the most talented people in society performing each job."[1] Paraphrasing somewhat, we may say that women's traditional preferences reduce both social productivity and women's individual enjoyment. Since both are important determinants of overall happiness, the utilitarian argument against the traditional preferences may seem very strong.

In fact, however, the situation is considerably more complicated than this. Although altering women's preferences would indeed promote the development of new talents, it would also drastically change the traditional division of society's labor. Because efficiency requires specialization as well as developed talents, it is far from obvious that such a change would increase overall productivity. Moreover, and more importantly for our purposes, it is also not clear that the change would increase women's individual enjoyment. On the standard assumptions of formal utility theory, enjoyment or happiness is not something over and above the satisfaction of preferences. Instead, one's happiness is defined by a utility function that is assigned on the basis *of* one's preferences as expressed under different assignments of probability to different states of affairs. On these assumptions, a woman whose utility function assigns a high ranking to her domestic life must be precisely as happy as a nontraditional woman whose life occupies a similar position in *her* utility function. Thus, to show that nontraditional preferences would bring more overall enjoyment, one must establish that they are on the whole more likely to be satisfied than traditional ones. But while this may be true in isolated instances, it is surely unlikely as a general rule. At the very least, no reason for accepting it has been provided. Of course this problem would not arise if the utilitarian were to drop either the assumption that happiness is defined in terms of satisfied preference or else the deeper assumption that only happiness has value. However, given the difficulty of providing a criterion of happiness that does not involve preference, the first suggestion does not seem promising. Moreover, if one adopts the second, then one must hold that of two equally satisfied sets of preferences, one may be worth more than the other. Since whether nondomestic preferences are worth more than domestic ones is precisely what is at issue, to assume this without argument would merely beg the question.

If the only preferences whose satisfaction could determine happiness were actual ones, then these objections to the utilitarian argument would be decisive. However, even if formal utility theory does imply this, a different tradition within utilitarianism connects happiness to preference-satisfaction in a more sophisticated way. In a famous passage in *Utilitarianism*, John Stuart Mill writes that "if one of . . . two [pleasures] is, by those who are competently acquainted with it, placed so far above the other that they prefer it, even though knowing it to be attended with a greater amount of discontent . . . we are justified in ascribing to the preferred enjoyment a superiority in quality so far outweighing quantity as to render it, in comparison, of small account."[2] Purged of rhetorical excess and restricted to single individuals, what this comes to is that the value of one's situation may depend not merely on how strongly one *does* prefer it, but on how strongly one *would* prefer it if one were "competently acquainted" with some alternative. The value of one's situation may depend not on its position in one's actual utility function, but rather on its position in the different utility function that would grow out of broader experience or more balanced judgment. If this "choice criterion of value" is acceptable, it will be of obvious application to women's traditional preferences. Although it will not guarantee that nontraditional lives are worth more than traditional ones for traditional women, it will at least open up this possibility. According to it, the value of a traditional life for a particular woman will depend not on her actual preferences, but rather on the preferences she would acquire if competently acquainted with nontraditional as well as traditional life styles. Moreover, whatever those preferences would be, the natural way of discovering them is simply to *make* her acquainted with the competing options. Thus, even where the choice criterion does favor a traditional lifestyle, it may still condemn any mode of social conditioning that precludes a competent acquaintance with other possibilities.

Although the issue is seldom framed in quite these terms, it seems clear that something like the choice criterion provides the appeal to utility with its best chance of success. However, even if that criterion is defensible in some contexts, its viability here is dubious at best. The competent acquaintance requirement is easy to satisfy when the competing alternatives are activities or states that can be sequentially performed or undergone and then compared from a neutral vantage point. However, when the alternatives are entire ways of life, the situation is vastly more problematical. The objection that some ways of life require lifelong immersion may perhaps be met by allowing that one's "acquaintance" with one or both competitors may be merely imaginative. However, even so, the ideal of the genuinely neutral standpoint will still be defeated whenever one of the competing ways of life requires a commitment that from the inside renders the other unattractive but from the outside seems merely incomprehensible. This is true of some forms of religious life, and it holds for at least some forms of domestic life as well. Because it does, no appeal to the choice criterion can succeed unless it disallows such committed lives as illegitimate. But to do this without further argument would again assume a version of what is to be shown. Thus embellished, the augmented appeal to utility would again be question-begging.[3]

I suspect that few feminists would be disturbed by this. Although utility is often invoked as a supporting consideration, a more basic complaint against the traditional preferences is that their perpetuation produces inequalities that are unjust. A widely accepted principle of justice states that all persons should be treated equally except when there is a relevant basis for inequality; and a system producing preferences that lead men and women to live very different lives may seem a blatant violation of this.[4] Yet here too problems arise. The strong presumption for equality applies only to modes of treatment that allocate benefits and burdens. Hence, to succeed, the egalitarian argument must assume that the traditional preferences deny women benefits or impose burdens upon them. But this assumption only reraises the difficulties encountered above. If benefiting someone is just raising his position as determined by his own utility function, then merely altering women's traditional preferences will not benefit them. On the other hand, if benefit involves more than this, then it implies a ranking of preferences which itself requires defense. Since this ranking is presupposed by the appeal *to* equality, it cannot be defended in terms *of* equality. Hence, the egalitarian argument threatens to be just as question-begging as the appeal to utility.

This objection applies not only to appeals to utility and equality, but also to appeals to all other principles for distributing goods. Hence, any criticism of women's preferences that appeals to such a principle may appear to confuse the question of how goods should be distributed with the question of which things are goods. But this conclusion, though tempting, is premature. The proponent of, say, equality may attempt to connect his distributional principle to a favored conception of the good by deriving the latter from the same considerations that support the former. If this can be done, and if women's traditional preferences do deprive them of equal amounts of the goods thus defended, then the egalitarian attack on those preferences will succeed after all. There is, moreover, at least one (moderately) egalitarian framework that seems to yield precisely this result. That framework is introduced by John Rawls; and it is to his account that we must now turn.

In *A Theory of Justice*, Rawls explicitly acknowledges that arguments for particular principles of justice should not presuppose any special conception of the good.[5] However, because he holds that the principles of justice depend on the choices that would be made by rational and self-interested parties who did not know their actual life circumstances or preferences, Rawls also cannot say that what counts as a good or benefit for a person is directly determined by that person's preferences. To resolve this dilemma and to provide a definite motivation for those in the "original position," Rawls introduces the notion of primary goods—of things whose possession can only help us to realize whatever (other) preferences we have. These primary goods, which include rights and liberties, powers and opportunities, income and wealth, and the social bases of self-respect, are things it is rational for us to want, whatever else we want. They would invariably be chosen by rational individuals in the original position, and it is this that confers on them their status as goods. Because that status flows from the same hypothetical choice procedure that yields Rawls's substantive principles of justice, the result is an egalitarian theory whose conception of benefit is internal to it. If this theory is correct, it may indeed allow egalitarians to criticize socially induced preferences without begging the question. In particular, it suggests (though Rawls himself does not assert) that women are treated unjustly if they are caused to develop preferences that prevent them from acquiring equitable shares of primary goods. Because primary goods acquire their status from choices made under ideal rather than actual conditions, this claim is not undercut by the fact that women with traditional preferences neither prefer more primary goods than they have nor have other preferences whose realization requires additional amounts of such goods.

Many feminists maintain that women's traditional preferences have caused them to acquire far less power than men.[6] Although power is a complicated notion, this claim may well be correct if power is interpreted politically and economically. If it is, the traditional preferences may indeed prevent women from acquiring equitable shares of an important primary good. The situation is complicated by the fact that Rawls himself does not include political and economic power among the primary goods. By "powers" he means only Hohfeldian abilities "to create by certain procedures a structure of rights and duties that courts will enforce."[7] Nevertheless, the idea that political and economic power are also primary goods is not implausible. Because it is not, the extension of Rawls's framework to demonstrate injustice in women's disinclination to seek such power is not implausible either.

Should we then agree that the conditioning that women undergo deprives them of their fair share of the primary good of power? Despite appearances, I believe we should not; for the idea that power is something it is rational to want whatever else one wants is belied by women's traditional preferences themselves. It is true that having more power outside her marriage would allow a woman with traditional preferences to satisfy some preferences that would otherwise go unsatisfied. However, it is also true that one cannot have such power without pursuing it, and that the character traits necessary for its pursuit are themselves incompatible with many sorts of traditional preferences. The successful pursuit of power demands aggressiveness and a taste for competition, and so would require drastic changes in the temperament and preferences of many traditional women. However, any such changes would inevitably preclude many quieter and more domestic pursuits and relationships. Hence, given the necessities of human psychology, any gains in political and economic power would be more than offset by what are, to many traditional women, satisfactions of far greater moment. Similarly, even if power is quite unequally distributed within many marriages, many traditional women will regard any rearrangement of this pattern as precluding the sort of relationship they value most deeply. Hence, here again, any shift in power may actually bring a net loss in preference-satisfaction. In view of this, the parties in the original position cannot automatically assume that their preferences in the actual world are best served by social arrangements that maximize their power. At best, they can assume this if they know that their actual preferences are not women's traditional ones. However, to build this assumption into the original position would of course be illegitimate. To do so would again beg the question against the very preferences whose value is at issue.

These considerations do not entirely discredit the idea that political and economic power should play an important role in any list of primary goods. Such power is often extremely helpful in getting what one wants, and nothing said here suggests that those in the original position should ignore this. However, given the sacrifices that acquiring power may involve, it does seem that what those in the original position should desire is not power simpliciter, but rather the absence of impediments to its acquisition when it *is* desired. Properly speaking, it is not power itself, but rather access to it, that really satisfies Rawls's definition of a primary good. Thus, Rawls's framework does not show that power should be distributed equally (or in a way that maximizes the power of the least powerful). At best, it shows that all persons should have equal access to power (or that any inequalities in access should maximize the access of those with the least access). Of course, the notion of equal access is itself problematical, and may be read as demanding anything from formal equality of opportunity to something much stronger. However, for our purposes, the crucial point is that it does not demand that all people's preferences should either require or yield similar amounts of power. A fortiori, it does not condemn women's traditional preferences for failing to require or yield as much power as others.

These remarks concern only inequalities of power, but similar considerations obviously hold for inequalities of wealth and income. Moreover, rights and liberties, as Rawls understands them, are basically absences of restraint on action (or protections against such restraint) and so are not made unequal by women's traditional preferences. In view of this, the only primary good whose unequal distribution may still tell against the traditional preferences is self-respect. According to Rawls, self-respect includes two main elements. It includes, first, "a person's sense of his own value, his secure conviction that his conception of his good, his plan of life, is worth carrying out. And, second, [it] implies a confidence in one's ability, so far as it is within one's power, to fulfill one's intentions."[8] If we lack self-respect, "then nothing may seem worth doing, or if some things have value for us, we lack the will to strive for them. All desire and activity becomes empty and vain, and we sink into apathy and cynicism."[9] Because self-respect thus affects not only one's ability to pursue one's goals, but also the value one attaches to them, it comes closer than the other primary goods to being something it is always rational to want whatever else one wants. Hence, if women's traditional preferences do bring significantly less self-respect than others, then the Rawlsian framework may indeed imply that they should be altered.

Do women's traditional preferences bring them less self-respect than men's? Given Rawls's account of self-respect, the operative questions here are (a) whether the traditional preferences cause women to downgrade their goals or themselves, and (b) whether those preferences reduce the likelihood that women will actually achieve their goals. Of these questions, the second can immediately be answered in the negative; for a woman whose central goals concern her home, husband, and family is surely no less likely to achieve them than a man (or woman) who prefers to be a corporate executive or an athlete. However, the answer to the first question is less clear; for the importance that women with traditional preferences attach to their goals (and themselves) may be said to be affected by several distinct factors. These factors include (1) the relative lack of difficulty of the tasks that the traditional preferences generate, (2) the internal structure of the traditional preferences, and (3) the fact that society attaches little prestige to women's domestic activities. Let us now consider each factor in turn.

The first factor, the relative lack of difficulty of the tasks generated by women's traditional preferences, is relevant to their self-respect because of a general principle of motivation, which Rawls calls the Aristotelian Principle. This principle asserts "that, other things equal, human beings enjoy the exercise of their realized capacities (their innate or trained abilities), and that this enjoyment increases the more the capacity is realized or the greater its complexity."[10] According to Rawls, activities that fail to satisfy the Aristotelian Principle "are likely to seem dull and flat, and to give us no feeling of competence or sense that they are worth doing."[11] Such activities are likely to reduce one's self-respect. Hence, if the traditional preferences do not generate tasks that tax women's ingenuity and skill, then the charge that they reduce women's self-respect may indeed go through.

Still, while it is true that some tasks required by women's traditional preferences are routine and mechanical, many others, such as cooking and child-rearing, can be performed in ways that are creative and challenging. For this reason, the Aristotelian Principle will at best predict not that women with traditional preferences must tend to find life dull and flat, but rather that they must tend to do these things in increasingly interesting and complicated ways.[12] But in fact, it is doubtful whether the principle predicts even this much. Although the Aristotelian Principle is proposed as a near universal description of how humans behave, it is very easy to find common-sense counterexamples, both male and female, to it. As Vinit Haksar has observed, "there are plenty of people who live well-regulated simple lives without becoming bored"[13] (and, we may add, without believing that they are less worthwhile than others). In view of this, the Aristotelian Principle at best describes a weak and easily overcome tendency in human behavior. But if this is so, then it is hardly strong enough to establish *any* conclusions about how women with traditional preferences are likely to act or feel.

The second way of working out the appeal to self-respect is very different. On this account, the crucial aspect of women's traditional preferences is not the complexity of the tasks they require, but rather the content of the goals they generate. It is often noted that a woman with traditional preferences aims largely at furthering the interests of other people. She is most concerned to support her husband's career and to look after the heath and well-being of her children. Because she does arrange her life to further the interests of others, it is tempting to describe her as minimizing or sacrificing her own interests. It is tempting to say, with Thomas Hill, Jr., that she "tends not to form her own interests, values and ideals; and when she does, she counts them as less important than her husband's."[14] If this is so, there is indeed a sense in which such a woman does not believe that she is as important as other people. This is true at least in that she systematically subordinates her own interests to those of others.

The claim that women with traditional preferences neglect or ignore their own interests is very common. It underlies not only many assertions that those preferences undermine self-respect, but also many assertions that those preferences are exploitative.[15] Yet despite its pervasiveness, the claim does not really take us any further forward. The difficulty is that its central assumption—that a preference to advance the interests of her husband and children cannot itself be an important element of a woman's own interest—is just as problematical as the disputed claim that a woman's traditional preferences are harmful or not worthwhile. We often do say that one's interests are constituted by one's basic religious, moral, or even recreational preferences; and so it is hardly obvious that they cannot also be determined by a preference to care for one's family. Thus, the proposed argument only replaces the question of how women are harmed by their traditional preferences with the equally difficult question of why such preferences cannot themselves determine women's interests. If we lack an answer to the latter question, we cannot invoke the content of women's traditional preferences to show that they reduce women's (Rawlsian) self-respect. If we have one, the appeal to diminished self-respect is no longer necessary.[16]

These considerations suggest that no intrinsic features of women's traditional preferences undermine self-respect. However, even so, it may still be held that those preferences have social accompaniments that produce the same effect. In particular, self-respect may be said to be undermined by the fact that women's traditional preferences bring them little prestige and few other social rewards. Because such rewards go largely to those whose activities are outside the home and family, they serve as a public announcement that our society places little value on women's traditional tasks and relationships. Thus, it may seem only natural for many traditional women to believe that they themselves have little value as well.

Unlike other versions of the appeal to self-respect, this one focuses squarely on the *social bases* of self-respect. It thus comes closer than the others to addressing what Rawls himself considers the relevant primary good. Moreover, although the notions of prestige and reward are themselves complex, there is clearly something right about the idea that our society does not currently place a high value on women's traditional preferences. The prevailing reward structure may indeed lead many traditional women to think less of themselves; and so too, ironically, may the recent pronouncements of some feminists. But what, exactly, should we conclude from this? The conclusion often advocated is that the determinants of the traditional preferences should be altered or abolished. However, if those preferences are not in themselves harmful and if the tasks to which they lead are worth doing and important, then this conclusion is perverse. Under these conditions, the more reasonable conclusion is that we should strive to change the inadequate and destructive reward structure that is presently *associated* with those preferences. If the only complaint against women's traditional preferences is that they reduce self-respect because they are inadequately rewarded, then the proper response is surely not to abolish them, but rather to reward them more adequately.

With this conclusion, we may finally abandon the claim that women's traditional preferences deprive them of equitable shares of primary goods. Because no other conception of the good that is internally connected to a distributional principle is available, the prospects for a successful appeal to equality or a related principle do not seem bright. However, even so, one other major argument against women's traditional preferences does remain. It is often held that the real problem with these preferences lies not in their distributional effects, but rather in the way they are acquired and perpetuated. What is really objectionable, it is said, is not the decisions they yield, but rather the fact that they are relentlessly conditioned by various aspects of the social environment. On this account, nothing wrong occurs when a woman rationally weighs her options under conditions of equal opportunity and then freely chooses to live a domestic life. However, when her decision stems from preferences shaped by expectations encountered since early childhood, then it is in an important sense not autonomously made. Since autonomous choice is among the most precious and distinctive of human activities, women are greatly harmed by being denied a capacity for it. Hence, to set things right, the forces that render women incapable of autonomy—the forces that cause them to acquire a single, stereotyped set of preferences—must now be altered.

If anything, this appeal to autonomy is even more common than the appeal to equality. However, even so, it is hard to assess, for its central notion is notoriously unclear. In this context, of course, autonomy must involve something more than merely doing what one prefers; but what that something more could be is far from obvious. To appreciate the difficulty, consider first the claim that women only choose autonomously if the basic preferences motivating their choices have not themselves been produced by social conditioning. As Sharon Bishop Hill puts it, women's autonomous choices must "express genuine interests of theirs which arise spontaneously under certain conditions [of psychological strength and rationality]."[17] There is an obvious danger that Hill's notions of psychological strength and rationality will covertly assume the very normative claims she wants to establish. However, given the recent emphasis on the effects of sex role stereotyping, Hill's central contention—that autonomy requires preferences that arise spontaneously rather than through social conditioning—does strike a familiar chord.

Can an appeal to autonomy, thus conceived, support a general attack on women's traditional preferences? Despite its familiarity, I believe it cannot. For one thing, if women's traditional preferences are largely or entirely shaped by sexual stereotypes, then one's character and preferences must be extremely malleable when one is young. But if so, then abolishing the prevailing stereotypes is likely only to clear the way for other, less systematic forms of conditioning. Hence, abolishing those stereotypes is unlikely to increase women's autonomy as Hill defines it.[18] In addition, even if eliminating stereotypes *did* increase autonomy in Hill's sense, the moral import of this would remain unclear. We value autonomy because we believe that people should control their own destinies; and Hill's definition at first seems attractive precisely because a conditioned preference is so plainly not within one's control. But on second glance, this is inconclusive; for however we interpret "spontaneous," it seems clear that a preference that arises spontaneously is also not within one's control. Whether it is caused by the agent's innate psychological tendencies or simply by nothing at all, the fact remains that such a preference arrives unbidden. Thus, replacing conditioned preferences by spontaneous ones would bring no real increase in women's control over their lives.

Given these considerations, those who argue that traditional preferences reduce women's autonomy cannot interpret autonomous action as action grounded in unconditioned preferences. Instead, they must interpret it as action grounded in preferences that stem more positively from the agent's choice or will. Generally speaking, such positive accounts of autonomy have taken two main forms. On the one hand, because choices concerning preferences are always grounded in further preferences, some philosophers have maintained that autonomous agents must be motivated by preferences that accord with their higher-order preferences—by preferences they prefer to have.[19] On the other hand, since higher-order preferences are themselves embedded in a broader context of interests, abilities, beliefs, and circumstances, other philosophers have understood autonomy as requiring reflection of a more broad-gauged sort. Because genuine control requires an understanding of all the values and presuppositions supporting one's preferences, these philosophers contend that one cannot act autonomously unless this entire complex of attitudes has been subjected to rational assessment.[20]

The first of these accounts will plainly not support the claim that women's traditional preferences must render them nonautonomous. If one accepts the two-level approach, one must concede that women with traditional preferences do not lack autonomy as long as they prefer to have and be motivated by those preferences; and there is no reason to deny that this may occur.[21] However, the second approach seems more promising. Women socialized to prefer domestic roles are often said to be incapable of ascending to higher planes of reflective awareness. Because they are so firmly anchored in a single view of their lives and themselves, they cannot raise questions about the appropriateness or desirability of their plans and aspirations. They cannot fully imagine alternative possibilities. Hence, they may indeed appear to lack autonomy in its second positive sense.

This version of the appeal to autonomy is plainly the strongest we have seen. Even so, I do not think it succeeds; for like the other arguments we have examined, it tacitly prejudges the very question it seeks to answer. The argument assumes that women with traditional preferences lack control of their lives because they cannot examine the presuppositions and values upon which their preferences depend. It is only by raising questions about these attitudes, and by imagining alternative ways of life, that they can freely decide to accept or alter their preferences. But if we accept the argument's premise that the traditional preferences preclude such questioning and imagining, then we must surely challenge its further assumption that such activity, if undertaken, would make possible a genuine choice between traditional and nontraditional preferences. If traditional preferences do involve a commitment that makes radical questioning impossible, then no woman can engage in such questioning unless her erstwhile traditional preferences are already so altered that a decision to retain them is no longer possible. To question in this way is already to have made one's choice; and so its justification cannot be that it alone makes real choice possible. Instead, the justification must again be that the resulting preferences are superior in some other dimension. If autonomy requires this sort of questioning, then Haksar may well be correct in asserting that the idea that people should be autonomous is itself a form of perfectionism.[22]

This point can be made in another way. To see that some alternatives must always lie outside the boundaries of genuine choice, consider a feminist attempting to imagine herself living a traditional life. Such a woman may indeed imagine herself remaining at home with her children while her husband works; but she can surely not imagine herself accepting all aspects of the traditional role. Given her penchant for exhaustive self-scrutiny, she cannot imagine herself entertaining a simpler and less self-conscious commitment to domestic life; and many related attitudes and values will elude her as well. A fully traditional outlook is no more a genuine option for her than her own outlook is for a more traditional woman. Hence, the difference between traditional and nontraditional preferences cannot be that only the former impose genuine restrictions on choice. The claim that such preferences interfere with autonomy may yet succeed; but the argument's center of gravity must again be shifted to another place.

It is, however, no longer clear what that other place could be. We have now examined all of the familiar arguments against women's traditional preferences; and each argument has been found to be either inconclusive or question-begging. In view of this, it seems safe to conclude that the case against those preferences has not yet been made. The possibility of making it receives continuing support from our common abhorrence of conditioned preferences for slavery and certain other forms of servitude. However, until this abhorrence is satisfactorily analyzed and accounted for, we cannot tell whether it stems from moral principle or simply from a deeply held ideal of the person. In the latter case, the reaction might still be defensible; but the strategy of attacking women's traditional preferences by invoking moral principles would be fundamentally misguided. Moreover, and even more important, until this abhorrence is explained, we also cannot tell whether consistency demands that we condemn the preferences of contented housewives as well as contented slaves. At least prima facie, the analogy seems very far from complete; for the traditional male-female relation is grounded in bonds of mutual attraction and affection, and in shared purposes and concern for common dependents, which the master-slave relation utterly lacks. However, many feminists will reply that the similarities outweigh the differences. Without a well-motivated account of what is relevant, the situation remains obscure.

In the end, its obscurity may not matter. Whatever we believe about well-integrated traditional preferences, there is clearly a problem when a woman's traditional preferences do not cohere with her other attitudes. When a woman is strongly attracted to domesticity yet hopelessly unsatisfied by it, or when she aspires to independence but lacks the drive or aggressiveness to achieve it, then the conditions that have shaped her character and preferences may indeed be criticized. Moreover, although there is no reason to believe that such tensions are inherent in women's traditional preferences, they do seem to be increasingly associated with them. Given the overwhelming testimony of unhappiness and bitterness that feminism has called forth, it seems clear that women with unmixedly traditional preferences are increasingly rare. Given the swirl of influences to which contemporary women are exposed, this is hardly surprising. Yet surprising or not, it suggests an important insight in the feminist position. We saw above that there is good reason to increase the prestige and rewards that attach to women's traditional preferences. However, if the traditional preferences are seriously at odds with other attitudes that many women hold, then some changes of a rather different sort may also be required. If the determinants of the other attitudes are pervasive and intractable, and if the lack of coherence produces deep conflict and unhappiness in many women, then there may indeed be a reason to alter some of the conditions that produce the traditional preferences at an early age. In that case, at least some efforts to change our traditional expectations and stereotypes may be called for on grounds of simple humanity.

This way of justifying efforts to alter the determinants of women's traditional preferences resembles some of the arguments considered above; but it also differs importantly from them. Unlike the earlier arguments, it appeals not to the nature or effects of the traditional preferences themselves but to their incompatibility with certain other preferences; not to timeless considerations but to the peculiarities of the historical moment; not to principles of distributive justice or respect for autonomy but to the humbler principle that suffering should be relieved. If it lacks the moral grandeur of the rejected arguments, it is at least grounded in a principle whose content and validity are uncontroversial. To be fully convincing, the argument would have to be supplemented by evidence that the current malaise will not dissipate on its own, and that particular efforts to relieve it will not cause unintended harm to women, their children, or others. These matters cannot be considered here. However, what can be said is that given the degree of self-consciousness that many women have already reached, neither stasis nor a return to past attitudes seems likely. The final irony is that some of the changes so often advocated in the name of freedom may be best defended as ways of accommodating a shift about which there is no real choice at all.

Notes

1. Jane English, "Introduction," in *Sex Equality*, ed. Jane English (Englewood Cliffs, N.J.: Prentice-Hall, 1977), 8. For remarks in a similar vein, see Alison Jaggar, "On Sex Equality," in *Sex Equality*, 106.

2. John Stuart Mill, *Utilitarianism* (Indianapolis: Hackett, 1979), 8–9.

3. For related criticism of the choice criterion, see Vinit Haksar, *Equality, Liberty, and Perfectionism* (Oxford: Oxford University Press, 1979), 206–31.

4. In "On Sexual Equality," Jaggar goes so far as to claim that a feminist must by definition believe "that justice requires equality between men and women" (94).

5. John Rawls, *A Theory of Justice* (Cambridge: Harvard University Press, 1971), 94; see also 325–32.

6. See, for example, B. C. Postow, "Thomas on Sexism," *Ethics* 90, no. 2 (January 1980): 254.

7. John Rawls, "Fairness to Goodness," *Philosophical Review* 84, no. 4 (October 1975): 542–43n.

8. Rawls, *Theory of Justice*, 440.

9. Rawls, *Theory of Justice*, 440.

10. Rawls, *Theory of Justice*, 414.

11. Rawls, *Theory of Justice*, 440.

12. As Rawls himself notes, "the forms of life which absorb men's energies, whether they be religious devotions or purely practical matters or even games and pastimes, tend to develop their intricacies and subtleties almost without end" (Rawls, *Theory of Justice*, 429).

13. Haksar, *Equality, Liberty*, 200.

14. Thomas Hill, Jr., "Servility and Self-Respect," in *Today's Moral Problems*, ed. Richard A. Wasserstrom (New York: Macmillan, 1979), 135.

15. See, for example, Judith Farr Tormey, "Exploitation, Oppression, and Self-Sacrifice," in *Women and Philosophy*, eds. Carol C. Gould and Marx Wartofsky (New York: Capricorn, 1975), 206–21.

16. There may appear to be an alternative route to the conclusion that women with traditional preferences believe themselves to be less important than other people. Instead of deriving this conclusion from the fact that such women neglect their own interests, one may attempt to derive it from the fact that the preferences that generate those interests are logically parasitic on the preferences of others. However, it is simply a non sequitur to infer from "X's preferences are logically parasitic upon Y's" to "X believes himself to be less important than Y."

17. Sharon Bishop Hill, "Self-determination and Autonomy," in *Today's Moral Problems*, 132.

18. Irving Thalberg makes a similar point in "Socialization and Autonomous Behavior," *Tulane Studies in Philosophy* 28 (1979): 30–32. Thalberg, however, does accept a different version of the autonomy argument.

19. See Gerald Dworkin, "Acting Freely," *Nous* 4 (1970): 367–83; Harry Frankfurt, "Freedom of the Will and the Concept of a Person," *Journal of Philosophy* 68, no. 1 (January 14, 1971): 5–20; and Gary Watson, "Free Agency," *Journal of Philosophy* 72, no. 8 (April 24, 1975): 205–20.

20. For a clear statement of this view, see William E. Connolly, *The Terms of Political Discourse* (Lexington, Mass.: Heath, 1974), 140–78.

21. Again, see Thalberg, "Socialization and Autonomous Behavior," 22–27.

22. See Haksar, *Equality, Liberty*, 172–84.

9

Predicting Performance

Equal opportunity requires (at least) that persons be selected for desirable positions on the basis of their qualifications.[1] To assess an applicant's qualifications, we must both predict how well he would perform if chosen and compare his projected performance with that of his rivals. Since we lack direct access to future performance (and since only those who are chosen will ultimately perform), all such predictions must be based on some past- or present-tense information about the applicants, together with some relevant supporting information. But is any and every way of predicting performance acceptable? Or are some methods of predicting improper even if they are more accurate than any available alternatives? And, if some methods of predicting are improper, which ones are those, and why?

I

To get a sense of what is at stake, let us briefly survey some of the ways in which employers or admissions officers might predict performance. To do so, they might use any of the following indicators:

1. Performance at tasks comparable to those the position requires—theatrical auditions, athletic tryouts, and the like.
2. An applicant's past record of performance, as revealed by grades, letters of recommendation, and the like.
3. A history of criminality, alcoholism, drug use, or any other behavior that adversely affects performance.
4. Performance on an entrance exam or other test of skills that is relevant to the position and that does not disproportionately affect any racial or sexual group.

5. Performance on a test of relevant skills that *does* disproportionately affect some racial or sexual group.
6. The fact that an applicant's age is statistically correlated with a reduced level of performance or a shorter work life.
7. The fact that an applicant's handicap is correlated with a reduced level of performance or a high level of absenteeism.
8. The fact that an applicant has personal commitments—for example, to children, aged parents, or a spouse with a separate career—that require periodic absences or otherwise distract attention from work.
9. The fact that an applicant is short or light, and thus is at a disadvantage in the sorts of physical conflict one may face in the military or the police.
10. The fact that an applicant belongs to a race, sex, or ethnic group whose performance is statistically below the norm.

Whether each factor ever *is* the best available predictor of performance (or, more plausibly, is an essential element of a larger information package that is the best available predictor) is of course an empirical question. However, to clarify the moral issues, we need not mount an empirical inquiry, but can simply ask what would follow if each factor *were* predictively significant. Thus, in what follows, I will proceed on the assumption that information about each factor does sometimes contribute to the best available prediction of performance.

II

Granting this assumption, which sorts of information may legitimately be used? Since many of the cited cases are controversial, appeals to intuition are unlikely to be of much help in answering this question. Rather, any adequate answer must appeal to moral considerations that are independently well grounded and, preferably, widely accepted. There are, of course, many such considerations. However, because the question concerns restrictions on attempts to implement equal opportunity, it is natural to begin with whatever considerations support that ideal itself.

This suggestion is complicated by the fact that the moral grounding of equal opportunity is itself not entirely clear. Nevertheless, one line of defense is sufficiently familiar and appealing to provide a plausible starting point. One main reason for providing equal opportunity is to give all persons as much control as possible over their own lives. By allocating positions competitively, we extend to each a chance to go as far as his own talents and desires will take him.[2] If we accept this justification, we will naturally seek methods of predicting performance that are in its spirit. Since no one can control either his fixed characteristics or the behavior of others, we may then be attracted to the principle that no prediction is acceptable unless it is based on information about the applicant's own past activities.

This proposal has in fact been made. In his discussion of equal opportunity, James Fishkin has written:

> I assume that a fair assessment of an individual's qualifications must rest, crucially, on his *own* past or present *actual performance* of relevant tasks, for example, exams, previous employment, or other relevant experience. Therefore a determination of qualifications should not rest simply on statistical inferences (derived from the behavior of others) about how one might expect a given person to perform. . . . an individual in a given group who is subjected to "statistical discrimination" in this way, would never have had a chance to compete, to prove his own competence. He would be judged entirely on the basis of the performance of *other* persons—persons who happen to share some arbitrary characteristic of him (or her).[3]

If we accept this principle, then predictions based on factors 1–5, which do involve the applicant's own actions, will be acceptable unless they are ruled out by some further restriction. However, predictions based on factors 6–10, which involve statistics about the performance of relevantly similar others, will definitely be unacceptable.

Should we accept the principle? Before doing so, we must look more carefully at its implications. Superficially, it may seem fully compatible with the ideal of choosing all and only those who would perform best. However, if applied consistently, the principle would rule out not only non-action-based predictions to which there are equally accurate action-based alternatives, but also non-action-based predictions that are far *more* accurate than the best action-based alternatives. Suppose we rank the predictive power of different methods according to their correlations with performance, where a perfect correlation is equal to 1.0 and no correlation is equal to 0. If an employer accepted the principle that we should use only action-based methods, he would have to use an action-based method of prediction with .5 predictive power even if he had access to a non-action-based method with .8 predictive power. He would also have to ignore any independent non-action-based evidence that the applicant with the best track record will suffer a decline in his powers before assuming the position or while discharging his duties. In view of this, applying the principle to disallow statistical information that is part of the best predictive package will clearly raise the probability of *not* selecting the applicant who will perform best. To square this with the ideal of selecting the best-qualified applicant, we would have to redefine "best-qualified applicant" to mean not the applicant who *would* perform best, but rather the one who *has* performed best at predictively relevant tasks.

By itself, this objection is not decisive. If the only point of equalizing opportunities were to give people maximal control over their lives, and if predicting solely on the basis of past performance were the best way to accomplish this, then Fishkin's principle could be defended as a consequence of the aim of selection by qualification itself. But are both premises acceptable? To decide, let us first ask whether predicting solely on the basis of past actions does significantly increase people's control over their own fate. This question is complicated by the fact that such predictions may be based either on all of an applicant's known past acts or else only on his performance on standardized tests open to all. In Fishkin's view, it is the wider interpretation that ought to prevail. However, if it did, an applicant might fail to receive a position simply because he had less opportunity than others to demonstrate his skills. For example, A's talents might be better known to an employer than B's because A had worked for that employer previously; or B might deservedly receive a stronger recommendation than A, only to have it discounted because A's recommender was more trustworthy. In these and other ways, predicting on the basis of all known past acts leaves far more to chance than using only standardized tests open to all. Thus, if either method of prediction is to give people maximal control over their lives, it must be the latter.

But does even selection by standardized exam significantly increase such control? Doubts are raised by the variety of outcome-affecting factors that remain *beyond* each test-taker's control. Most obviously, even perfectly fair exams are little help to those whose talents are meager. Even if all persons are given the same training, some are far better equipped than others to utilize it. Hence, the more talented may have a decisive advantage in any subsequent competition. For the untalented, selection by standardized test is apt to bring no real gains in control.[4] Less obviously, the gains seem minimal even for the more talented; for whether a talented person is selected depends not merely on factors within his control, such as how much effort he exerts to develop his talents and to do well on the test, but also on such externalities as which other persons choose to take the test and how much effort *they* choose to exert. In addition, because different talents are valued by different sorts of societies, the options open to us depend on both the degree to which our society values our particular gifts and the magnitude of the rewards it attaches to their successful exercise. Needless to say, the availability of positions requiring just the talents one has, and the fact that these positions are rewarding enough to be desirable, are also beyond one's control.[5]

These considerations do not show that basing predictions solely on applicants' past acts does not afford some persons some additional control over their lives. What does follow, however, is that any resulting gains are apt to be restricted to comparatively few persons and to be insignificant on any reasonable metric of overall control. Hence, the proposed principle will at best be derivable from the aim of selection by qualification if that aim is *exclusively* to maximize people's control over their lives. But there are surely a number of other important reasons for selecting by qualification, and these uniformly favor the use of all available predictive evidence. First, even if an employer's hiring practices are properly subject to moral or legal restraint, he retains a strong and legitimate interest in who is chosen. Given his aim of finding the most productive employee, he has every reason to select the applicant who actually will perform best. Moreover, since choosing best future performers raises overall utility, the utilitarian case for selection by qualification also favors using all available evidence. But not all arguments for selection by qualification are appeals to consequences. By considering qualifications, we also select those who, in one important sense, *deserve* to be chosen. Prima facie, it may not be clear that the basis for desert here is potential future performance rather than past performance on qualifying exams. However, if the basis of desert were not potential future performance, we would not be able to say that qualifying exams themselves are, in good measure, administered precisely to establish who *is* most deserving. Since anyone who takes seriously the desert of the best-qualified will want to say this, it seems that the real desert basis must be logically prior to the outcome of any test. Thus, the aim of selecting the most deserving applicant will also favor the use of all available indicators of future performance.[6] Given these and related considerations, the aims of selection by qualification plainly do not compel the reinterpretation of qualifications in backward-looking terms. Hence, they also do not support a principled rejection of statistical predictions of performance.

III

So far, I have tried to distinguish legitimate from illegitimate predictions by considering the degree to which different predictive methods permit persons to control their lives. This presupposes that the relevant moral units are precisely the individuals who will exercise the control.

However, it can also be maintained that the relevant moral units are not (only) these individuals, but (also) the groups to which they belong. If so, then one criterion of a prediction's legitimacy will presumably be its effect on the relevant groups. By this criterion, even some non-action-based predictions may be legitimate, while even some action-based predictions may be illegitimate. Thus, a non-action-based prediction may be acceptable if it is based on a characteristic—for example, being overweight—that is distributed roughly equally across all races, sexes, and ages. A prediction based on a standardized test, however, may be unacceptable if the test disproportionately disqualifies minorities or women.

Like its predecessor, this proposal is familiar. There is little doubt that something like it underlies the intuitions of those who object to such qualifying tests as strength trials for prospective firefighters. Although these tests are at least prima facie job-related, they disqualify most women applicants because women tend not to be as strong as men. Given this disproportionate effect on the group of women, critics argue that the tests should be revised or replaced. And—though here the waters are muddied by questions about what constitutes a qualification and about the tests' predictive accuracy—some take a similar position toward the tests that determine promotion in police departments when these have a disproportionate impact on blacks or Hispanics.

Yet despite the allegiance it has commanded, a prohibition on predictive methods that disproportionately affect specific groups would raise two serious problems. First, and most obvious, the claim that these groups have independent moral standing is itself problematical. Unlike individual humans, the groups do not have organized bodies, consciousness, or the capacity to make or carry out decisions. They cannot strive to achieve goals or be thwarted in their pursuit; they cannot undergo suffering, satisfaction, or joy; and they cannot have or lack self-esteem. Because the groups lack these and other prerequisites of well- or ill-being, there is, at least, a heavy presumption against the view that they have independent moral standing.[7] But, second, if we did ascribe moral standing to some groups and consequently forbade all predictions that would harm them, we would again have to abandon our commitment to selecting those who are most likely to perform best. For example, we would be forced to choose even a non-group-affecting method with a predictive power of (say) .55 over a group-affecting method with a predictive power of much nearer 1. Moreover, in this case, we could not plausibly redefine the notion of qualification in a way that preserves our commitment to selection by qualification. Combining both difficulties, we may say that a principle restricting group-affecting predictions would have to rest on a premise that seems both extremely hard to defend and in tension with equal opportunity itself.

Yet, here again, the difficulty is not decisive as it stands. Before rejecting a prohibition on group-affecting predictions, we must consider the possibility of deriving the rationale for such a prohibition from some aspect of our actual predictive practice. More specifically, we must consider the possibility that because statistical predictions are unavoidable, and because such predictions tie an individual's fate to his membership in a group, they themselves confer upon groups a moral importance they might otherwise lack. This, I think, is the underlying idea when Lester Thurow remarks that

> since employers will of necessity use groups in their decision-making, the state must necessarily become involved in the definition of what is a legitimate, or an illegitimate, group. The option of prohibiting all decisions based on group characteristics simply isn't possible since the price of efficiency would be too high.[8]

and, again, that

> every society has to have a theory about which groups are legitimate and which illegitimate, as well as about when individuals can, and when they cannot, be judged on the basis of group data.[9]

In these passages, Thurow seems to appeal only to the practical unavoidability of basing predictions on statistics about groups. But the necessity goes deeper, for even information about an individual's own performance supports predictions only because our experience *with others* suggests that such predictions are reliable. This point reinforces Thurow's position. If his idea can be worked out, we may indeed arrive at a prohibition on (some sorts of) group-affecting predictions that is both firmly grounded and internally connected to the practice of selecting the best-qualified.

But can the idea be worked out? Does the practical or theoretical necessity of using statistical predictive methods compel us to adopt a "theory" of which groups, or group-affecting predictions, are illegitimate? This does follow in the trivial sense that anyone who bases his predictions on group membership must at least *consider* the question of whether all such predictions are equally legitimate. But to raise this question is not to resolve it in any special way. In particular, raising the question is consistent with answering it by adopting the "theory" that the classes of illegitimate groups, and of illegitimate uses of group data, are empty. Thus, the mere fact that we must use group data in predicting does not by itself rule out any group-affecting predictions.

However, let us grant, for purposes of argument, that a focus on group characteristics renders group-affecting predictions at least suspect. Since *any* predictive method will disproportionately affect some groups—for example, the group of all those not chosen—it still remains to be shown why disproportionate effects on some groups are more objectionable than disproportionate effects on others.[10] This requires an account of *which* groups the relevant principle should protect. Although Thurow himself is noncommittal about how these groups are to be singled out, it is not clear that he can afford to be agnostic on this point. The great attraction of his approach is that it promises to reveal some internal connection between a prediction-limiting principle and our predictive practice. But if that practice singles out no specific groups as requiring protection, then no principle derived from it will have any content. Thus, to preserve what is most interesting about his suggestion, Thurow must indeed show how our use of statistical predictions can determine the identities of the "protected" groups.

Yet, given the resources at his disposal, it seems clear that Thurow cannot show this. If all we have to go on is our use of group-defining characteristics in predicting performance, then the only groups our predictions could single out are precisely the ones that the characteristics define. But if all predictions affecting *these* groups were illegitimate, we would not be able to use statistical predictions at all. Moreover, even if we accepted this conclusion (as Thurow does not), additional problems would be posed by our use of *action-based* predictions with disproportionate impact on groups. As we just saw, predictions based on strength trials, which do measure actual performance but which in practice exclude most women, are presumably among those that the proposed principle aims to exclude. However, if strength trials single out any group, it is that of the physically weak. Thus, the proposed criterion for whether a prediction illegitimately affects a given group—that is, does it turn on the characteristic that defines that group?—provides no reason for concluding that such predictions illegitimately affect women. Although the group of women substantially overlaps with that of the physically weak, there is nothing *in the method of prediction itself* that suggests that its impact on just this overlapping group (as opposed to some other, or none) should be held against it.

Given all this, there are two serious problems with Thurow's remark that

Since employers are interested only in macro-efficiency, they will make the trade-off in favor of efficiency and in favor of unfair individual treatment unless they are restrained from using certain group classifications. As a result the state is forced to establish categories of illegitimate groups (such as sex, age, or race).[11]

This remark is a non sequitur, first, because the fact that employers are interested exclusively in efficiency appears only to raise, but not to settle, the question of whether their decisions should be constrained and, second, because nothing about the decisions employers would make if unconstrained tells us why the illegitimate groups should include races, sexes, and age groups, but not groups of other sorts. It is of course possible that some further premises might support these inferences; but until such premises are advanced, we may reject the move from the need to make statistical predictions to any principled restrictions on group-affecting predictions.

IV

Yet it is hard to believe that this is the end of the story. If it were, there would be no objection even to a case in which

> the dean of a medical school is charged with the task of maximizing the number of M.D.'s for some given medical school budget. In the process of carrying out this mandate he notices that 99 percent of all male admissions complete medical school and that 99 percent of all male graduates go on to become doctors, but that the corresponding percentages for females are each 98 percent. As a consequence, each male admission represents .98 doctors and each female admission represents .96 doctors. Seeking to be efficient and obey his mandate to maximize the number of practicing doctors, the dean establishes a male-only admissions policy.[12]

Quite obviously, the dean's decision is marred by his assumption that he need not consider the quality of the doctors produced (and, more subtly, by his assumption that males ranked lower in the pool are as likely as higher-ranked males to go on and become doctors). But it is hard to believe that these are the *only* things wrong with his decision. If something else is wrong, there are indeed likely to be some constraints on the efficient predictors of performance we may use.

In the remainder of this paper, I will try to provide a more positive account of these constraints. In so doing, I will not try to defend any hard-and-fast prohibitions on specific sorts of predictions. Rather, in this section, I will enumerate several considerations that weaken the case for using the most accurate predictive method. In the next and final section, I will discuss some aims that legitimately compete with the aims that are served by selecting the best-qualified. Clearly the relative importance of these competing aims will increase as the case for using the most accurate predictive method grows weaker. Thus, to establish constraints on the use of best predictions, the obvious strategy is to plot the points at which the competing aims begin to dominate.

What, then, are the factors that weaken the case for using the best available predictive method? Given the example just cited, one relevant variable seems clear. A good part of the force of the medical school case derives from the triviality of the difference between the success rates of males and females. In that example, the method of selecting best-qualified applicants of both sexes is said to produce almost as many doctors as filling all the seats with best-qualified male applicants. Hence, even if we grant that the point is simply to maximize the number of doctors, a shift from the best to the second-best method is apt to bring little loss of overall utility. In an employment situation, a similar shift is apt to bring little loss of expected profit. Under these conditions, the consequentialist case for using the best predictive method will be easily outweighed by countervailing consequentialist considerations. In addition, even when there are no countervailing utilities, the obligation to use the predictive method that yields the best consequences seems weak when that method's consequences are only marginally better than those of the alternative.[13] Given all this, the consequentialist case for using a marginally better predictive method does not appear strong. But if this is so, then the overall case for using the best method, which draws considerable support from consequentialist considerations, must also have less force than it otherwise might.

If a best predictive method's *relative* accuracy can affect the strength of the case for using it, can its *absolute* accuracy have a similar effect? Is the case for using the best available method any stronger when that method's predictive power is, say, .9 than when it is only .6? Because a best method's advantage in promoting productivity and utility stems solely from its greater relative accuracy, this suggestion does not in any obvious way draw support from consequentialist considerations. But when we turn to non-consequentialist considerations, the situation is different. As we saw earlier, a good part of the overall case for selecting by merit is that those who would do the best job deserve to be chosen. However, as the absolute accuracy of our predictive methods declines, we move progressively farther from the ideal of treating each applicant as he deserves. As this ideal recedes, its moral pull can be expected to weaken. Thus, the overall case for using the best predictive method can be expected to weaken as well.

These determinants of the strength of the case for using the best method are features of the methods currently available to the predictor. But an additional factor to consider is surely the ease or difficulty of developing *better* methods. In some instances, the only barrier to more accurate predictions of performance is a lack of information of a kind that is already known to be statistically significant—for example, information that can be obtained by running (more) tests. In other instances, the problem is to establish better statistical correlations. In either case, the expected cost of generating more accurate predictions may range from prohibitively great to very small. Quite clearly, as the expected cost of developing more accurate alternatives declines, the consequentialist case for sticking with the best currently available method becomes less compelling.

There may seem, finally, to be a variable of a very different sort. Up to now, I have construed the problem as that of specifying the sorts of knowledge that can legitimately be used to predict performance. But the assumption that prospective employers *know* the exact predictive significance of different factors—that they have clear statistical information about how well persons with specific characteristics or histories are likely to perform—is, of course, only an analytically useful fiction. In the actual world, even the most scrupulous employer must often base his choice on factors whose connection with future performance is not documented. Thus, a small businessman who seeks a new shipping clerk may have nothing more to go on than his impression that one applicant is more alert than the others; while a faculty search committee may need to make an intuitive leap beyond the evidence provided by recommendations, interviews, writing samples, and lectures. Because such exercises of judgment are often inevitable, they do not invalidate the decisions to which they lead. However, because judgments of the significance of evidence can be more or less well grounded, they may seem to provide an additional dimension along which the strength of the case for using the best predictive method can vary.

Yet on inspection, this cannot be right. To use the best available method is precisely to make whichever prediction is in fact supported by the totality of one's evidence, and to rest as much credence in it as the evidence warrants. Thus, if someone makes a different prediction, he simply is not *using* the best predictive method available to him. Because of this, the unreasonableness of his prediction has no bearing on the strength of the case for selecting among applicants on the basis of what is in fact the best method. There is, of course, great practical value in ascertaining which sorts of cues warrant which predictions of performance to which degrees. By investigating this, we may hope to increase both our own predictive accuracy and our assessments of the justification for others' predictions. Nonetheless, such questions enter not by determining the strength of the case *for* selecting among applicants on the basis of the best available prediction but, rather, at the prior stage of determining what the best prediction *is*. Thus, no discussion of the case for using the best available prediction need address the difficult question of how justified our actual predictions tend to be.

V

We have seen that the case for selecting the applicant who is likely to perform best is weakest when (1) the evidence for the prediction is itself weak, (2) there is little difference between his projected performance and that of other applicants, and (3) there is good reason to believe that more accurate predictions could be obtained at reasonable cost. These conclusions are both intuitively satisfying and theoretically defensible. Yet even when the case for selecting the best applicant *is* weak, it may still be decisive if there are no countervailing considerations. Hence, to complete our discussion of the moral limits on such selection, we must examine the range of properly competing aims.

In the process, we discover salvageable elements in the rejected proposals of both Fishkin and Thurow. First, (re)consider Fishkin's contention that "a determination of qualifications should not rest simply on statistical inferences (derived from the behavior of others)." As presented, this contention appeared to rest on a principle—that persons should have as much control over their own destinies as possible—that is neither fully compatible with the aim of selecting the best performer nor the main rationale for our commitment to equal opportunity. I therefore rejected a blanket prohibition against decisions grounded in non-action-based predictions. Yet even if they are not prohibited, such predictions may remain less desirable than others. It undeniably *is* important for persons to have as much control over their lives as possible, and I have conceded that basing employment decisions on actual performance does give some applicants some control they would otherwise lack. Hence, if predictive method A utilizes data about the applicants' own activities while method B uses only statistical information about others, this will indeed count in favor of A. And where B yields the better predictions but the case for using B is weakened by its imprecision or its small margin of superiority, the balance may tip to favor A.

A similar line of thought supports a chastened version of Thurow's suggestion that we consider the impact of our predictions on racial and sexual groups. Although there is little reason to assign moral standing to these groups themselves, it clearly is possible for a sequence of decisions with a disproportionate cumulative impact on a given group to have adverse collateral effects on many group members. In particular, persons may suffer serious psychic harm when they repeatedly observe that other members of a highly visible group to which they belong, and with which they strongly identify, are conspicuously absent from positions of prestige or authority. By observing the absence of others like himself, a person may internalize the damaging conclusion that he too is not competent or is otherwise unworthy of inclusion. Correlatively, persons biased against the group may have their low opinion of its members confirmed. Although these facts are sometimes advanced as elements of a justification of preferential treatment,[14] one need not accept this use of them to acknowledge that the goal of disrupting damaging patterns can *compete* with the aims of selection by merit. If the goals do compete, then when predictive method A is less likely to perpetuate a damaging pattern than method B, this counts in favor of A. Hence, where B yields the better predictions, but these are either imprecise or only marginally superior, the balance of reasons may again favor using A. Alternatively, when the most cost-effective predictive method relies on gross statistical information about the performance of group members, the balance of reasons may favor replacing it with a finer-grained but more costly method.[15]

Thus far, we have found two aims that may compete with the case for selecting the applicant who will perform best. But these aims hardly exhaust the field. Also relevant are claims to compensation for the effects of past discrimination, rights of privacy that may be violated when employers test for drugs or inquire about applicants' marital status or personal histories, and (no doubt) various other considerations. With each addition, the problem of evaluating the challenge to the weighty case for selection by merit, and thus too of evaluating the overall case for using the best predictive method, grows more complex. However, at no point does the problem's logic change.

To what degree, finally, does this analysis carry over to situations in which persons must use statistical information to make *other* sorts of decisions—for example, decisions about who should pay which insurance rates or how to design legislation that will reduce highway fatalities? Although these issues really require separate treatment, the short answer is that the problem's underlying logic often is the same. In each of the cited cases, there is both an important aim or set of aims to be achieved and a need to use statistical data to come as close as possible to achieving it. However, in each case, too, we find familiar objections of principle to the use of certain *sorts* of statistical data. In the insurance case, some object to rate schedules that reflect the comparative longevity of men and women, or the incidence of AIDS among unmarried men, because using such data will adversely affect a group such as women or homosexuals. In the driving case, some object to raising the drinking age to reduce alcohol-related accidents involving teenagers because such legislation would be insensitive to differences in individual behavior. Given what has been said, it seems that these principled objections, too, must fail. Here again, the issues are better decided by first considering the strength of the case for using the best available data (as measured by the importance of the aim to be achieved, the data's relative and [perhaps] absolute predictive accuracy, and the cost of developing better data), and then weighing this case against whatever countervailing considerations are relevant. For example, in the case of the drinking age, the countervailing considerations will surely include a presumption in favor of personal liberty.

With each such extension of the proposed account, the reasoning it requires becomes yet more complicated and disorderly. Indeed, on that account, the real challenge posed by statistical predictions is exactly to recognize and assign due weight to each of what may be indefinitely many relevant considerations. This complexity renders the account far less elegant than any appeal to a single principle. But such inelegance is perhaps to be expected in an area of moral theory which is rendered problematic precisely by our inability to know enough about persons to treat them as the individuals they are.

Notes

1. According to many, equal opportunity requires in addition that persons be given equal chances to *develop* their qualifications—that they enjoy equally favorable developmental conditions and access to training. See, for example, Bernard Williams, "The Idea of Equality," in his *Problems of the Self* (Cambridge: Cambridge University Press, 1973); John Rawls, *A Theory of Justice* (Cambridge: Harvard University Press, 1971), chap. 2; and James Fishkin, *Justice, Equal Opportunity, and the Family* (New Haven, Conn.: Yale University Press, 1983), chap. 2. In the present paper, I will not be concerned with this further claim.

2. The idea of increasing people's control over their lives pervades discussions of equal opportunity. Its influence can be discerned both in the familiar view that providing opportunities consists precisely in removing obstacles to the achievement of goals (see, for instance, Robert Fullinwider, *The Reverse Discrimination Controversy* (Totowa, N.J.: Rowman and Littlefield, 1980), chap. 7) and in the claim, cited in note 1, that the obstacles to be removed include not only legal barriers but also the lack of preparation and training. Yet despite the pervasiveness of the idea of control, its justificatory role is not often brought into the open. In the published defenses of equal opportunity that I have read,

the most straightforward statement of this that I have found is William Galston's remark that "equal opportunity may be defended on the grounds that it is conducive to *personal satisfaction*. Within the limits of competence, individuals are permitted to choose their lives' central activity" (William A. Galston, "Equality of Opportunity and Liberal Theory," in *Justice and Equality Here and Now*, ed. Frank S. Lukash [Ithaca, N.Y.: Cornell University Press, 1986], 100). Ironically, a more forceful statement is presented by critic John Schaar, who correctly notes that a good part of the appeal of equal opportunity is that it purportedly "(does not) set artificial limits on the individual. On the contrary, it so arranges social conditions that each individual can go as high as his natural abilities will permit" (John Schaar, "Equality of Opportunity, and Beyond," in *Equality; Nomos IX*, ed. J. Roland Pennock and John Chapman [New York: Atherton Press, 1967], 233).

3. Fishkin, *Justice, Equal Opportunity*, 24.

4. For discussion of the implications of these facts, see Schaar, "Equality of Opportunity"; Rawls, *Theory of Justice*, secs. 12, 17, 48, and passim; and my "Effort, Ability, and Personal Desert," *Philosophy and Public Affairs* 8, no. 4 (Summer 1979): 361–76 (chapter 5 of this volume).

5. This point is made by Schaar in "Equality of Opportunity."

6. Of course, this aim will only be worth pursuing if the desert of the best qualified has real normative force—if there is good reason for an applicant to *get* the job he deserves. In my book *Desert* (Princeton, N.J.: Princeton University Press, 1987), I argue that such desert claims do have normative force and that they draw this force from an obligation to treat all persons as agents rather than mere recipients of largesse or passive links in causal chains. Roughly, the argument is that in hiring those who actually will perform best, we focus on the difference the applicants' own actions can make in the world. By thus taking seriously their ability to influence events through their own intentional acts, we take them—the originators of these acts—seriously as well. If correct, this argument will obviously deepen the case for saying that the real basis of an applicant's desert is his potential future performance itself.

7. For elaboration of this argument, see my "Groups and Justice," *Ethics* 87, no. 2 (January 1977): 174–81 (chapter 4 of this volume).

8. Lester Thurow, "A Theory of Groups and Economic Distribution," *Philosophy and Public Affairs* 9, no. 1 (Fall 1979): 30.

9. Thurow, "Theory of Groups," 31.

10. If we assume that our use of group characteristics to predict performance is what confers moral standing on groups, it may follow that the only groups that can have moral standing are those whose defining characteristics *support* predictions. This in turn may seem to imply that an arbitrary collection of individuals, such as the group of all those not chosen, lacks moral standing, and thus that its disproportionate exclusion is not objectionable. But in the current context, what defines this group is precisely its members' lack of whatever characteristics license the selection of members of its complement. If the possession of these characteristics is predictively significant, then the fact that an applicant lacks them while others possess them surely is also. Thus, on the suggested account, the group of those not chosen can have moral standing.

11. Thurow, "Theory of Groups," 30.

12. Thurow, "Theory of Groups," 29–30.

13. Here I assume that the strength of one's obligation to produce good consequences depends on how good the consequences are compared to those of alternative acts. Although this assumption is controversial, I believe that it underlies, and is needed to explain, our judgments about how much weight to assign to consequentialist obligations when these conflict with non-consequentialist obligations.

14. See, for example, Thomas Nagel, "Equal Treatment and Compensatory Discrimination," *Philosophy and Public Affairs* 2, no. 4 (Summer 1973): 348–63.

15. Upon members of which groups is "underrepresentation" in professions actually likely to inflict psychic damage? Although blacks and women are the two groups most often mentioned, I am skeptical about the parallel between them. Besides occupying comparatively few positions of security or authority, blacks often must endure miserable housing, do without amenities that others take for granted, and depend in humiliating ways on the decisions of bureaucrats. By contrast, women observing other women find no such gross failure to procure a share in life's goods. Given this difference, I suspect the message conveyed by the "underrepresentation" of blacks is far more undermining than any message conveyed by comparable "underrepresentation" of women. I suspect, too, that when predictive methods do contribute to a group's "underrepresentation," their harmfulness will vary with such factors as the visibility of those who occupy the contested positions, the prestige that attaches to those positions, and the shamefulness of not possessing the abilities that constitute qualifications for them. Since the last two factors are largely absent in the case of firefighters, it seems unlikely that strength tests for aspiring firefighters are harmful. But given this paper's theoretical purposes, these (admittedly controversial) issues may be set aside. We can agree that contributing to a psychically damaging employment pattern tells against a method of predicting performance without agreeing which methods do in fact have that effect.

10

What Makes a Lottery Fair?

It is generally agreed that when two or more people have equal claims to a good that cannot be divided among them, the morally preferable way of allocating that good is through a tie-breaking device, or *lottery*, which is fair. Intuitively, we have little difficulty recognizing which lotteries are fair. Tossing ordinary coins, drawing straws, and picking numbers from one to ten are all clearly fair, whereas awarding goods on the basis of personal preference, of flips of "loaded" coins, or of racial or religious characteristics are generally not. However, the principle behind these intuitions is not nearly as clear as the intuitions themselves. When one is asked about this principle, one is apt to reply that a lottery is fair provided that it affords each claimant an equal chance of obtaining the contested good; but this is helpful only to the extent that the relevant notion of equal chances can then be specified in its turn. Failing such specification, it will not be clear why lotteries based on personal preference or racial characteristics do not afford *their* entrants equal chances; and neither, conversely, will it be clear how coin tosses or straw drawings can offer genuine chances to any but their eventual winners. In this paper, I shall try to develop an adequate account of the principle that underlies our intuitions about fair lotteries. This will involve asking (*a*) exactly what conditions are necessary and sufficient for a lottery to be fair, and (*b*) why it should be morally preferable to allocate indivisible contested goods through lotteries that satisfy these conditions.

I

Suppose that n, o, and p are persons with equal claims to a good G, and that G cannot be divided among them. If any member of this group is to have G, then someone will have to institute a lottery L to determine

143

who it will be. Assuming that *m* is entitled to institute the required lottery (and waiving the interesting question of how *m* acquires this entitlement), let us begin by asking what determines whether the lottery established by *m* is fair. We have seen that *L*'s fairness depends on its affording all claimants an equal chance; but what exactly does it mean to say that *L* affords equal chances in this context?

A first possible way of interpreting "equal chances" here is to say that *L* affords such chances if and only if its outcome is not at all fixed in advance. Because the crucial procedure's outcome is not predetermined, the identity of the winning entry will be simply a matter of luck. This interpretation has the virtue of reflecting the common belief that in a fair lottery, the outcome rests on "the luck of the draw." Nevertheless, despite its familiarity, the proposed interpretation of "equal chances" could not possibly explicate our intuitive notion of fairness. If a lottery's fairness did depend on its outcome not being predetermined, then *all* lotteries would be unfair if determinism were true. In fact, however, the truth of determinism would simply not imply that coin tosses, straw drawings, and all similar devices are unfair.

In light of this difficulty, a different interpretation of "affording equal chances" is plainly called for. Because the notions of chance and probability are so closely connected, the obvious next move is to say that *n, o,* and *p* have equal chances of winning if and only if the probability of winning is equal for each. Moreover, because the events whose probability is at issue are single occurrences, the most natural way to interpret probability here is in terms of degrees of confirmation by available evidence.[1] If we do interpret probability in this way, then our proposal will become

> P1: A lottery *L* held at *t* is fair if and only if the hypotheses that the different claimants will win are all equally well confirmed by the totality of evidence available at *t*.

Because it construes a lottery's fairness as relative to what is known when the lottery is held, P1 implies that the fairness of a particular type of lottery may change as our state of knowledge increases. That this is so is confirmed by the intuition that an ordinary coin flip would cease to be fair if the person calling it became able to predict its outcome from a set of causal laws and statements of antecedent conditions.[2]

P1 is clearly a step in the right direction. Nevertheless, a closer look reveals that it requires modification in at least two ways. An immediate difficulty with P1 is that it does not specify *which* persons must know at *t* that the entrants' probabilities of victory are equal. Because it is silent on this point, P1 implies that a lottery may be rendered unfair even by the foreknowledge of someone whose interest in the situation is merely academic, and who does not intend to communicate his predictions to anyone. However, this implication seems highly counterintuitive. We are not inclined to say that an otherwise fair lottery is rendered unfair by the mere existence of a hidden Laplacian calculator who does not plan to publish his predictions. To avoid such judgments of unfairness, we must modify P1 so that it applies only to certain relevant persons. These persons will include those responsible for deciding which lottery is to be held and also those whose choices (of particular straws, heads or tails, etc.) will determine the chosen lottery's outcome. Since the feature common to all these persons is that each can at some moment affect the contested good's allocation, the natural way of restricting P1 is to make it apply only to those persons who exercise *control* over L's outcome at a given moment.[3]

A second difficulty with P1 is raised by a lottery whose controlling parties know *nothing* about the entrants' respective probabilities of victory. To illustrate this difficulty, let us imagine that n, o, and p are all about to undergo surgery and that m, knowing nothing about their medical histories, decrees that G will be awarded to whichever claimant has some physical characteristic (say, the smallest liver) which will be discovered during the surgery. Although this lottery is somewhat bizarre, it does not intuitively seem unfair. However, it is unclear whether m's ignorance warrants *any* conclusion about the entrants' respective probabilities of victory, and so it is *a fortiori* unclear whether the lottery satisfies P1. M *will* be warranted in believing that the entrants are equally likely to win if he is permitted to invoke the principle of indifference; but because this principle is widely held to be suspect, we will do better to reformulate P1 in a way that makes an appeal to it unnecessary. To accomplish this, we must replace P1's positive evidential requirement with something a bit weaker. Instead of demanding that the controlling parties must *have* evidence that the entrants' probabilities of victory *are* equal, we must require only that the controlling parties *lack* evidence that the entrants' probabilities of victory are *not* equal.

When both of the suggested modifications are incorporated into P1, the result is

P2: A lottery L is fair if and only if, for every time t and every person q with control over L at t, there is nothing that q knows at t that confirms the hypothesis that one claimant will win any more highly than it confirms the hypothesis that any other claimant will win.

Since P2 has been arrived at through successive refinements of the notion of equal chances, it expresses clearly the suggestion that fair lotteries are just those that offer all their entrants an equal chance of winning. However, once this suggestion is clarified, it is readily seen to be false. Although P1's conditions are indeed (roughly) necessary for fairness, they fall far short of sufficiency; there are many lotteries that do afford equal chances in the way specified by P2, but which nevertheless remain clearly unfair. As one example of this, we may imagine a case in which n, o, and p are persons of unknown racial and religious backgrounds and in which m decrees that G will be awarded to whichever one of them is discovered, through a genealogical search, to have the fewest Jewish ancestors. Although this lottery conforms to our amended P2 and is formally analogous to the smallest-liver lottery, it raises intuitions of unfairness as the previous lottery did not. Moreover, similar intuitions are also raised when we imagine m to decree that the contested good will be awarded to whichever entrant turns out to belong to the highest (or lowest) social class, to be the most intelligent, or to be the most attractive. If these intuitions are to be accommodated, then some further restriction on P2 will obviously be required.

What is most immediately striking about the unfair lotteries just described is that their victory criteria all involve characteristics that significant segments of society hold to be either positive or negative in value. Because this is so, the most obvious way of ruling them out is to augment P2 with a clause prohibiting lotteries with victory criteria involving such characteristics. In fact, however, we cannot simply rule out all such lotteries, for there would be nothing unfair about a lottery in which (*a*) each entrant designated some proxy about whose racial background he was ignorant, and (*b*) G was then awarded to the entrant whose proxy turned out to have the fewest Jewish ancestors. To complete our account, we must establish why this proxy Jewish ancestor lottery is fair while the original Jewish ancestor lottery is not.

The answer to this question is not difficult to discover. Although both Jewish ancestor lotteries have victory criteria that *involve* characteristics that are value-laden, the mode of involvement is radically different in the two cases. In the case of the original Jewish ancestor lottery, any person who satisfies the relevant victory criterion must himself possess the associated value-laden characteristic, while in the case of the proxy Jewish ancestor lottery, nothing like this is true. Taking our cue from this, let us distinguish between those value-laden victory criteria whose satisfaction *does* imply the possession of the associated value-laden characteristic (call these *primarily* value-laden victory criteria) and those others whose satisfaction does not imply this (call these *secondarily* value-laden victory criteria). Besides "being the claimant with the fewest Jewish ancestors," the class of primarily value-laden victory criteria will also include such specimens as "being the claimant whose mother and father have the fewest Jewish ancestors" and "being the claimant with the fewest ancestors who observed the Jewish laws." Of these further criteria, the first guarantees the possession of a value-laden characteristic via an analytic connection, while the second implies the possession of such a characteristic via a well-known empirical generalization. Given the distinction between primarily and secondarily value-laden victory criteria, the way we must modify P2 to rule out the original Jewish ancestor lottery is clear. What we must add is simply that no fair lottery can have a victory criterion that is primarily value-laden.[4]

When this final modification is incorporated into P2, what we get is

P3: A lottery L is fair if and only if
    a. For every time t and every person q with control over L at t, there is nothing that q knows at t that confirms the hypothesis that one claimant will win any more highly than it confirms the hypothesis that any other claimant will win; and
    b. L's victory criterion is not primarily value-laden.

Unlike our earlier attempts, P3 does specify conditions that, at least for the most part, are satisfied by just those lotteries we intuitively consider fair. In this respect, P3 constitutes a major advance in our discussion. Nevertheless, P3 still remains deficient in at least two ways. First, its requirements for fairness are not related in any obvious manner. There is little apparent connection between P3a's strictures on knowledge and P3b's restrictions on admissible victory criteria, and so P3 leaves unexplained the unity that our notion of fairness appears to possess. Furthermore, and even more damaging, P3's requirements for fairness are not airtight. There are, as we shall see, a number of odd cases that violate P3 without any intuitive loss of fairness, and these must somehow be accommodated if our account is to stand. In the next section, both of these difficulties will be explored. They are, of course, not unrelated.

II

To see that P3 is not airtight, consider the following anomalous cases:

1. m knows in advance that lottery L will lead to n's victory, but m has no special preference for this outcome. m does select L, but he

does so on some basis that is totally independent of, and unaffected by, his foreknowledge of *n*'s victory.

2. *m* knows in advance that *L* will lead to *n*'s victory, and *m* does want *n* to win. However, *m* uprightly and successfully refuses to let his desires determine his decisions on such matters. Thus, *m* chooses *L* on some basis that is totally distinct from his preference for *n*.

3. *m* has no racial or religious preferences at all. However, for entirely independent reasons, he decrees that *G* will be awarded to whichever claimant turns out to have the fewest Jewish ancestors.

4. *m* is biased against Jews and promulgates a lottery whose victory criterion does in fact imply non-Jewishness. However, *m* is unaware of this implication and selects the lottery on other grounds entirely.

5. *m* is biased against Jews and so decides to award *G* to whichever claimant has the fewest Jewish ancestors. Because claimants *n*, *o*, and *p* all share *m*'s bias, they all willingly acquiesce in his decision.

Of the lotteries just described, 1 and 2 violate P3's first clause, while 3, 4, and 5 violate its second. However, none of them is intuitively unfair. By discovering *why* these violations of P3 are not unfair, we may hope to deepen our understanding of what it is for a lottery to be fair.

Let us begin by considering counterexamples 1 and 2. These lotteries both have outcomes foreseen by controlling parties; and yet neither lottery is unfair. Because this is so, it cannot be merely the controlling parties' foreknowledge that is responsible for the unfairness of most violations of P3a. Instead, the operative factor must be something that usually *accompanies* foreknowledge, but is strictly distinct from it. Given the fairness of 1 and 2, this further factor is not hard to find. The salient fact about 1 and 2 is that although their initiators do *know* the outcomes of the crucial procedures, they do not *use* this knowledge to guide them in their choice of lotteries. Unlike most predictable lotteries, 1 and 2 are not instituted with the aim of awarding the contested good to any claimant whom a controlling party happens to favor. Because this is so, it must be not the controlling parties' foreknowledge, but rather their use of that foreknowledge to channel goods to favored claimants, which really renders most predictable lotteries unfair. Strictly speaking, foreknowledge is not a sufficient condition for unfairness at all, but rather is a necessary condition for, and a reliable sign of, a further condition—manipulation to favor a preferred claimant—which is genuinely sufficient for unfairness in its turn. In light of these considerations, P3's first clause must plainly be recast. Properly expressed, this clause must assert not that it is the controlling parties' foreknowledge, but rather that it is the meshing of this foreknowledge with the controlling parties' preferences to guide their actions, that really determines a lottery's unfairness.

This reorientation of P3's first clause naturally suggests a corresponding reorientation of its second as well. P3's second clause rules out primarily value-laden descriptions as victory criteria for fair lotteries. Because the pertinent values are those of the controlling party's society, and because someone who values a given characteristic will ceteris paribus prefer to award goods to the type of person who has it, P3's second clause in effect makes it unfair for controlling parties to award contested goods to any of the types of claimants they are most likely to favor. Because this is so, we can bring P3a into line with P3b by saying that just as most violations of P3a are unfair because they are intended to award goods to *individuals* favored by controlling parties, so too are most violations of P3b unfair because *they* are intended to award goods to *types* of individuals favored by controlling parties.[5] If this suggestion can be defended, then the underlying conception of fairness in lotteries will indeed be a unified one. In the last analysis, a lottery will be fair if and only if those who control it have not exercised their power in any of the ways they prefer.

The proposed revision of P3b is easily seen to be confirmed by counterexamples 3 and 4. Of these counterexamples, 3 is a racial lottery whose initiator lacks racial preference, while 4 is a racial lottery whose initiator is biased but unaware that his victory criterion is primarily racial. If value-laden victory criteria are themselves sufficient for unfairness, then the fairness of these lotteries will be hopelessly anomalous. However, their fairness will make good sense if what determines a lottery's unfairness is not simply the value usually attached to its victory criterion, but rather the intention with which the person initiating it has *adopted* that criterion. If the real determinant of unfairness is a controlling party's effective aim of awarding the contested good to a preferred type of claimant, then 3's fairness will be a straightforward consequence of the fact that *m* has no preference for claimants of the chosen race, while 4's fairness will follow just as naturally from the fact that *m*'s racial preference is not effective in determining his choice of what is in fact a racial lottery.

Given the ease with which the revised P3b explains these counterexamples, there is clearly a strong case for the view that a lottery is fair if and only if no one has exercised control over it in any of the ways he prefers. However, before we can accept this view, we must deal with a problem that is raised by our final counterexample, 5. This counterexample, we recall, is a racial lottery that is agreed to by a set of claimants whose racial preferences coincide. Like the other counterexamples, 5 is fair even though it violates P3. However, unlike the other counterexamples, 5 *is* chosen with the aim of aiding a favored type of claimant, and so violates our new conditions for fairness as well as the older conditions they replace. Because this is so, and because the new conditions are clearly superior on other grounds, the best way of accommodating 5 is through an appropriate restriction on the new conditions' scope. The exact strength of this restriction is not immediately obvious, for it is not entirely clear whether 5's fairness is due to (*i*) the fact that its victory criterion is *agreed to* by all claimants, or (*ii*) the fact that *m knows* that his preference accords with those of all the claimants, or (*iii*) the fact that *m*'s preference *just does* accord with those of all the claimants. To decide among these alternatives, we must imagine two further variations of 5, the first of which satisfies only (*ii*) and (*iii*) and the second of which satisfies only (*iii*). Our intuitions about these further lotteries may be somewhat hazy; but I do not think we would consider either of them unfair. If this is so, however, then only the weakest of the three possible restrictions on our new principle would be called for. Properly amended, that principle will state that any lottery initiated to aid a preferred claimant or type of claimant is unfair *unless its initiator's preference is shared by all the claimants involved.*

This concludes our discussion of the counterexamples to P3. The outcome of that discussion is that our intuitions about these counterexamples all fall into place once we suppose that a lottery is fair if and only if no one has exercised his control over it in any way that he, but not all the claimants, prefers.[6] More precisely, our intuitions about the counterexamples fall into place once we reject P3 and accept in its stead

P4: A lottery L is fair if and only if there is no person q such that
   a. q desires that L's contested good be awarded to a particular claimant or type of claimant, and
   b. q's desire is not shared by all the claimants to L's contested good, and
   c. q knows that his performing an action of type A will increase the probability of his desires being satisfied, and
   d. q performs an action of type A on the basis of this desire and the belief-component of this item of knowledge.

Setting aside certain well-known difficulties with "know" and "on the basis of" (which are standard problems of epistemology and action theory, and so need not be decided here), P4's conditions for fairness are not open to any further counterexamples that I can envision. Furthermore, P4's clauses bring together, in an extremely natural way, all the disparate elements of our previous discussion. Of these clauses, *a* brings out the underlying unity of P3's seemingly disjoint requirements by stressing the continuity between the different desires that they in effect proscribe. Clause *b* incorporates the refinement, brought to light by counterexample 5, that such desires are pernicious only insofar as they are not shared by all the claimants to the contested good. Clause *c* captures a basic insight of section I, that fairness in lotteries has an ineliminably epistemic component; and clause *d* connects knowledge and desire by specifying a relationship in which each plays an essential role. Taken together, *a–d* fuse all the earlier strands of our discussion into a single natural whole. These considerations strongly suggest that P4's conditions for fairness are the correct ones, and I shall hereafter accept them as such.

III

Having clarified the conditions under which a lottery is intuitively said to be fair, we may now turn to the moral grounding of the intuitions we have regimented. Granted that all and only those lotteries that satisfy P4 are fair, one may still wonder why it is morally preferable to *use* such lotteries to allocate indivisible goods to which several persons have equal claims. Because fair procedures are ceteris paribus definitionally preferable to unfair ones, there may be a minimal sense in which P4 itself provides a reason for adopting the sorts of lotteries it describes. Nevertheless, the moral preferability of these lotteries would obviously be grounded more deeply if it could be deduced from other, more general moral considerations. To complete our discussion, we must now ask whether any such deeper derivation of P4 is possible.

To see why it is morally preferable to use lotteries conforming to P4 to allocate indivisible goods to which several persons have equal claims, let us begin by examining the assertion that someone has a (strongest) claim to a good. It is no part of our concept of strongest claims to goods that a person with such a claim is entitled to delegate the relevant good as he prefers. Many claims to goods, such as claims to jobs or admission to competitive institutions, are nontransferable. It *is* part of our concept of strongest claims to goods, however, that when someone has such a claim, no one *else* is entitled to enjoy or dispose of the relevant good as he alone prefers. If n has the strongest claim to G, then any other person who either arrogates G to himself or delegates it to another on the basis of a preference different from n's is ipso facto infringing on n's rightful claim to it. Given this conceptual truth, the rationale for ruling out the allocation of contested goods on the basis of personal preference should not be hard to see.

For suppose, again, that n, o, and p all do have equal (strongest) claims to an indivisible good G. In this case, all but one of their claims to G will have to be canceled or overridden if any claim to G is legitimately to be satisfied. It is extremely difficult to specify the exact circumstances under which, or the mechanism through which, such claims are legitimately canceled;[7] but what we can say with confidence is that the strength and equality of the initial claims impose severe limits on the permissible ways in which this can be done. More specifically, since it is part of the concept of claims to goods that no one without the strongest claim to G may delegate G as he pleases, the mere fact that n, o, and p share strongest claims to G must itself entail that no person different from them can legitimately take any step aimed at awarding G to a person or type of person whom he, but not all the claimants, favors. Any non-claimant who took such a step— including the step of advancing a lottery with this aim—would ipso facto violate at least some claimant's strongest equal claim to G. Furthermore, given the equality of their claims, it also follows that no member of n, o, and p may *himself* take any step towards directing G to a person or type of person whom he, but not all the others, favors. Any claimant who took such a step—including again the step of advancing a lottery with this aim—would necessarily violate the others' equal claims by attempting to impose his preferences on them. Taken together, these considerations entail that no person at all may legitimately advance any lottery with the purpose of awarding the contested good to a person or type of person whom he, but not all the claimants, favors. This conclusion, however, is identical to the principle whose grounding we have been trying to understand. Since this is so, our account leaves little mystery about the moral preferability of fair lotteries. Given the conditions for fairness we have sketched, the moral preferability of using fair lotteries to allocate indivisible contested goods is merely an analytical consequence of the lottery situation itself.

Although this derivation of the moral preferability of fair lotteries seems adequate for the range of cases we have considered, it may be wondered whether this range has been quite broad enough. Our discussion to this point has focused entirely on lotteries whose purpose is to allocate indivisible *goods*. There are, however, also cases in which lotteries are called for to allocate indivisible *burdens*. One example of a burden that may best be allocated in this way is the burden of military service. Because our account has derived the demand for fair lotteries from the concept of claims to goods, it may seem unable to account for the demand for fairness in lotteries that distribute burdens rather than goods. To suppose this, however, would be to overlook the internal connection between the concepts of burdens and goods. If B is a burden for n, then escaping from B is necessarily a good for him. Moreover, the mere fact that there is a moral problem about allocating a burden among a group of people implies that each of them has an equal claim not to bear that burden. Given these facts, there should be little difficulty in extending our account to explain the demand for fairness in lotteries distributing burdens. To do this, we need only view such lotteries as devices for distributing the goods of avoiding these burdens.

Notes

1. For a comprehensive elaboration of this logical conception of probability, see Rudolf Carnap, *Logical Foundations of Probability* (Chicago: University of Chicago Press, 1950).

2. Although Pl has been couched in terms of the logical rather than the frequency approach to probability, nothing important rests on this choice. A frequentist who is willing to countenance single-case probabilities can formulate an analogous principle by saying that a lottery is fair if and only if each entrant would win equally frequently in an indefinitely long sequence of trials. Since Reichenbach has shown that single-case probability estimates lead to difficulty if they are not relativized to the narrowest known reference class, the relationship between a lottery's fairness and what is known when it is held would on this account be captured by the fact that the hypothetical sequence in question must incorporate all the features of L about which statistics are known at t. For discussion of Reichenbach's rule in particular, and the frequentist approach in general, see Hans Reichenbach, *The Theory of Probability* (Berkeley: University of California Press, 1949).

3. For a useful discussion of the various ways in which control can be exercised, see Nicholas Rescher, "The Concept of Control," in his *Essays in Philosophical Analysis* (Pittsburgh: University of Pittsburgh Press, 1969).

4. An interesting test case for this addition is the practice of awarding indivisible inheritances to the first-born. Hobbes considers this practice to be an acceptable form of lottery (Thomas Hobbes, *Leviathan* [New York: Collier Books, 1962], 121; but I suspect many readers will disagree. Some of our intuitions of its unfairness may stem from the facts that few inheritances are genuinely indivisible and that primogeniture was often restricted to males. However, a further source of unfairness may well be the value that has traditionally been attached to the property of being born first.

5. Of course, *any* lottery is intended to award its contested good to one type of claimant—namely, the type of claimant who wins. However, this intention cannot reflect the initiator's independent preference, because the "type" in question cannot be fully specified without mentioning the lottery itself. In

what follows, such trivial "types" should be understood as excluded from consideration.

6. It has been suggested to me that there is one further counterexample that may resist such treatment. This is a case in which m does not know in advance who will win in L, but claimant n foresees that he will lose, and so declines to participate. If m initiates L over n's objections, then there may be some temptation to view the lottery as unfair to n even though m has not initiated it to further his own aims. However, if n is permitted to exercise a veto on the basis of his foresight, then the choice of any alternative lottery may seem unfair to those claimants who lack n's gift. In light of this, I am inclined to view the lottery in question as not unfair, but rather merely as a case in which one of the losers knows his fate a bit sooner than the others.

7. If it could be shown that claimants concerned to maximize their legitimate access to goods could only gain from the implementation of fair lotteries, it might be possible to explain how such lotteries eliminate claims by invoking the fact that all the claimants either have consented to them or would consent if they were rational (see Thomas Nagel, "Rawls on Justice," in *Reading Rawls*, ed. Norman Daniels [New York: Basic Books, 1974], 5–6). However, it is simply false that all claimants concerned to maximize their legitimate access to goods can only gain from the implementation of fair lotteries. We can easily imagine a situation in which n and o have equal strongest claims to G, but in which getting G is of less value to n than is o's failing to get G. In such a case, it would be irrational for n to consent to a fair lottery; yet such a lottery, if held, would still eliminate all but one strongest claim to G. In light of these considerations, I suspect that a satisfactory explanation of the binding force of fair lotteries must await the construction of a full theory of the grounding of obligations.

11

Subsidized Abortion: Moral Rights and Moral Compromise

Most philosophical discussions of abortion have addressed such issues as the personhood of the fetus, the omission-commission distinction, and the rights of women to control their bodies. But as central as these issues are, they do not exhaust the moral problems connected with abortion. Further problems, less noticed by philosophers, are raised by society's role in the affair, and specifically by the fact that the government may not only tolerate abortions, but also may fund them through programs such as Medicaid or welfare. Of the questions thus raised, one is whether women have a right to be provided with abortions that they want but cannot afford, while another is how society should respond to the deep moral disagreement about abortion that divides its constituent groups. In this essay, I shall discuss these questions and the connections between them. Although my main aim is to bring philosophical order to an often undisciplined public debate, I also hope to shed reflected light on some broader issues of rights and moral compromise.

I

The distinction between elective and therapeutic abortion is not exclusive. A woman may elect to have an abortion for purposes wholly or partly related to her health. Nevertheless, the issues that concern us here emerge most clearly when the aim is entirely nontherapeutic; and I shall consider only such polar cases here. For similar reasons, I shall adopt narrow definitions of health and therapy, so that, for example, poverty and a hard life are not themselves states of ill health that could be mitigated by abortion. While it may be tempting to say that abortions performed for these reasons are therapeutic, this tactic would gain us no real ground. If we adopted it, our distinction between therapy and non-therapy would merely reappear as a distinction between *types* of therapy.

Given the view of elective abortions outlined here, should we say that poor women have a moral right to be provided with them? Prima facie, it may seem impossible to answer this question without first ascertaining the moral status of abortion itself. If elective abortions are seriously wrong, then poor women cannot have a right to be provided with them. But on further inspection, this suggestion is not fully satisfactory. Whatever their ultimate moral status, elective abortions are now widely available in the United States, and their availability has been found by the Supreme Court to be constitutionally guaranteed. Because abortion is thus officially tolerated by our legal system, its permissibility for us as a society is no longer an open question. In condoning elective abortion for women who can afford it, we have in effect reached a societal judgment that the practice is not seriously wrong. Moreover, despite some continuing controversy, we also seem to be moving toward a decision to provide basic medical care for those who cannot afford it. In view of this, a right to be provided with elective abortions may seem to follow from the more general right to consistent and nondiscriminatory treatment. Given our tolerance of elective abortions and our funding of other medical services, how can we refuse to provide funding for elective abortions? To be consistent, must we not either fund abortion as we do other medical procedures, or else reverse our judgment that abortion is permissible for those who can afford it? If we do otherwise, then are we not merely discriminating against the poor?

There is plainly something right about this argument. Given the societal judgment that abortion is morally permissible, we cannot consistently refuse to fund abortions for the poor on the grounds that they (alone) are morally wrong. To do this would be to indulge in the worst sort of hypocrisy. However, it is one thing to say that *this* sort of refusal to fund elective abortions is indefensibly inconsistent, and quite another to say the same for *any* refusal to fund such abortions. To say the latter would be to invoke an inappropriately rigid standard of consistency in policy making. It is true that society tolerates abortions and funds appendectomies, and true also that both are performed by medical personnel in a clinical setting. Still, as long as appendectomies differ from abortions in significant ways, it is no more inconsistent for government to fund the former but not the latter than it is for government to provide coupons for the purchase of food but not sweaters, or tax credits for insulation but not other home improvements. Moreover, whatever their moral status, abortions plainly do differ from appendectomies in many significant ways. Even if they are morally permissible, abortions remain distasteful in a way that appendectomies are not. Moreover, elective abortions are not aimed primarily at improving health, while appendectomies are. Given these and other differences, the case for government funding of elective abortions cannot be made on grounds of formal consistency alone. And neither, I think, can it be made on the related grounds that to permit abortions without funding them is to discriminate against the poor, for precisely the same is true in *every* instance where we permit the enjoyment of an amenity without subsidizing it for everyone.

The claim that it is consistent to fund appendectomies but not elective abortions establishes very little. A policy may be consistent and yet violate any number of other substantive rights. But which other rights, exactly, could ground the right to be provided with elective abortions? The right to be provided with medical care is inappropriate because of the fact, already noted, that elective abortions are not typically aimed at the maintenance or improvement of health. The right to privacy is another possibility; but despite what the Supreme Court has said about it, its connection with abortion seems too tenuous and indirect to be credible. In view of this, the most promising basis for a right to be provided with elective abortions may seem to be a kind of generalized welfare right: a right to have one's basic needs met by society if one cannot meet them oneself. Of course, since welfare rights are positive rights—rights not merely to be left alone, but rather to be provided with goods or services supplied by others—their very existence is a matter of controversy. But we cannot resolve this controversy here, and so I shall simply assume that some such rights exist. Granting this, how plausible is it to suppose that the right to be provided with elective abortions falls among them?

Since welfare rights are rights to be provided with what one needs but cannot afford, the question of whether they include the right to elective abortions depends on whether elective abortions satisfy basic needs, and this depends on our interpretation of basic needs. If basic needs encompass only the requirements for biological survival, then a general welfare right will dictate some therapeutic abortions, but no purely elective ones. However basic needs may also be construed more broadly, as encompassing all the requirements for effective functioning in contemporary society; and on this interpretation, the case for a right to elective abortions looks more promising. Given the limitations imposed by children one cannot afford, it seems reasonable to suppose that an abortion is often as necessary for a poor woman's effective functioning as access to transportation, education, or some discretionary income. Of course, while one cannot avoid the need for transportation, education, or money, one *can* avoid encumbrance by an unwanted child by simply giving it up for adoption. However, given the strength of parental feelings, the request that one give up a child already brought to term seems neither reasonable nor humane. Thus, the proper conclusion seems to be that elective abortion is lower than the most essential items, but higher than many others, on the overall scale of basic needs for the poor.

Given this conclusion, the right to be provided with elective abortions may seem to follow from a liberal, yet not implausible, interpretation of welfare rights. But on closer inspection, even this liberal interpretation does not secure the desired result. If the purpose of providing elective abortions is to enable poor women to function effectively within society, then that purpose will be equally well served by providing them with enough additional money and ancillary services to support their unaborted children. If such additional support is provided, then they will not be thrust into unmanageable poverty by those children. Hence, a right to the prerequisites for effective functioning does not automatically yield a right to elective abortions. Instead, it yields at best a disjunctive right to be provided with either additional support *or* abortion. Of course, the additional support is apt to be considerably more costly than abortion; but whether society can or should absorb this cost is a separate issue. The present point is only that if society does choose to absorb it, it violates nobody's rights.

This conclusion might be disputed. What we have missed, it may be argued, is that even if a woman is not thrust deeper into poverty by her unwanted child, that child can drastically restrict her freedom of movement. It can drastically reduce her vocational, geographic, and personal options, and so impose a real limitation on her liberty. In view of this, the right to be provided with elective abortions may seem to flow from a more general right to be provided with the prerequisites of liberty and self-determination. And this more general right may be defended either as being fundamental or as being an important corollary of the right to have one's basic needs satisfied.

If this argument were sound, it would indeed establish a categorical right to be provided with elective abortions. But even apart from any difficulties with the alleged general right to be supplied with the prerequisites of liberty,[1] the argument is highly problematical. On any reasonable interpretation, the proposed general right will not require the protection of liberties that are threatened by the prior exercise of liberty itself. If one's options are foreclosed by the foreseeable and easily avoidable consequences of one's own past choices, and not by uncontrollable externalities, then any right to the prerequisites of liberty has already been satisfied. But given the easy availability of reliable contraception, precisely this appears true of most unwanted adult pregnancies. Setting aside the young and uneducated, for whom special provision might be made, most women who become pregnant without wanting to appear to do so because they neglect to take rudimentary contraceptive precautions (or to see that such precautions are taken). But if so, then a right to be provided with elective abortions is not derivable in the standard case at all.

There is, moreover, a further difficulty with the attempt to ground a right to elective abortions in a more general right to the prerequisites of liberty. Even where pregnancy is due to the unavailability or ineffectiveness of contraception, and not to mere carelessness, it is by no means obvious that a woman's liberty *will* be drastically restricted if she is not provided with an abortion. Her liberty would be so restricted if women had to raise all the children they bore. However, as we noted above, it is always possible to give an unwanted child up for adoption. It is not humane to make a woman's material well-being depend on her willingness to give up her child. But where the issue is not her material well-being, but rather her preference for a life without the child, the case looks quite different. Here any right to liberty seems well enough served if she is allowed to choose between the child and the style of life she wishes to have after the child is born. Of course, the choice is apt to be considerably more difficult then; but difficult choices, far from impeding the exercise of liberty, are part and parcel of it. One might perhaps counter that complete liberty requires the ability to prevent the formation of desires (for example, maternal ones) that one believes will lead to the abandonment of one's present plans. However, while our relation to our future selves is puzzling and difficult,[2] it seems implausible to say that a person's freedom is seriously restricted by the inability to manipulate future desires. In view of this, it seems unlikely that a categorical right to be provided with elective abortions can be derived from a right to the prerequisites of liberty.

II

So far, we have focused entirely on the claim that the poor have a moral right to be provided with elective abortions. We have considered and rejected three distinct attempts to establish such a right. But even if all appeals to this right are mere inflated rhetoric, it hardly follows that the government has no reason to fund elective abortions. Given the enormous financial cost of providing adequate support for all unaborted children, given the manifest undesirability of further overpopulation, and given the carnage wrought by illegal abortions performed under unsanitary conditions, there is obviously a strong utilitarian case for government funding. Of course, utilitarian arguments are often overridden by the fact that maximizing utility would violate someone's rights; but here, as before, the appeal to the fetus' right to life seems to be blocked by the prior societal decision that there is no such right. Thus, the utilitarian case for government funding may at first appear quite overwhelming.

But even if the utilities do strongly favor government funding, there is a further dimension to the problem. To bring this out, we need only recall that the decision to tolerate abortion is by no means unanimous. Even if society as a whole *has* accepted the permissibility of abortion, many members of it emphatically have not. To these individuals, the legalization of abortion represents a serious moral error, and a government policy of paying for it merely compounds the error. For them, any appeal to society's collective decision is vitiated by the conviction that that decision is badly mistaken. But what exactly does this mean? Given their own moral views, must these persons continue to oppose abortion with every tactic that they believe appropriate to its gravity? Or is there a more general and independently grounded moral principle that tells against this? If there is, does it require that those who tolerate abortion make any concession in return? To ask these questions is to raise the difficult issue of compromise among parties with radically divergent moral views; and it is to this issue that I now turn.

One argument against continuing opposition by anti-abortionists can be dismissed at the outset. It is often maintained that those who oppose abortion are acting properly when they themselves refuse to abort, but not when they attempt to prevent others from aborting as well. When they try to ban *all* abortions, the argument goes, they overstep the bounds of tolerance by imposing their own moral views upon others. But the principle that underlies this argument—that all morally controversial decisions should be matters of individual conscience—is plainly untenable. Even the most ardent proponents of tolerance would deny that wife-beating, slavery, or murder are matters of individual conscience; and their position would hardly be affected by the discovery that some or most other persons consider such practices morally permissible. The abortion issue is clouded by the fact that some who oppose abortion do so on religious rather than purely moral grounds. However, as long as the conservative position on abortion can be articulated in purely secular terms—as I believe it can—the basic point remains. If an act is seriously wrong, we may well be obligated to prevent others from performing it. Hence, those who believe that abortion is murder are hardly overstepping the bounds of tolerance when they try to prevent others from aborting.

Given these considerations, the opponents of abortion appear to be doing exactly what they should be doing when they seek its total abolition. Indeed, given the enormity of the wrong that they believe abortion to involve, what is puzzling is why they are not doing even more. Where systematic murder is concerned, not only political pressure, but also relentless civil disobedience and other forms of extralegal resistance seem called for.[3] Of course, such actions are not really justified unless abortion really is murder; but since we have no direct access to moral facts, this observation is not particularly helpful. What is important is that from their own perspective, conservatives seem obligated to wage a no-holds-barred campaign against abortion, while from their perspective liberals seem equally obligated to resist those tactics that they view as outside the bounds of political legitimacy. If each side acts consistently on principles conscientiously arrived at, the result will apparently be an unending, acrimonious, and lawless contest of wills.

Now there may be some disputes whose contending factions are committed by their principles to just this sort of strife. It may even be that the abortion dispute is among these. But before we accept this pessimistic conclusion, we will do well to examine an alternative possibility. It seems possible to combine even a stern deontological code of ethics with a higher-order moral principle that moderates what one is required to do when one's efforts to act morally conflict with the similarly motivated efforts of others. By accepting a principle of this sort, we acknowledge both our own fallibility and the status of others besides ourselves as moral agents. But if some such principle is acceptable, then the parties to the abortion debate may not be locked into an endless and no-holds-barred struggle. Instead, even if the legal status of abortion continues to divide them, definite limits may be introduced into the conflict. Tactics that are permissible to prevent murder (or to defend against the unwarranted use of such tactics by others) may no longer be permitted. The conflict may be de-escalated.

It is not easy to specify precisely the conditions under which one can compromise one's moral convictions without compromising oneself.[4] However, one plainly relevant factor is the complexity and uncertainty of the subject. If one's convictions involve principles whose grounding is itself problematical, if the opposing view is also supported by plausible-sounding arguments, and if thoughtful and intelligent persons are unable to agree about the issues, then only a dogmatist will deny that he may well be mistaken, and his adversary correct. But once this acknowledgment is made, such considerations as respect for one's opponent and the value of mutual accommodation may permit (or even require) adjustments in behavior that would otherwise be inappropriate. Moreover, precisely these features are present in the abortion dispute. Such issues as the possibility of imaginative identification with the fetus and the moral significance of potential personhood are as obscure and difficult as any in the moral sphere; and neither liberals nor conservatives have produced a powerful general account of the moral personhood of normal adult humans.[5] In view of this, the abortion dispute is quite unlike such apparently related questions as whether contraception is permissible. Concerning abortion, but not contraception, both liberals and conservatives must in candor admit that the opposition has a genuine chance of being right.

Given all of this, the case for moral compromise in the abortion dispute appears promising. But what form, exactly, might such a compromise take? Because abortion is now widely available and because a total ban on it would violate a strong presumption against unnecessary government interference with citizens' activities, it does not seem reasonable to ask liberals to accept a proposal to make all abortions illegal. However, what does seem reasonable is to ask them to accept measures whose effect is to diminish the number of abortions *without* undue government interference. Such measures might include expanded programs of contraception, expanded adoption facilities, and perhaps also laws limiting abortions to the stages of pregnancy at which personhood is least certain. On the other side, since conservatives consider abortion a form of murder, it seems unreasonable to ask them to relinquish their efforts to make it totally illegal. However, what we may reasonably ask of them, in return for measures limiting the number of abortions performed, is that they (continue to) abjure the more extreme responses that would normally be called for by an officially sanctioned policy of murder. It is one thing to apply political pressure, quite another to firebomb an abortion clinic. Even if the conservative forswears only the latter tactics—tactics that would have been quite appropriate if employed in Hitler's Germany—his concession will be a major one and the gain in civility substantial.

With this in mind, we may now return to our original topic of government funding of elective abortion. Because both sides of the abortion dispute may have good moral reasons to compromise their positions, the natural question to ask about such funding is what role it might play in a reasonable compromise between them. Because an acceptable compromise will limit abortions without forbidding them entirely and because not subsidizing abortions seems to violate no one's rights, the obvious suggestion is that a proper compromise will include no government funding of elective abortions. This impression is confirmed, moreover, by two further considerations. First, any policy of government funding for abortions must draw upon tax monies collected from conservatives as well as liberals; and this must place conservatives in a position of actively supporting abortions rather than reluctantly tolerating their performance by others.[6] Second, such a policy must amount to an implicit government endorsement of abortion, and so must provide it with a symbolic legitimacy that conservatives wish to withhold. On both grounds, a compromise that includes government funding of elective abortions may not be one that conservatives can reasonably be asked to accept.

If this is so, then even a stalwart liberal may have a good (second-level) moral reason not to press for government funding of elective abortions. By relinquishing his claims in this area and attending to the needs of the poor in other ways, he may hope to reach an accommodation with the conservative that is not otherwise possible. This accommodation may indeed be more costly than providing abortions for all who want them; but if the accommodation is genuinely called for on moral grounds, its cost should not be prohibitive. And, of course, the liberal who accepts it may still contribute voluntarily to private organizations providing free abortions to the poor. The more difficult question is whether conservatives should accept even this type of compromise. We have presented some considerations in favor of it; but there are arguments on the other side as well. More specifically, it may be contended that (1) the propriety of a moral compromise should not depend on such morally irrelevant facts as the baseline determined by the current wide availability of abortions, that (2) we can morally compromise our own interests but never our duty to protect the interests of others, or that (3) the greater concessions should be made by the side whose actions are potentially the more seriously wrong—in this case, the liberal side. If one of these replies is correct—and it would take a full-fledged theory of moral compromise to evaluate them all—then the liberal's restraint concerning government funding will warrant no answering concession by the conservative. However, in that case, the conservative will justifiably view his position as more nearly uncompromisable than the liberal's; and so the liberal's restraint may still be called for. Some conciliatory gestures are appropriate even though they will be neither acknowledged nor reciprocated.

Notes

1. One problem with the alleged right concerns its intelligibility. Because it treats liberty as a single item, and not as the absence of particular restraints on particular activities, the right as stated seems incompatible with Gerald

MacCallum, Jr.'s widely accepted triadic analysis of freedom. For details, see Gerald MacCallum, Jr., "Negative and Positive Freedom," *Philosophical Review* 76, no. 3 (July 1967): 312–34.

2. For an interesting discussion of the way our relation to our future selves is connected to our moral obligations, see Derek Parfit, "Later Selves and Moral Principles," in *Philosophy and Personal Relations*, ed. Alan Montefiore (London: Routledge & Kegan Paul, 1973), 137–69.

3. Some extra-legal resistance to abortion has surfaced in the years since *Roe v. Wade*. As one magazine article reported, "Many . . . women (have) had to cross picket lines to obtain abortions; some subsequently received telephone calls charging them with murder. Abortion clinics in every region of the country have been disrupted repeatedly and more than a dozen have been fire-bombed. In St. Paul, Minn., where Planned Parenthood has spent $284,000 repairing fire damages, staffers continue to cope with arson, attempted bombings, bullets fired at the clinic, windows smashed with cement blocks, walls sprayed with graffiti (including swastikas and Ku Klux Klan initials), door locks sealed with glue, pickets, boycotts of businesses associated with Planned Parenthood's board of directors, prayer vigils, and kidnap threats." Helen Epstein, "Abortion: An Issue That Won't Go Away," *The New York Times Magazine*, March 30, 1980, 45. But as striking as such activities are, they hardly begin to approach what might be done to combat (what conservatives must consider) the many millions of murders of unborn persons committed since 1967.

4. This apt formulation is introduced by Arthur Kuflik in his article "Morality and Compromise," *Nomos XXI: Compromise in Ethics, Law, and Politics*, ed. J. Roland Pennock and John Chapman (New York: New York University Press, 1979), 38–65. Throughout this section, I have drawn heavily on Kuflik's illuminating discussion.

5. The recent literature on these issues is voluminous. Several of the more important articles are reprinted in *The Rights and Wrongs of Abortion*, ed. Marshall Cohen, Thomas Nagel, and Thomas Scanlon (Princeton, N.J.: Princeton University Press, 1974). Also worthwhile are Jane English, "Abortion and the Concept of a Person," *Canadian Journal of Philosophy* 5, no. 2 (October 1975): 233–43; and H. M. Hare, "Abortion and the Golden Rule," *Philosophy and Public Affairs* 4, no. 3 (Spring 1975): 201–22.

6. The point I am making here is *not* that tax monies should never be used to support policies with which some segments of the population disagree. Although this principle is sometimes invoked against subsidized abortion, it is implausible on its face. If government never funded policies that were unpopular or controversial, it would be unable to do much of anything. The point I am making is much narrower and applies only to cases in which public policy is contested on moral grounds. Furthermore, the principles underlying the disagreement must be both supported by reasonable arguments and serious enough to justify extra-legal activity.

12

Deserved Punishment Revisited

In my book *Desert*,[1] I examined the normative underpinnings of various claims about desert, including, prominently, the claim that wrongdoers deserve to be punished. The account I proposed—a variant of the familiar view that punishment is deserved when, and because, it rectifies an unfair distribution of benefits and burdens—has since been criticized in a number of places. Here I shall first summarize the account's main elements and then reconsider it in light of two especially probing objections. In so doing, I shall try to clarify the account where it remains adequate and to improve it, if possible, where it is not.

I

The view that punishment rectifies an unfair distribution of benefits and burdens has its roots in the retributive theories of Kant and Hegel and was given its definitive modern statement by Herbert Morris. According to Morris, it is unfair not to conform to a system of conduct-limiting rules when most others conform and when general conformity benefits everyone; for

> A person who violates the rules has something others have—the benefits of the system—but by renouncing what others have assumed, the burdens of self-restraint, he has acquired an unfair advantage. Matters are not even until this advantage is in some way erased. Another way of putting it is that he owes something to others, for he has something that does not rightfully belong to him. Justice—that is punishing such individuals—restores the equilibrium of benefits and burdens by taking from the individual what he owes, that is, exacting the debt.[2]

Putting Morris's point in (yet) another way, we may say, first, that anyone who disobeys the rules acquires an extra benefit, because he benefits once from the conformity of others and again from his own lack of conformity; second, that his victim similarly acquires an extra burden, being burdened once by his own conformity and again by the rule-breaker's failure to conform; and, third, that because punishing the rule-breaker imposes an additional burden upon him, it offsets his extra benefit and so restores a fair(er) balance of benefits and burdens.

Because everyone agrees that benefits and burdens should be distributed fairly, this elegant theory has an obvious appeal. However, to complete the theory, we must specify exactly what the relevant benefits and burdens are; and it is here that we encounter problems.

For suppose, first, that we take a criminal's extra benefit to be whatever wealth or gratification he gains by breaking the law. This proposal is problematic because many law-breakers gain neither wealth *nor* gratification. Some are not seeking financial gain while others fail to attain it, and there is no necessary, or even any very close, connection between criminal activity and happiness. Given these obvious facts, this proposal implies that many who commit serious crimes do not deserve to be punished and that many others deserve only minor punishment. Conversely, because even some trivial crimes are profitable and satisfying, it also follows that some petty criminals deserve very heavy sentences.

To avoid these implications, we must understand the rule-breaker's extra benefit differently; and one way to do so is to see it as an extra degree of *freedom*. The most common version of this idea, suggested by Morris's phrase "the burdens of self-restraint," is that each rule-breaker gains extra freedom to indulge his inclinations. This proposal provides a natural measure of *how much* freedom each rule-breaker acquires, for it implies that the stronger the inclination someone indulges, the more extra freedom he gains. Unfortunately, this measure itself has counterintuitive implications: as Richard W. Burgh has observed, most people "have a greater inclination to cheat [on their income taxes] than they ever have to murder."[3] Thus, if how much punishment a rule-breaker deserves depends on how much extra freedom he gains and if that in turn depends on the strength of the inclination he indulges, then tax evaders will generally deserve more punishment than murderers.

Because this implication, too, is unacceptable, anyone who takes rule-breakers to gain extra freedom must interpret their extra freedom differently, and in *Desert*, I tried to do just that. What I proposed was, first, that we measure the rule-breaker's gain in freedom, not by the strength of the impulse he has indulged but by the strength of the constraint he has violated, and, second, that we take the relevant constraints to be moral rather than legal. Of these proposals, each will be discussed in more detail below. However, because deserving punishment is so often linked with breaking the law, the decision to focus on moral rather than legal constraints requires some explanation now.

My main reason for not couching the account in terms of legal constraints is that we are under an equal (legal) obligation to obey *every* law. Because this is so—because legal constraints do not differ in strength—allowing the amount of extra freedom that a rule-breaker gains to depend on the strength of the legal constraint he violates would mean holding that all rule-breakers gain *equal* amounts of freedom. That would have the unacceptable implication that all criminals from shoplifters to serial murderers deserve equal amounts of punishment. By contrast, because some acts are more wrong than others, the constraints imposed by moral rules are evidently *not* all equal in strength. Thus, if the amount of extra freedom that a rule-breaker gains is determined by the strength of the *moral* constraint he violates, then different rule-breakers—or, as we may now more accurately say, different wrongdoers—will indeed gain different amounts of freedom. In each case, the amount of freedom gained will be proportional to the wrongness of the act performed.

Unlike other ways of completing the benefits-and-burdens account, this one nicely captures our intuitions about how much punishment different wrongdoers deserve. For example, because murder is more seriously wrong than tax evasion, the current proposal implies that murderers gain more extra freedom than tax evaders. That in turn implies that it takes a greater burden—a more severe punishment—to offset a murderer's extra benefit. To right the balance, the victim (or some agent of society acting on his behalf) must be freed from a constraint on his behavior toward the wrongdoer that is approximately as strong as the one the wrongdoer himself has violated. Thus, what determines the magnitude of the deserved punishment is the requirement that each wrongdoer be treated in a way that is ordinarily as wrong as what he himself has done.

Even by itself, the proposal's ability to capture our intuitions about proportionality would have considerable weight. But in addition, it offers a plausible account of the complex relation between deserved punishment and the law. On the one hand, by detaching desert of punishment from all facts about actual legal systems, we become able to say that those systems must themselves be sensitive to desert. Unlike theories that take the law and its penalties to determine who deserves what punishment, the current proposal implies that a legal system can itself be unjust if it punishes wrongdoers more (or perhaps less) harshly than they deserve. In addition, the current proposal explains how persons can deserve punishment even for acts that are *not* illegal—for example, how high-ranking Nazis could deserve to be punished despite the fact that they violated no laws. In these and other ways, the proposal captures the intuition that desert of punishment is pre-institutional.

But, at the same time, it also suggests some important *connections* between deserving punishment and violating the law. For one thing, because many of the same acts that violate laws also violate moral rules that help to justify the laws, the proposal nicely explains why so many who deserve to be punished are (also) criminals. In addition, by augmenting the proposal with Locke's observation that private punishment often elicits resentment and reprisals,[4] we can understand the case for replacing such punishment with an impartial criminal justice system that acts on the victim's behalf. Although state-inflicted punishment does not fully restore a fair distribution of benefits and burdens, it represents a step in the right direction for two distinct reasons: first, because it symbolically lifts the moral restraints on the victim and, second, because it actually treats the wrongdoer in a normally impermissible way. Thus, all in all, the proposed account locates desert of punishment at just the right distance from the legal system.

II

Or so, at any rate, I believe. However, the account has drawn a good deal of critical fire—far more than was directed at any other aspect of *Desert*—and I now want to examine what some critics have said. The objections that seem most telling are, first, that the proposed account is somehow question-begging—that in the end it presupposes rather than justifies the idea that wrongdoers deserve to be punished—and, second, that it cannot explain how wrongdoers who themselves were previously wronged can now deserve punishment. Let me consider these objections in turn.

That my account is question-begging has been suggested by several critics. For example, Michael J. Zimmerman objects that the account "seems simply to constitute a restatement, rather than a justification, of the *lex talionis*."[5] A bit more specifically, Bernard Gert complains that

> freedom seems to be doing no work at all here; we can leave it out and get the same conclusion simply by saying that violating a prohibition of greater force deserves greater punishment.[6]

And, again, Jeffrie Murphy has written that

> We were supposed to get our intuition that serious wrongdoers deserve serious punishment explained and justified in terms of excess advantage; but, if the concept of excess advantage itself can be explicated only in terms of that very intuition, we have not moved very far ahead.[7]

Murphy's account of what I say about the wrongdoer's excess advantage is inaccurate; for in fact, I presuppose not that serious wrongdoers deserve serious punishment, but only that some acts *are* more seriously wrong than others. However, this misstep aside, Zimmerman, Gert, and Murphy are right to complain that my account of the wrongdoer's extra benefit—the claim that "what he gains is freedom from the demands of the prohibition he violates"[8]—requires more elaboration than I have provided. Let me now try to remedy this lack.

Wrongdoers violate moral constraints, and constraints by definition constrain. Thus, one way to understand the wrongdoer's extra freedom is to equate it with the *lifting* of the violated constraint. If we take moral constraints to be factors that render acts impossible or hard(er) to perform—if we think of them on the model of locked doors, physical limitations, and inadequate financial resources—then the lifting of a moral constraint will make a wrongdoer more free by increasing his ability to perform the proscribed act (or, perhaps, by increasing his ability to perform other tokens of the proscribed act-type). By contrast, if we emphasize the *normativity* of moral constraints—that is, if we see them as constraining agents not primarily by making any acts impossible or harder to perform, but rather by commanding that certain actions not *be* performed—then the lifting of a moral constraint will make a wrongdoer more free by exempting him from whatever requirements the lifted constraint would otherwise impose.

But if a wrongdoer's gain in freedom is understood in either of these ways, then few wrongdoers will actually receive such gains; for, as Jorge Garcia correctly points out,

> the wrongdoer does not, by her immoral act, gain the physical or psychological ability to perform it, for she must have that in advance. But then neither does she thereby gain the moral freedom to perform such an act, for she possesses that neither before nor after her wrongdoing.[9]

Garcia's observations show that a wrongdoer's extra freedom cannot consist of the lifting of the relevant constraint. But if not, then how *can* I unpack my claim that wrongdoers gain freedom from the constraints they violate?

What this comes to, I suggest, is that for the wrongdoer but not for the moral person, the violated constraint is simply *not effective*. It is ineffective not in the manner of an impediment that can be overcome, such as a surmountable hurdle or a manageable shortage of resources, but rather in the manner of a command or prescription that goes unheeded. For because morality is essentially practical, its constraints are commands directed at an agent's will. In placing certain acts off limits, they seek to circumscribe the options from which the agent may choose. And, taking my cue from this, I want to argue that a wrongdoer is more free than a moral person because, in doing what morality forbids, he exercises an option that is *unavailable* to the moral person.

The obvious question about this proposal is why we should suppose that the option of acting wrongly is unavailable to a moral person. Zimmerman, for one, thinks we should not make this supposition:

> The wrongdoer doesn't *have* options that others don't have; those who do right *have* the option of doing wrong and so are no less free in this respect. What the wrongdoer does is to *choose* an option that others don't choose. Why should this be thought especially liberating? After all, those who do right likewise choose an option that the wrongdoer doesn't choose.[10]

There is clearly something to Zimmerman's point. In particular, it is clearly correct to say that when someone does the right thing because he takes morality seriously, he retains the option of *not* taking morality seriously right up until (and, of course, again after) he acts. The harder question, though, is whether the mere existence of this option should be said to have an effect on the moral agent's *other* options. That is, given that someone who takes morality seriously at *t* then has the option of not taking it seriously, are his other options at *t* exhausted by what morality permits, or do they include the further options that he would have if he *took* the option of not taking morality seriously?

We do not, in general, deny that someone has the option of doing *A* merely because he does something else, *B*, which is incompatible with his doing *A*. As Zimmerman implies, when this situation arises—when, for example, someone takes the freeway instead of a local route—the right thing to say is not that the agent lacks the option of taking the local route, but rather that he chooses the freeway *over* the local route. But it is significant that in this example, taking the freeway and taking the local route are straightforward competitors. When the agent chooses the freeway, he simply concludes that whatever reason he has for doing so—for example, that it will get him to his destination sooner—outweighs whatever reason he has for going locally. By contrast, when someone chooses *A* over *B* for moral reasons, the two alternatives are *not* straightforward competitors. Here the agent's rationale is not that the reasons for doing *A* *outweigh* the reasons for doing *B*, but is rather that given the demands of morality (and, perhaps, given the reasons for taking the demands of morality seriously), whatever reasons there are for performing the morally proscribed *B* are simply *not in play*. Although the agent could choose *not* to take morality seriously, the fact that he does choose to take it seriously means that any reasons for doing what it forbids are from the start excluded from his calculations.[11] Thus, from the moral agent's own perspective—and if we want to specify his options, this is surely the relevant perspective— the acts that morality forbids are *not* available as options.

III

Here, then, is a clear sense in which wrongdoers do have options that moral persons lack. But can we really analyze a wrongdoer's extra freedom in *terms* of such extra options? To show that we can, I must do three things: first, specify more precisely how the analysis might run; second, explain why those whose acts are more seriously wrong gain *more* of the relevant form of freedom; and, third, explain why extra freedom, so conceived, is always a benefit. I shall attempt these tasks in order.

(1) In a recent discussion of the theory of punishment that I advanced in *Desert*, Phillip Montague wrote that if wrongdoers gain extra freedom by ignoring moral restraints, then extra freedom must also accrue to "people who have divested themselves of *moral* self-restraint, but who refrain from wrongdoing out of concern for their own interests."[12] Thus, if punishment is required to offset the wrongdoer's extra freedom, then those who reject morality "should be punished even though they engage in no wrongdoing."[13] Although Montague does not make his reasoning explicit, he seems to be arguing that someone who rejects morality but refrains from wrongdoing out of self-interest gains just as much extra freedom as a wrongdoer because his rejection of morality provides him with just as many extra options. If this is what Montague means, he must take the theory I advanced in *Desert* to rest on an "extra-options" account of freedom. And because I am here elaborating the theory in just such terms, Montague's objection may seem right on target.

In fact, however, it is not, for extra freedom can be analyzed in terms of extra options in either of two ways. We can say that a wrongdoer has more freedom than a moral person either because he *has* more options than such a person or because he actually *exercises* one of his extra options. If sound, the argument of the preceding section shows that wrongdoers both have *and* exercise extra options, so nothing yet said distinguishes between these alternatives. However, Montague's objection is only damaging if my theory of deserved punishment presupposes the first analysis, while there is independent reason to take it to presuppose the second. For because punishing is *itself* the exercising of a normally forbidden option, punishing a wrongdoer can only offset his extra freedom if that extra freedom, too, consists of his actually exercising an extra option rather than merely possessing it. Hence, to answer Montague, we need only note that those who reject morality without acting wrongly gain *no* extra freedom of the relevant sort, and so, according to the benefits-and-burdens account, do not deserve to be punished.

(2) The next question is how, if wrongdoers gain extra freedom by exercising extra options, an act's degree of wrongness can have any bearing on an agent's *amount* of extra freedom. This question arises because morality forbids both more and less seriously wrong acts— both grave transgressions such as murder and relatively minor offenses such as shoplifting. Because someone who takes morality seriously will refuse to consider either the reasons to murder *or* the reasons to shoplift, won't a murderer and a shoplifter each exercise exactly one option that a moral person lacks? On the proposed analysis, won't they therefore both gain the same amount of extra freedom? And, hence, won't the current proposal, too, have the unacceptable implication that all wrongdoers from shoplifters to murderers deserve the same amount of punishment?

Because this objection relies on the inference from "each wrongdoer exercises exactly one extra option" to "each wrongdoer gains the same amount of extra freedom," the first thing to point out is that this inference is a non sequitur. It is perfectly consistent to say that *whether* an agent gains any extra freedom depends on whether he exercises an option that a moral person lacks, but that *how much* extra freedom he gains depends on some further fact about his extra option. And, indeed, the idea that some options contribute more to freedom than others is a commonplace of political philosophy.

Thus, whatever else is true, my proposal leaves ample room for the claim that how much extra freedom a wrongdoer gains depends on how seriously wrongly he acts. But is there any positive reason to accept this claim? To see that there is, consider what we imply when we say that A is more seriously wrong than B. To say this is to imply, among other things, that A's wrongness provides a reason for discounting the reasons for doing A that is stronger than the reason for discounting the reasons for doing B that B's wrongness provides. That in turn implies that if someone believes both that A's wrongness is not sufficient to warrant his rejecting A as an option and that B is even less wrong than *A*, then he cannot consistently hold that *B*'s wrongness *does* warrant his rejecting *B* as an option. By contrast, if someone believes that *B*'s wrongness does not warrant his rejecting *B* as an option but that *A* is *more* wrong than *B*, then he *can* consistently hold that *A*'s (additional) wrongness warrants his rejecting *A*. It is inconsistent to allow oneself to resort to murder while balking at shoplifting, but not at all inconsistent to allow oneself to shoplift while drawing the line at (or well before) murder.

These implications provide the key to understanding how an act's degree of wrongness can affect the amount of extra freedom that a wrongdoer gains; for they suggest that even though a murderer and a shoplifter each exercises only one extra option, the amounts of leeway that they allow themselves are very different. For when someone commits murder, he displays not only his willingness to disregard the reasons for rejecting murder as an option, but also, and a fortiori, his willingness to disregard the reasons for rejecting acts of any lesser degree of wrongness. He is, in this way, admitting each less wrong act, including shoplifting, into his current option-range. By contrast, when someone shoplifts, he displays only his willingness to disregard the relatively weak reasons for rejecting shoplifting as an option, and so he admits far fewer other acts—and certainly not murder—into his option-range. Hence, murderers gain more extra freedom than shoplifters because the extra option a murderer exercises is part of a far greater range of associated (though unexercised) extra options.[14]

(3) I described wrongdoers in *Desert* as gaining freedom *from* the constraints they violate, while here I am explicating their extra freedom in terms of extra options. Because my original formulation was negative while this one is positive, the two formulations may appear to express quite different conceptions of freedom. I think, in fact, that the difference is only superficial—it is, after all, precisely a wrongdoer's freedom from (self-imposed) moral constraints that *gives* him his extra options[15]—but I shall not argue that point here. Instead, to end this part of my discussion, I shall simply note that the new "extra-options" formulation provides a convincing answer to Zimmerman's complaint that "even if it is granted that wrongdoing is especially liberating in some way, I cannot see why it must also be granted that such liberty constitutes a benefit."[16]

For whatever we say about freedom from moral constraints, there is little doubt that agents are made better off by having (and a fortiori exercising) additional options. Other things being equal, having a given option makes someone better off by providing him with another way of achieving his goals, while actually exercising an option means taking a step toward achieving a goal that, at least in the agent's own eyes, is preferable to any available alternative. It is, of course, well known that other things are *not* always equal—that agents can be immobilized by having too many options, can do themselves harm by exercising bad options, can make mistakes about which options will best advance their aims, and so on—but none of this shows that having and exercising extra options does not, in general, make agents more able to achieve their goals. And, hence, to explain why the wrongdoer's extra freedom constitutes a benefit (and why those who act more wrongly gain *more* extra benefit), we need only note that each increase in an agent's willingness to disregard the requirements of morality leaves him in a better position to accomplish the goals that partially determine his interests.[17]

IV

The other main objection that I want to discuss concerns the status of wrongdoers who themselves have previously been wronged. Such wrongdoers, having already been burdened by others' lack of moral restraint, now appear to have sustained both extra benefits *and* extra burdens of the relevant sorts. Thus, if punishment is deserved when it *offsets* a wrongdoer's extra benefit, these wrongdoers may appear to deserve no punishment. This is disturbing because many previously wronged wrongdoers intuitively *do* deserve to be punished. Even more disturbingly, if fairness requires that the benefits and burdens of moral restraint be equalized, then previously wronged persons who have *not* yet acted wrongly may now be entitled to "free" transgressions.

In *Desert*, I argued that whether a previously wronged wrongdoer Y now deserves to be punished depends on whether his current victim is the very person X who previously wronged him or some further person Z. In the first case, Y deserves no punishment because "if Y's ordinarily wrong act harms the X who has previously wronged Y, then Y's act will in effect be X's deserved punishment."[18] Here it is inaccurate to call Y a wrongdoer at all. But if Y has been wronged by X and now wrongs Z, then punishment still is required; for in its absence

> the original wrongdoer X is still left with the double benefit of moral restraint upon others plus his own freedom from such restraint; and the current victim Z is left with the double burden of moral restraint on his acts plus the absence of restraint on the acts of (some) others. Thus, the original unfairness is not removed but merely displaced.[19]

Although critics have objected to both responses, I think what I said about the first case can stand with only minor modifications.[20] However, the objections to my treatment of the second case are more serious, and it is these that I now want to consider.

The central objection, advanced independently by both Jorge Garcia and Stephen Kershnar,[21] is that what I said about this case simply misses the point. Although Garcia and Kershnar do not deny that the unwronged wrongdoer X deserves to be punished, Garcia correctly notes that "the relevant question is whether [I] can, consistently with [my] account, justify punishing Yolanda [Y] on the grounds that *she* deserves it."[22] Moreover, as Garcia continues,

> It appears not, for Yolanda has gained no "double benefit," and thus punishing her cannot be justified on the grounds that it restores a just distribution by removing such extra benefit.[23]

That is, because the extra benefit that Y now gains by wronging Z is still offset by Y's past extra burden of being wronged by X, the original objection—that according to my theory, Y does not deserve to be punished—remains unanswered.

A further difficulty, suggested by C. L. Ten,[24] reinforces this point. Ten asks us to envision a variant of the original X, Y, Z case in which the circle of wrongdoing is closed:

> Suppose that A assaults B, B assaults C, and C assaults A. In each case, an equivalent harm is inflicted on the victim. So we have three distinct acts of equal wrongdoing which proceed in a nice circle, balancing the benefits from moral restraint that each person receives. If the balancing of benefits and burdens is crucial to punishment, there should be no punishment.[25]

Closing the circle gives us two additional wronged wrongdoers while eliminating the twin distractions of the unwronged wrongdoer and the innocent victim. It thus underscores the objection that if wrongdoers can deserve to be punished even though their extra benefits are already offset, then their deserved punishment can hardly be justified on the grounds that *it* will offset their extra benefits.

I think Garcia, Kershnar, and Ten are right to suggest that I have not met the original difficulty; but I also think the difficulty rests on the unargued assumption that the relevant principle of fairness governs the distribution of benefits and burdens among *groups* of individuals rather than between *pairs* of them. For if instead the principle applies to pairs of individuals—if what it says is that for each two people, it is unfair if the first exhibits moral restraint toward the second while the second does not exhibit comparable restraint toward the first—then the fact that Y was previously wronged by X will simply have no bearing on the unfairness that results when Y wrongs the innocent Z. The new unfairness—the fact that Y has acquired a double benefit relative to Z and Z a double burden relative to Y—will only be rectified when Z acquires an appropriate extra benefit relative to Y and Y an appropriate extra burden relative to Z. Thus, a fair distribution will not be restored until Z, or someone acting on his behalf, punishes Y. Mutatis mutandis, the same will hold for the more complicated case in which X wrongs Y, Y wrongs Z, and Z wrongs X.

Thus, the crucial question concerns the scope of the relevant principle of fairness. If what the principle governed were the benefits and burdens associated with obedience to law, a collective version of it might indeed be plausible; for in that case, the benefits would not be available in the absence of a legal system whose effective functioning requires the cooperation of many. Because most attempts to ground punishment in fairness *do* focus on the benefits and burdens of obedience to law, I suspect that this accounts for much of the current objection's appeal.

But, as I have repeatedly stressed, my own argument concerns the benefits and burdens of conformity to *moral* requirements; and where these are concerned, the case for regarding the relevant principle of fairness as collective is much weaker. First, even if morality is in some sense a social construct, its requirements clearly do not presuppose the existence of any legal system or other institutional structure that is sustained by the contributions or sacrifices of many. Also, even if no one can enjoy the important benefit of security unless most others exercise moral self-restraint, each individual's self-restraint yields many other benefits which are not similarly dependent on what others do. Even if others rob or assault me, I remain better off if you, at least, respect my rights; and especially if others do not come to my aid, I am better off if you, at least, act charitably toward me. Because the benefits of moral behavior are not mainly collective, there is little reason to regard the relevant principle of fairness as collective either. By contrast, because morality itself is standardly thought to be a set of rules that govern each person's treatment of each particular other person, there is considerable reason to regard the relevant principle as dyadic. Thus, all in all, the dyadic interpretation of fairness is clearly preferable here.

But if we adopt it, then we can indeed explain why even previously wronged wrongdoers deserve to be punished. The explanation is that what is unfair when one person wrongs another who has not wronged him is not the overall balance of benefits and burdens but precisely the balance *between these particular individuals*. When that balance is upset, the wrongdoer's previous burdens at the hands of others, even if themselves unfair, are not capable of rectifying it. Only an extra burden that gives the current victim an extra advantage relative to the wrongdoer—only punishment administered by or on behalf of the victim—is capable of doing that.

In proposing this solution to the problem of the wronged wrongdoer, I have (further) differentiated my own benefits-and-burdens argument not only from the justifications of punishment advanced by Morris and others, but also from attempts to ground political obligations in the "principle of fair play." Unlike these other arguments, which treat failures to obey the law or otherwise support the state as forms of free riding, the argument advanced here treats wrongdoing as a failure of reciprocity between individuals—as a breakdown in mutuality.[26] Given the many other ways in which morality and mutuality are linked, this implication is one I welcome. However, the transition to a dyadic notion of fairness also has a less welcome implication, and I shall end by briefly discussing the problem it raises.

The problem, in a nutshell, is that this notion of fairness stands in some tension with my earlier claim that each wrongdoer receives a double benefit. Above, I explicated that claim by saying that each wrongdoer benefits once by exercising an option that is not available to a moral person and again because others refrain from exercising that option in their dealings with him. But although it is plausible to say that each wrongdoer benefits from the fact that *some* others refrain from exercising morally forbidden options in their dealings with him, it is far less plausible to suppose that each wrongdoer benefits from the fact that *his own victim* refrains. For when a wrongdoer's victim has not acted wrongly toward him, the reason may be not that the victim is committed to morality, but simply that he has not (yet) had the inclination or the opportunity to act wrongly.

This objection—a variant of Montague's—would not be troublesome if we could assume that each victim's commitment to morality would have prevented him from exercising the relevant option if he *had* had the inclination and the opportunity. If we could make this assumption, we could say that just as homeowners benefit from insurance protection that they never use, each wrongdoer has benefited from the unactivated protection against being wronged that his victim's commitment to morality affords him. But, in fact, we *cannot* make the assumption; for, human nature being what it is, there are obviously some victims who are *not* committed to morality and who would *not* resist an inclination to act wrongly if given the opportunity. When a wrongdoer's victim is not committed to morality, his past failure to wrong the wrongdoer is due *only* to his lack of opportunity or inclination.

Because such cases can arise, we cannot say that each wrongdoer has benefited once from his victim's self-restraint and again from his own lack of restraint. But what we can say, and what seems sufficient for our purposes, is that each wrongdoer has benefited once from the fact that his victim has *not failed* to restrain himself in the way that morality requires and again from his own lack of restraint. Even when only the latter description applies, the wrongdoer still has received a double benefit in relation to his victim, although his victim, who himself is unencumbered by morality, has borne no double burden relative to him. Punishing the wrongdoer, which provides him with an extra burden but also provides the victim with an extra benefit, thus does not fully right the balance. However, because the extra benefit that punishing provides the victim is largely symbolic in any case, this does not significantly decrease the degree to which punishment moves us closer toward rectifying the imbalance.

Notes

1. George Sher, *Desert* (Princeton, N.J.: Princeton University Press, 1987).

2. Herbert Morris, "Persons and Punishment," in his *On Guilt and Innocence* (Berkeley and Los Angeles: University of California Press, 1976), 33–34.

3. Richard W. Burgh, "Do the Guilty Deserve Punishment?" *Journal of Philosophy* 79, no. 4 (April 1982): 209.

4. John Locke, *The Second Treatise of Civil Government* (New York: Hafner, 1969), secs. 13, 124–26, and passim.

5. Michael J. Zimmerman, "Review of Peter A. French, *Responsibility Matters,* Jeffrie G. Murphy, *Retribution Reconsidered: More Essays in the Philosophy of Law,* and George Sher, *Desert,*" *Nous* 29, no. 2 (June 1995): 258.

6. Bernard Gert, "Review of George Sher, *Desert,*" *Ethics* 99, no. 2 (January 1989): 427.

7. Jeffrie Murphy, "Review of George Sher, *Desert,*" *Philosophical Review* 99, no. 2 (April 1990): 282–83.

8. Sher, *Desert*, 82.

9. Jorge Garcia, "Deserved Punishment," *Law and Philosophy* 8, no. 2 (August 1989): 272. David Dolinko, in "Thoughts About Retribution," *Ethics* 101, no. 3 (April 1991), makes the same point in a bit more detail when he writes: "In one sense, the lawbreaker has perhaps revealed that he has a kind of 'freedom' by exercising it—by demonstrating that he is able to violate the prohibition. In this sense, however, he must have been 'free' from the prohibition even before his lawless act (or he could not have committed it!), and, presumably, many law-abiding citizens are equally 'free' (in this sense) to violate the prohibition. In another sense, we may ask whether the criminal's wrongful act has released him from a constraint upon his actions which the prohibition imposes on the actions of his fellows. One would think the answer should be 'no' " (p. 547).

10. Zimmerman, "Review," 258.

11. In saying that a moral agent excludes from his calculations the reasons

for doing what morality forbids, I do not mean to suggest that he must *ignore* those reasons. There is, indeed, a good moral reason for him to remain aware of them; for without such awareness, he cannot be sure that they have not become so strong that the acts they support are now morally permitted or required. Also, if someone's commitment to morality is less than absolute, he may want to assure himself that the reasons for acting immorally have not reached the threshold at which the case for remaining committed to morality is no longer decisive. But none of this affects my claim that as long as someone *is* committed to morality, the reasons for doing what it forbids are excluded from his calculations.

12. Phillip Montague, *Punishment as Societal Defense* (Lanham, Md.: Rowman & Littlefield, 1995), 82.

13. Montague, *Punishment as Societal Defense*, 82.

14. Because I have sought only to vindicate the claim that those who act more wrongly gain more extra freedom, I have taken no position on what *determines* an act's degree of wrongness. However, if this depends in part on how harmful the act is, then my account will imply that wrongdoers who inflict more harm deserve more serious punishment.

15. Here I draw on Gerald A. MacCallum, Jr.'s suggestion that "freedom is . . . always *of* something (an agent or agents), *from* something, *to* do, not do, become, or not become something; it is a triadic relation. . . . When reference to one of these three terms is missing in such a discussion of freedom, it should be only because the reference is thought to be understood from the context of the discussion" (Gerald A. MacCallum, Jr., "Negative and Positive Freedom," *The Philosophical Review* 76, no. 3 [July 1967]: 314).

16. Zimmerman, "Review," 258.

17. The qualification "partially" is necessary because the goodness of a person's life is also affected by certain objective features of it, including, arguably, the moral goodness of his behavior and character. For defense of this claim, see my *Beyond Neutrality: Perfectionism and Politics* (New York: Cambridge University Press, 1997), chap. 9.

18. Sher, *Desert*, 85.

19. Sher, *Desert*, 85.

20. For criticism of the first response, see C. L. Ten, "Positive Retributivism," *Social Philosophy and Policy* 7, no. 2 (Summer 1990): 194–208. The gist of Ten's criticism is that by making punishment by the victim so central to my account, I turn punishment into retaliation and leave it unclear how anyone but the victim can legitimately punish. I think, in fact, that my account *does* legitimate a form of retaliation, but I regard this not as a criticism of my account but rather as evidence that retaliation has received bad press. I am less certain about why Ten thinks the state may not punish on the victim's behalf. At least in part, his reasoning rests on the claim that "punishment does not confer any special rights on victims, nor does it remove any obligations which they have in common with others" (p. 199). However, if this claim is not backed by some further argument, it will simply beg the question against my appeal to fairness.

21. Garcia, "Deserved Punishment"; Stephen Kershnar, "The General Justi-

fication of Deserved Punishment," *Southern Journal of Philosophy* 33, no. 4 (1995): 477–78; and Stephen Kershnar, "George Sher's Theory of Deserved Punishment, and the Victimized Wrongdoer," *Social Theory and Practice* 23, no. 1 (Spring 1997): 75–91.

22. Garcia, "Deserved Punishment," 274; emphasis added.

23. Garcia, "Deserved Punishment," 274.

24. Ten, "Positive Retributivism."

25. Ten, "Positive Retributivism," 198. Kershnar, in "George Sher's Theory," proposes a similar example to block a possible solution to the problem of the previously wronged wrongdoer.

26. This is, of course, not the only difference between my argument and the "fair play" defense of political obligations. For an enumeration of some further differences, see *Desert*, 88–89, n. 27.

Index

About the Author

George Sher is Herbert S. Autrey Professor and Chair of the Philosophy Department at Rice University. He holds a B.A. from Brandeis University (1964) and a Ph.D. from Columbia University (1972), both in philosophy. He began his teaching career at Fairleigh Dickinson University in 1966, moved to the University of Vermont in 1974, and joined the Rice faculty in 1991. He has been a fellow at the National Humanities Center in Research Triangle Park, North Carolina, and a visiting member at the Institute for Advanced Study in Princeton, New Jersey.

Sher is the author of numerous essays and two previous books: *Desert* (Princeton University Press, 1987) and *Beyond Neutrality: Perfectionism and Politics* (Cambridge University Press, 1997). In addition, he is the editor of *Moral Philosophy: Selected Readings* (Harcourt Brace, 1987; 2nd ed. 1996) and a co-editor of *Reason at Work: Introductory Readings in Philosophy* (Harcourt Brace, 1984; 2nd ed. 1990; 3d ed. 1996). Another co-edited work, *Political and Social Philosophy* (Harcourt Brace), will appear in 1998.